W9-CAO-929

DATE DUE

MAR 2 7 2015	

Understanding the Chiapas Rebellion

Understanding the Chiapas Rebellion

MODERNIST VISIONS AND THE INVISIBLE INDIAN

Nicholas P. Higgins

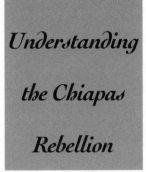

University of Texas Press

AUSTIN

Requests for permission to reproduce material from this
work should be sent to Permissions, University of Texas
Press, P.O. Box 7819, Austin, TX 78713-7819.

⊚ The paper used in this book meets the minimum
requirements of ANSI/NISO Z39.48-1992 (R1997)
(Permanence of Paper).

Library of Congress Cataloging-in-Publication Data
Higgins, Nicholas P. (Nicholas Paul), 1971—
    Understanding the Chiapas rebellion : modernist
visions and the invisible Indian / by Nicholas P. Higgins.
        p.   cm.
Includes bibliographical references and index.
    ISBN 0-292-70294-9 ((cl.) : alk. paper) —
ISBN 0-292-70565-4 ((pbk.) : alk. paper)
    1. Mayas—Mexico—Chiapas—Politics and govern-
ment.   2. Mayas—Mexico—Chiapas—Government
relations.   3. Mayas—Civil rights—Mexico—Chiapas.
4. Marcos, subcomandante.   5. Ejército Zapatista de
Liberación Nacional (Mexico)   6. Chiapas (Mexico)—History—Peasant Uprising, 1994—   7. Chiapas
(Mexico)—Politics and government.   8. Chiapas
(Mexico)—Ethnic relations.   I. Title.
    F1435.1.C48H54   2004
    323.1197'4207275—dc22
                                                        2003027034

to dad, mum, and moni

My problem is essentially the definition of the implicit systems in which we find ourselves prisoners; what I would like to grasp is the system of limits and exclusion which we practice without knowing it; I would like to make the cultural unconscious apparent.

—MICHEL FOUCAULT, *RITUALS OF EXCLUSION*

Contents

Preface

As those who have written one will know, a book is always vulnerable to correction or further amendment. At some point, however, a line must be drawn and the writing shared and opened to the scrutiny of a public. This book is no different, especially as it is born of a doctoral thesis completed some three years ago.

Although further contributions to our understanding of the Chiapas conflict have appeared since I first completed my doctorate, I still consider the central tenet of my thesis to remain unchanged.

It has always been my intention to provide an alternative understanding of the Zapatista conflict, and to do so initially required an intellectual journey through the highways and byways of social theory and political philosophy. It has perhaps been an idiosyncratic journey, in many ways peculiar to the academic study of international relations, but I believe the inclusion of this journey within the final text remains instructive and also explains why I hope this book will have a multidisciplinary relevance.

Questions of knowledge, of ethics, and of political culture remain as pertinent now as they then seemed to a young doctoral student. Nevertheless, I feel conscious that certain readers may find such an inquiry into methodology and epistemology unappealing, and so I suggest to those readers that they skip the heavily theory-laden introduction where these issues are explored and that they instead begin with chapter 1.

Following the text from chapter 1 through chapter 6 should provide a coherent historical narrative. The conclusion will make certain assertions concerning the relationship between the modern Mexican state and the Indian. History, like politics, is essentially contested. Nobody contests Mexico's modern history more dramatically than today's rebel Maya. I hope this book will make a contribution toward our understanding of how and why this current political contestation is taking place.

Finally, as I write this preface I am conscious of one recent event that has perhaps reconfigured the world of global politics more than any other and thus has a bearing on this text. The terrible attacks of September 11 on the United States of America have undoubtedly led to the dominance of a security discourse over the economic discourse that dominated the last two decades of the twentieth century.

I hope that in its own small way, this book will remind readers that history runs deep, and while government administrations may come and go, *govern-mentalities* persist. Peace, and its concrete realization, requires the renegotiation of such embedded mentalities and not their reassertion under the guise of self-defense or national security.

In light of this, Mexico as a multiethnic nation-state currently laboring under an incomplete peace process should remain especially sensitive to the long-term historical injustices that the Zapatista rebels first brought to the world's attention. It appears to me that leaving spaces for the evolution of a cultural humanism has become more important than ever as an alternative political project for the twenty-first century.

NICHOLAS P. HIGGINS
April 2003
Department of Politics
University of Glasgow
Scotland, U.K.

Acknowledgments

This book has been a long time coming, and as a result, I owe much gratitude to many people. In geography alone, I have found myself living in Canterbury, London, Mexico, and Glasgow at various times during its development. I have also been fortunate to have presented my work to diverse academic audiences in Paris, London, Vienna, Los Angeles, and Hull. Through all these twists and turns, it has always been people rather than books who have made my research worth doing. As is customary, and as a token of my appreciation, I shall now attempt to put some names to the kindness and companionship that I have received along the way.

I must thank my lecturers at the University of St. Andrews, John Skorupski and Vivienne Jabri, for their encouragement and exemplary tuition before I even arrived in Canterbury. As chance would have it, Vivienne also moved south, and she has been a good mate ever since. In the Department of International Relations at Kent, the singular Stephen Chan first provided supervision for my doctoral thesis. His humor, insight, and support, then and now, are much valued. After this initial period, Stefan Rossbach took over supervision. It is difficult to summarize the nature of Stefan's contribution, for like several others in my academic trajectory, he has become a good friend. As a consequence, recalling Stefan's enthusiasm, rigor, and imagination falls far short of describing the fellowship from which both I and my work have benefited.

The Department of Politics and International Relations at Kent and the London Centre of International Relations have also at various times offered challenging and entertaining environments within which to try out ideas. In particular, the staff and students who participated in the Critical Theory Reading Groups should be thanked. Exchanges with Mervyn Frost, Jeff Huysmans, and Cirino Hiteng remain most memorable. During the early days of the London School of Economics workshop on postmodernism, I also enjoyed the input of Mark Hoffman, Michael Banks, and Molly Cochrane, among others. Presentations to and within the BISA Working Group for Contemporary Research in International Political Theory also provided a supportive environment for experimentation. Around this time, my work also profited from the critical commentaries of Chris Brown, Andrew Linklater, and Quentin Skinner. Their intellectual generosity was much appreciated.

The beauty of international conferences is international audiences. In Paris I was lucky enough to meet Roland Bleiker and Christine Sylvester. Later presentations in Vienna and Los Angeles have been that much more pleasurable by virtue of their warm companionship. Again, thanking Roland for his honesty and sensitivity is insufficient acknowledgement for someone who has been a good friend. More recently in the world of Latin American studies, I must thank the knowledgeable Mexicanists David Stansfield, John Gledhill, and Neil Harvey for their encouragement and feedback. I must also offer considerable thanks to the selection committee of the Leverhulme Trust for 1997, without whose generous award of an eighteen-month scholarship I would never have been able to immerse myself in Mexican life and politics. I also gratefully acknowledge two smaller grants, the BISA research award and the Gilbert Murray Trust International Studies research award.

In Mexico I must first thank the Center for Historical Studies at the Colegio de México, Mexico City, where I was a visiting researcher between 1997 and 1998. I should also especially mention Javier Garciadiego and Anne Staples for their kind assistance during my time at the center. I will always fondly remember the librarians of the Biblioteca Daniel Cosío Villegas, not only for their characteristic professionalism, but for their generous habit of addressing me as "Professor Higgins," an academic promotion that eased considerably the feelings of historical vertigo that those early months at the Colegio were wont to provoke. For sharing their Mexico with me and showing unforgettable hospitality in the process, I cannot thank enough my good friends Martine, Malcolm, Anders, Ray, Raymond, Henry, Terri, Agñes, Grisel, Phillipe, Jorge, Alex, and Lisette.

During my regular visits to Chiapas I have also become indebted to certain individuals for keeping me both safe and well informed. I owe thanks therefore to members of the Center for Human Rights Fray Bartolomé de Las Casas; the Diocese of San Cristóbal de Las Casas; Pablo Cassanova of the Centro de Investigaciones Humanísticas de Mesoamérica y el Estado de Chiapas; Enlace Civil; and various others too numerous or anonymous to mention. In particular, though, I will never forget Henry's friendship and example. Mariano, John, Yutta, Jan Rus, Marta Durán de la Huerta, and latterly Bishop Samuel Ruiz and Miguel Alvarez were all extremely generous with their time and intimate knowledge of a complex situation.

I must also thank the University of Glasgow's Department of Special Collections for their generous loan of several illustrations. Throughout the book I have made all possible efforts to secure permission for the photographs and maps used, and I would like to thank in particular Pedro Valtierra and Yen Nomikos for their generous permission to use their images. Thanks also go to the estates of Gertrude Blom and Gustavo Schiebe, and for the loan of maps, to Jan Rus and the journal of indigenous studies *Akwe:kon.*

Outside of the world of academia, and the project itself, the friendship, laughs, and support of good friends Elsa, Barry, Emily, Gerry, and Helena have been inestimable. More recently, warm thanks go Abigail for her assistance with the final preparation of the manuscript. My sister Monica has been, as the Aussies would say, a legend. Sadly, my father did not live to see the completion of this book; whatever is good in this work I undoubtedly owe to him. His memory and example will always shine strongly. Last but never least, to my mother, who continues to ask tough questions—with love and respect—here are the answers so far.

And finally, since this book was completed I have returned to Mexico and Chiapas several times, most recently to make a documentary film concerning the Acteal massacre. I continue to feel humbled by the warmth and courage of the people I encounter there. I will forever remain in their debt.

Understanding the Chiapas Rebellion

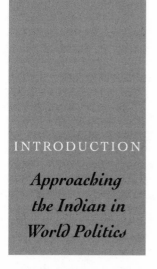

*Approaching
the Indian in
World Politics*

Over the Christmas and New Year break of 1993–1994 I sat in a cold and damp cottage on the outskirts of St. Andrews, Scotland, writing up my master's thesis. I was trying to make sense of the fact that a war between two Marxist-inspired rebel armies in eastern Africa had concluded with the establishment of two democratic states. I remembered a conversation with one rebel–turned–government minister during my fieldwork in the region some months earlier. He had expressed frustration and shock at discovering that if a new state, such as Eritrea then was, wanted international financial support, it had to adopt both free-market economics and multiparty democracy. At the time, this financial conditionality was promoted by the donor governments of the West under the policy of "good governance." Just as I was coming to conclude that the role of nongovernmental relief organizations had been central to the success of this policy, I heard the news that a rebellion had erupted in southern Mexico.[1]

What caught my attention about this latest rebellion was that the rebels were mostly indigenous Maya Indians and their struggle claimed to fight against the very type of "good governance" being so reluctantly embraced by the former rebels of East Africa. Calling themselves the Zapatista Army of National Liberation (EZLN), they claimed that Mexico's latest "development," the North American Free Trade Agreement (NAFTA), was "nothing more than a death sentence for the indigenous ethnicities of Mexico, who are perfectly dispensable in the modernization program of Salinas de Gortari [the Mexican president at the time]."[2] Their appearance seemed to raise several important questions to me, and over the next weeks I put a Ph.D. proposal together as a means of studying my hunches. This book is the result of that study.

The fact that these indigenous rebels openly contested an international neoliberal package, so much more advanced in Mexico than in East Africa, led me to believe that perhaps they had some lessons to teach me—not just about Mexican politics, an arena about which I knew precious little, but about world politics, an arena about which, as a graduating master's student, I supposedly knew much more.

I say I knew little about Mexican politics, but that's not to say I knew nothing of southern Mexico. Only two years earlier I had spent my summer vacation traveling through Central America and Mexico, following what tourists will know as La Ruta Maya (the Mayan route). Like many before me and surely many to follow, I had spent countless hours scaling and sitting atop the spectacular Maya temples of Tikal, Cobán, Chichén Itzá, Tulum, and of course, Palenque. I thus thought I knew something about Maya culture. I had, after all, been reading several accounts of the preclassic, classic, and postclassic Maya—as the archaeologists have come to delineate the culture prior to the Spanish conquest. I had even read something of the more contemporary Maya, in particular the supposedly classic studies of Egon Votz on the highland Maya of Chiapas. But even armed with this knowledge, and informed by my own experience of the living Maya who populate the villages that surround the temples (and who sell their artifacts to "culturally sensitive" tourists like me), I had not suspected that I might discover the most organized and convincing challenge to international neoliberalism witnessed so far.

If any interested individual were to look back to what was obviously visible during the late 1980s and early 1990s—that is, if she were to look in both the international and Mexican national press, or listen to the proclamations of the Mexican government itself, above all those of the self-promoting then president, Carlos Salinas de Gortari—she could easily be forgiven for believing that Mexico was a country poised on the verge of a deliciously attractive precipice. Moreover, if she were to consider the economic indicators of that period, and allow such statistics to be her point of departure for analyzing Mexico's condition, again she would be forgiven for supposing that Mexico was tantalizingly close to joining the coveted green pastures of that international plateau called the developed world. Scholars of international relations, where the study of institutions, treaties, and alliances has long been considered of key academic concern, may also have considered the presence of

Mexico among the OECD countries (Organisation for Economic Co-operation and Development), combined with its successful inclusion in NAFTA and its subsequent close alliance to the United States of America, as powerful signals that Mexico was indeed a wealthy, confident, developed, modern nation-state assuming an international role that reflected its newly acquired status.

This is what was obviously visible to sensitive tourist and interested individual alike. But the obviously visible was about to be displaced by the hidden invisible. When the Zapatista rebels erupted onto the international scene on New Year's Day, 1994, the question that seemed to pose itself most strongly to me was, how? How had these complex, politically motivated Indians stayed invisible for so long? How had these same Indians come to recognize an international governmental logic as a threat to their very survival, and how had they become so marginalized from Mexico's supposed success? And how, therefore, was this now openly contested relationship between the Indian, the Mexican state, and the international to be best understood? How, then, was one to approach the Indian in world politics?

International Relations and the "Real"

Perhaps coincidentally, around the same time that questions and accusations surrounding the marginalization of the Indians of Chiapas were first being raised in the wake of the Zapatista uprising, the academic discipline of international relations also faced a challenge to its dominant mode of study. Raised by Christine Sylvester, the charge was leveled at the methods of the "realists" in international relations, who, it was argued, had effectively rendered the subject devoid of people.[3] Through a concentration on the high politics of international actors — the agreements made by anonymous states and their famous representatives — the subject, Sylvester claimed, had forgotten, if not actually erased, the existence of a myriad of lesser-elevated realities. The realities to which Sylvester referred were in the main those of women, and in particular women of the third world, but the profound methodological point she advanced had relevance for the millions of human subjects who live international relations instead of merely studying it.

Ever since the foundation of the discipline in the years after the First World War, the subject of international relations has embodied a twofold methodological bias. First, as one of the founding professors, E. H. Carr, was astute enough to recognize, every new scholarly discipline comes into being in response to some social or technical need. In this respect, international relations was no different, except perhaps that in this instance the need was nothing less than "the passionate desire to prevent war." In Carr's opinion, this need "determined the whole initial course and direction of the study," leading him to argue that since its inception, "the *science* of international politics has been markedly and frankly utopian."[4] The second bias was a result of Carr's own reaction to such "utopianism." In labeling his critique of the liberal institution-building of the Wilsonian era "realist," Carr initiated a dichotomy that would have a lasting impact on what was to prove a burgeoning discipline.

The fact that Carr's own brand of critique involved what might be called an early variant of ethnocentric awareness and, as such, a conscious recognition of theoretical relativism, has been all but forgotten.[5] In his own opinion, "theories of social morality are always the product of a dominant group which identifies itself with the community as a whole, and which possesses facilities denied to subordinate groups or individuals for imposing its views of life on the community." Subsequently, "theories of international morality are, for the same reason and in virtue of the same process, the product of dominant nations or groups of nations."[6] As a result of this belief, which he associated with the Machiavellian dictum that "morality is the product of power," Carr's realist methodology actually involved an attempt to historicize the then widely promulgated theory of a "harmony of interests."

Carr should therefore be remembered for offering the young discipline an alternative foundation to the liberal-scientific approach to war prevention with which it was first burdened. His work instead promotes both the insights of political theory and the utility of historical research as a means to better understand the analysis of contemporary political problems and their political solutions. That Carr is only rarely remembered for these suggestions, and that the discipline studiously ignored such methodologies, has much to do with Carr's own unfortunate adoption of the rhetorical garb of realism.

In the aftermath of World War II, the more subtle dialectical relationship behind Carr's rhetorical opposition between realism and idealism found itself reinvented as a strict and often vulgar dichotomy between "rational" realists and "woolly-thinking" liberals. The reasons for this appear to be twofold and self-reinforcing: first, the increased influence of positivism as a marker of methodological rigor, and second, the growing diplomatic interpretation of the world along bipolar lines.

The two individuals who best exemplify these new influences on the discipline are Karl Popper and George Kennan. With a concentration on the "facts" and the rule-based demands of falsifiable theory, Karl Popper and his contemporaries sought to deny the utility of historicism and provide a firm scientific basis for all departments within the social sciences. Furthermore, with his publication of *The Open Society and Its Enemies* in 1945, Popper attempted to link his particular "scientific rationalist" approach to the more overtly political practices of a liberal democratic society. One year later, George F. Kennan, then U.S. chargé d'affaires in Moscow, provided an analysis of Soviet thinking that made the consequences of the politicization of rationality and its association with realist interpretation only too clear. He accused the Soviet Union of being "impervious to the logic of reason" and instead viewed the socialist regime as one "highly sensitive to [the] logic of force." This analysis led him to recommend the employment of "strong resistance" when confronted with Soviet expansion.[7]

By 1947, the wartime cooperation of the western liberal democracies with the Soviet Union had mutated into a cold war of theory, practice, and rationality. International relations, the discipline, thus found itself dominated by both American academic ideas and their direct preoccupation with Soviet expansion and threat, manifesting itself most clearly in what was often a poorly articulated theory of realism. As the years passed and the Soviet threat became less pressing, theories of realism took on a greater methodological rigor. The books of Hans Morgenthau and Martin Wight are now considered classics, while later work by Kenneth Waltz is viewed as an attempt to reinvigorate this perspective after behavioralist criticism.[8] Irrespective of increased theoretical sophistication, the concentration on the state as the principal, and essentially rational, actor in an amoral or anarchic system of international relations remained the key component of a dominant realist approach for the majority of the postwar years.[9] In an attempt to contest this dominance and to place the variety of approaches within the discipline on a more even footing, Michael Banks proposed a new interpretation of the role of theory within IR. In the early 1980s he argued that

> it is wrong to think of 'theory' as something that is opposed to 'reality.' The two cannot be separated. Every statement that is intended to describe or explain anything that happens in the world society is a theoretical statement. It is naive and superficial to try to discuss IR solely on the basis of the 'facts.' This is because whatever facts are

selected — any at all — are literally abstract. They are chosen from
a much bigger menu of available facts, because they are important.
The question is: why are they important? And the answer to that is:
because they fit a concept, the concept fits a theory and the theory
fits an underlying view of the world.[10]

Banks called these "underlying views" paradigms, breaking the discipline down into three: realism, structuralism, and pluralism. However,
while such a move was intended to create new spaces and legitimacy for
long-subjugated strands of thinking within the discipline (consider, for
example, the work of Mitrany and Deutscher), it could also be seen as
running the risk of excluding those that are not, or cannot be, accommodated by the definition of norms peculiar to each paradigm. Just
as Kuhn was aware of the implications of translation, which he saw as
"always involving compromises which alter communication," so too has
Michael Banks, by his adoption of a Kuhnian rhetoric outside of the
Kuhnian context, altered the meaning that can be attached to the term
"paradigm." Other theorists such as Michael Nicholson, in a similar
way, have attempted to introduce the Lakatosian criteria for "appropriate research strategies" in lieu of what Nicholson refers to as Banks's
"imaginary paradigms."[11] Although they disagree in method, Banks
and Nicholson are united in their desire to see some kind of disciplinary matrix or grid accepted within the discipline. What they dispute, of
course, are the terms that might legitimate the academic field of inquiry.
Both thus believe that generalizations are possible, but they disagree
over the terms of normalcy and the requirements of coherence and
rigor for the social science of IR. Calling them "paradigms" or "appropriate research strategies" does not, however, alter the attempt to place
parameters on the field of inquiry and thus set the agenda for present
and future members of the IR community. While such innovation has
been widely welcomed as a useful teaching aid, the question remains,
can IR really be said to have paradigms? Is there a set of disciplinary
norms that can be identified as constituting the concerns of "normal" or
"real" international relations?

I have already mentioned the perils involved in such an identification process, and not surprisingly, Banks has had to face the criticism
of those who feel they have been marginalized by his categorizations.
Steve Smith thus castigates Banks for the introduction of the paradigm
concept because "it anaesthetises the discipline by offering a 'pick and
mix' solution, a superficial liberalism which implies that you can choose

a paradigm which best explains the things you are interested in."[12] He considers the inter-paradigm debate to be "just another gate-keeping device for maintaining the status-quo, despite the clear intentions of people like Banks to use it as a way of liberating the discipline"; for this reason, then, Smith welcomes the recent resurgence of normative work within international relations because, he believes, "what is commonly treated as marginal, illegitimate or optional becomes central."[13] Smith even goes so far as to call this resurgence "the post-positivist revolution," revealing his own attraction to the Kuhnian rhetoric while all too readily ignoring the concerns of those excluded in his own act of identifying what is "central" to international relations. Nevertheless, undoubtedly Smith is right to recognize a new strand of thought in international relations that has, to a certain extent, out-maneuvered the early attempts, such as the three-paradigm debate, to open up the discipline.

Postpositivism or postmodernism has, since the late 1980s, attempted to introduce to international relations ways of thinking that not only take issue with realism but, to a large extent, take issue with international relations as an enlightenment practice in its own right. Postmodernism, borrowing Chris Brown's definition, is a body of thought that holds the belief that all the varieties of social and political thought dominant in the West since the Enlightenment—the discourses of modernity—are in crisis.[14] As this belief is also shared by critical theorists, by whom I principally mean the followers of Jurgen Habermas and the Frankfurt school, a further distinction is necessary: postmodernists are antifoundationalist, while critical theorists believe new foundations can be constructed for their beliefs.[15] While we might accept these as working definitions, clearly there are a multitude of approaches within these two strands of theorizing. Rather than attempt a summary or assessment of these perspectives, I will instead locate my own position within this broad church of theory, or what I have previously suggested might best be viewed as a new critical pluralism for international relations.[16]

Re-describing Knowledge

The attempt to provide extraneous justifications and foundations for what we know is what antifoundationalist philosopher Richard Rorty views as the epistemological and metaphysical quest of the Enlightenment.[17] This quest, he suggests, was captivated by the metaphor of philosophy as the "mirror of nature," and thus philosophical debates ever since have concerned the accuracy of representation to reality. Such a distinction, Rorty claims, takes as its source the mind-and-body dualism first set in play in the work of René Descartes in the seventeenth century. This distinction, he claims, also continues to provide the basis for what in philosophy has become known as the correspondence theory of truth, a theory that holds that words or facts correspond to an "antecedently determinate" reality.[18]

For a scientist, or a social scientist, statements are only true or factual in this strict sense, insofar as they match the world. Truth is thus determined by its correspondence to the world. However, for this theory of truth to hold, a perspective from outside of "the world," what we can call the transcendental perspective, is vital. Following in the spirit of René Descartes, Thomas Nagel calls this view "the view from nowhere."[19] For it is only by viewing the world from outside that we can confirm or refute whether people and the representations they create correspond with the world. As a consequence, Nagel argues that only on the basis of a transcendental perspective can we feasibly make a claim to such a thing as objectivity. Without any such claim, our "normal" understanding and "rational" basis for scientific knowledge since Descartes would appear to be in crisis. Our traditional and essentially modern understanding of knowledge and progress has, after all, been seen as a history of increasing sophistication in knowing and, importantly, seeing how the world "really" works.

If, however, we have several competing accounts of how the world works, as in the case of Banks's misappropriated paradigm approach, we are faced with the puzzle of how to choose among rival representations. This, in fact, was exactly the kind of question Thomas Kuhn posed in *The Structure of Scientific Revolutions*.[20] As just explained, for the correspondence theory of truth to be maintained, it would appear that we need some further external perspective to provide objective grounds upon which to judge among the now multiple conflicting approaches that offer competing "truths" or "representations" of how the world works. For Descartes, this further transcendental perspective was God; for contemporary philosophers of science like Thomas Kuhn, this further perspective would need to take the form of a "universal algorithm." Such an algorithm would thus provide the explanation and rational foundation for why certain scientific theories appear to "work" better than others.

Kuhn was to conclude that no such algorithm existed, and he thus famously claimed that major scientific revolutions, such as massive changes in perspective like the Copernican revolution, did not occur in the manner of a revolutionary "discovery." Instead, Kuhn claims, Galileo's theory that the world revolved around the sun was not immediately received as "objectively right." Rather, the reception of Galileo's theory was a "revolutionary moment" only insofar as the Copernican theory changed from one of illegitimate and "abnormal" scientific discourse to one of legitimate and "normal" scientific discourse. This "paradigm shift," as Kuhn was to label it, had more to do with relatively gradual and unpredictable historical and cultural factors — such as the changing role of the church in the eighteenth century — than with the discovery of any external and objective algorithm. Thus, Kuhn can be said to undermine our "modern" approach to understanding knowledge. His argument instead supports a more holistic conception of "truth" and scientific inquiry that places scholars' beliefs and representations firmly within the historical and cultural contexts of their scientific communities.

This holism can be better conceived of as "a coherence theory of truth and knowledge," as Donald Davidson argued in his essay of the same name.[21] A coherence theory of truth refutes the Cartesian dualism by denying the existence of any external and objective perspective or law, while still maintaining a conception of "truth." It maintains a conception of truth because it recognizes that there are causal connections between what the scientist describes and actual events on earth. Thus, Davidson claims, it follows that some laws must exist. These laws, however, are what could be called internal laws, rather than external, objective laws, and it is this internalism that characterizes Davidson's "anomalous monism." Furthermore, Davidson claims, laws are laws only insofar as they are described as such.[22] Like Kuhn, then, Davidson is not suggesting a reductive argument whereby "truth" or "laws" are internal to language; rather, he argues that their acceptance as truth or laws has more to do with historical, societal, and disciplinary factors, and thus with irreducible social conditions, than with any external "objective" criteria as such.

Contemporary pragmatists, such as Richard Rorty, have recently taken up this conception of truth as coherence, in recognition of its relationship to both society and politics, and in so doing have come to consider "truth" as the quest for a community of free inquiry and open encounter.[23] With this quest in mind, Rorty has argued that the existing system of political organization best suited to the desired end is that of liberal democratic political representation. Rorty writes,

> an anti-representationalist view of inquiry leaves one without a
> skyhook with which to escape from the ethnocentrism produced by
> acculturation, but that the liberal culture of recent times has found

a strategy for avoiding the disadvantage of ethnocentrism. This is to be open to encounters with other actual and possible cultures and to make this openness central to its self-image. This culture is an *ethnos* which prides itself on its suspicion of ethnocentrism — on its ability to increase freedom and openness of encounters, rather than on its possession of truth.[24]

Redescribing Politics

While Rorty's antifoundationalism may provide us with an ethos or sensibility with which to conduct research, we are still left with the question of how this liberal democratic attitude either progresses or confronts challenges. The provision of a normative basis, which many in the discipline interpret as the result of the "post-positivist revolution," thus still leaves open the question of how future change might occur or on what basis we might support one political movement over another.[25] In other words, questions concerning both politics and ethics, which by this argument now appear central to the discipline, still remain open. In order to understand the nature of such a self-consciously ethnocentric approach to politics, it is perhaps instructive, therefore, to proceed via consideration of an example of antifoundationalist politics in action. One example available to us concerns the sociocultural movement of feminism. In addressing this issue, we find revealed certain limits on Rorty's approach to politics, and thus we are able to consider the limits of one antifoundationalist project in order to suggest the possibilities of another.

In focusing on the feminist problematique in his 1991 Tanner Lecture on Human Values, Richard Rorty clearly identified feminism as the contemporary social issue with the greatest revolutionary potential for resulting in positive moral and ethical change within the existing liberal communities of the North Atlantic democracies today.[26] In keeping with his pragmatic historicist perspective, however, Rorty did not approach feminism in the manner of a free-floating sociopolitical project. On the contrary, he firmly located feminism as the latest in a long line of harbingers of intellectual and moral progress. Thus, Rorty came to situate feminism within the broader historical parameters of a much larger, and continually evolving, political and ethical project, one that I have called Rorty's "postmodern liberal humanism."[27] Feminism viewed from this perspective thus avoids what Rorty believes would be the pitfalls of an essentialist movement, that is, a movement concerned solely with the emancipation of the female subject. It accomplishes this because, from within the setting of a postmodern liberal humanism, feminism plays a much more inclusive sociocultural role, one that goes beyond gender distinctions and aims instead at "the production of a better set of social constructs than the ones presently available, and thus at the creation of a new and better sort of human being."[28]

In regarding feminism in such an evidently progressive light, Rorty indicates that his postmodern liberal humanism bears very little relation to the classical universal liberal construct of the rational male individual, a construct that feminist theory, among others, has done so much to deconstruct. This is because Rorty's humanism is metaphysically hollow; it does not claim to be universal in any useful sense. Rather, its content derives solely from the cultural and social context within which a human being might attempt to make the nature of her humanity intelligible. Such a stance, therefore, recalls the unavoidably ethnocentric nature of any human construction of identity, and as a consequence, Rorty's postmodern humanism denies the validity of questions concerning the absolute ontological, or metaphysical, constitution of the human subject. This stance is in keeping with a pragmatic dismissal of other modernist ideologies, including liberal metanarratives that base their political agendas on such metaphysical constructs.[29] For without an intrinsic nature, Rorty argues, the question of human identity becomes a highly contested issue, yet such contestation shares a contingent reliance on the cultural, social, and historical resources within which rival interpretations can only make themselves understood. Rorty's humanism is thus firmly situated within a pragmatic philosophical tradition that provides no extrasocial or extracultural perspective from which the nature of its humanity could be settled once and for all.

It is this very open-ended nature of Rorty's humanism that also informs the character of his liberalism. In much the same way that his humanism cannot be addressed without recourse to ethnocentrically situated historical and cultural resources, so too does his liberalism come to function as the minimal sociological structure within which such resources might have the political space to coexist and blossom. Rorty's liberalism thus stands as a loose political framework within which various human natures might have the freedom to pursue their various self-interpretations, untrammeled by the imposition of one version of what humanity can be shown to be. Unlike the liberals of the Enlightenment, Rorty does not seek justification for democracy by an appeal to any transcultural criteria of rationality. Rather, in the spirit of liberal philosophers such as John Stuart Mill, John Dewey, and Thomas Jefferson, Rorty gives priority to the pragmatic and procedural nature of democracy over and above any philosophical claims.[30] However, unlike the cold utilitarian rationale of Benthamite liberal democracy, Rorty's democratic impulse recalls the romantic and aesthetic aspect of Mill's more sensitive political liberalism.[31] Liberal democracy in this respect functions as a means of limiting the interference of the state in the personal life projects of the individual. This limitation is desirable, the logic runs, because if there is no one correct way of being, then individuals should be free, in a romantic manner, to "create themselves anew." The liberal structure does, of course, impose limits on the influence such life projects can assume. These limits, for Rorty, are considered both community and individual safeguards, manifesting themselves in the classic liberal construct of an institutional division between the realms of the public and the private. The private domain, in this analysis, provides the cultural space within which philosophers and poets can continue to work freely on the creation of novel self-descriptions of what it means to be a human being. The public domain, in contrast, demands that the role of creativity adopt a self-consciously pragmatic and communal nature. Public politics thus comes to adopt the reformist and practical character appropriate to a political ethos whose contemplation of social problems does not include the radical restructuring of the central mechanisms of governmental organization.[32]

Rorty's liberalism and humanism are thus closely interlinked, making little attempt to describe life within a postmodern North Atlantic democracy beyond endorsing the necessary double bind of the sociological distinction between the public and the private. This distinction is necessary because, if there is no ahistorical human being whose potential could be fully realized if only we were to apply the correct plans and policies, government and politics must be limited to a self-consciously defined public space. It is a double bind because many of the life projects of individuals are concerned with creating stories about who we are, stories that, because they cannot be considered true or valid in any strong metaphysical sense, must have their cultural impact limited to the private domain of their creators. Pragmatic liberals, like Rorty, thus hope to insulate the central political institutions of the state from the adoption of exclusionary political vocabularies that run the risk of subverting a liberal pluralism in the name of some extracultural or ahistorical truth. Nevertheless, while Rorty's postmodern conjuncture of a liberal humanism might provide a convincing antifoundationalist political framework with which support for our existing liberal democracies might continue in lieu of a better alternative, it is still far from clear how this pragmatic perspective can explain the achievement of the moral and social progress implicit in his support for a feminist attempt to create "a new and better sort of human being."

Language and Society

Although he agrees with Chris Weedon that "one should not view language as a transparent tool for expressing facts but as the material in which particular often conflicting views of facts are constructed," Rorty nevertheless wishes to claim that such conflicts occur in a positive dialectical manner.[33] This is because it has been Rorty's contention that moral and intellectual progress will only be achieved if "the linguistic and other practices of the common culture . . . come to incorporate some of the practices characteristic of imaginative and courageous outcasts."[34] According to this belief, such outcasts have to break away from mainstream linguistic practices because, as we have learned from other progressive movements in the past, "had there been no stage of separation there would have been no subsequent stage of assimilation."[35] Rorty cannot, however, provide reasons why a new language, such as a feminist language, might come to be assimilated into wider American culture, and this is because he has foregone the once "comforting belief that competing groups will always be able to reason together on the basis of plausible and neutral premises."[36] Therefore, "prophecy . . . is all that non-violent movements can fall back on when argument fails."[37] Yet for such prophecy to be confirmed, our approach to the history of the future must also conform to Rorty's whiggishly dialectical account of how historical change, via the role of language, has come to take place. As a consequence, Rorty admits that he cannot provide any analysis of how "the new language spoken by the separatist group may gradually get woven into the language taught in the schools," at least not one that does not start to look increasingly circular. In fact, all he can offer on the back of his antifoundationalist pragmatism is hope.

Could it be possible that Rorty has overplayed the extent of cultural agency available within the "fashioning of new names"? For in holding that "all awareness is a linguistic affair," does not Rorty suggest the presence of a cultural and linguistic idealism at work within his analysis, that is, an individualist idealism that exaggerates the moral and social possibilities of freedom within his project of redescription? Even without adopting her Gramscian analysis of the political, we might have more than a little sympathy with critics such as Nancy Fraser, when she attempts to engage with some of the institutional structures that influence the realm of possible redescriptions for contemporary woman.[38] Might not woman be especially subject to the limitations of identifications determined by, for example, the American welfare state? And even while refusing to make an invidious distinction between appearance and reality "in favour of a distinction between beliefs which serve some purposes and beliefs which serve other purposes — for example, the purposes of one group and those of another," might we not still wish to contest that the playing field upon which such groups confront each other is not one of equality but one permeated with the differential effects of power?[39] After all, are critics like Fraser not correct in thinking that some of our cultural institutions and social practices do have more power in the fashioning of names than others? Although Rorty might provide a convincing explanation of how language comes to shape our thoughts about ourselves — a position, borrowed from Wilfred Sellars, that he calls psychological nominalism — he nonetheless fails to provide any account of how such social practices and personal thoughts have come to interact.

Interestingly, it is also Wilfred Sellars who appears to recognize the sociological failings present in Rorty's oscillating philosophical stance, when he writes, "one seems forced to choose between the picture of an elephant which rests on a tortoise (what supports the tortoise?) and the picture of a great Hegelian serpent of knowledge with its tail in its mouth (where does it begin?)." Dissatisfied with both of the options available, Sellars concludes that "neither will do."[40] So might there be another route through the philosophical minefield of history and metaphysics? Ian Hacking believes there is. Calling attention to Rorty's own reliance on the historical influence of Descartes for his subsequent explanation of the dominance of a particular style of philosophical reasoning — that is, one preoccupied with the search for foundations — Hacking wonders whether "perhaps Richard Rorty's *Philosophy and the Mirror of Nature*, with its central doctrine of 'conversation,' will some day seem as linguistic a philosophy as the analysis emanating from Oxford a generation or two ago."[41] For although Rorty's linguistic stance is the result of a historicist approach to the practice of philosophy, Rorty has failed to recognize that a historicist approach to other cultural and social practices may yet reveal the durability of other historically specific styles of reasoning and naming.

This persistence is what leads Ian Hacking to assert a "literal belief in the creation of phenomena, [which] shows why the objects of the sciences, although brought into being at moments of time, are not historically constituted."[42] What *is* historically constituted is the way we use such objects and how we come to describe them — but not the objects themselves. Hacking makes a vital distinction between what he calls "making things up" and "making people up."[43] Thus, Hacking does not so much deny Rorty's attempt to create a community of liberals; rather, he calls attention to the historically persistent presence of certain phenomena whose existence, although lacking ahistorical philosophical foundations, nevertheless has an effect on the *practical* possibilities for creating a "community of free enquiry and open encounter." It is in this sense, then, that the practical existence of institutions and mentalities can place very real limitations on the ability of Rorty's project of antifoundational redescription to engender the kind of societal change for which he argues.[44]

The Limits of Self-Redescription

While not claiming to reveal any ahistorical truths, Hacking proposes that an inquiry into the history of certain practices, rather than simply into the history of modern philosophy, may just provide novel interpretations of how certain social practices have come to dictate the human and institutional parameters for the possibility of redescription in the present.[45] One of Hacking's examples is the history of statistics.[46] He writes, "the bureaucracy of statistics imposes not just by creating administrative rulings but by determining classifications within which people must think of themselves and of the actions that are open to them."[47] Hacking's disagreement with Rorty is therefore not related to Rorty's claim that a new type of being can be created through a project of redescription — the very project with which Rorty has come to characterize feminism — for Hacking, too, believes that "categories of people come into existence at the same time as kinds of people come into being to fit those categories, and there is a two-way interaction between these processes."[48] However, Hacking would have to contest Rorty's extension of the new philosophical freedom created by the acceptance of the pragmatist tradition within the discipline of philosophy to the whole of society. While it would be difficult to identify limits in the creative and imaginative attempt to redescribe women in the uninhibited realm of language, critics like Nancy Fraser may well have a strong case for arguing that all the self-redescription in the world will not transform the governmentally mediated relationships of power within which many woman *and* men currently find themselves subject.[49]

In this particular instance, I suspect that the answer lies in the tension between Rorty's picture of *the self* as a centerless and contingent web of beliefs and desires, and his separate endorsement of the overriding desire of women to unite such contingencies into a unifying story about *oneself*.[50] In this respect, it seems appropriate to think of the writing of Marie Cardinal, whose international best-seller, *The Words to Say It*, describes her personal experience of seven years of psychoanalysis.[51] Echoing Rorty, Cardinal writes of the personal freedom that she has come to value through creating a personal vocabulary from within which she has been able to articulate what it means to be a woman. Like Rorty, however, Cardinal then goes on to extend this very personal experience of the liberating effects of language, as discovered through countless hours of therapy, to the more collective enterprise of a feminist politics. She writes, "speech is an act. Words are objects. Invisible, palpable, revealing . . . Men hermetically sealed these words, imprisoned women within them. Women must open them if they want to survive. It is an enormous, dangerous and revolutionary task that we undertake."[52]

Cardinal's writing thus makes explicit what Rorty assumes. For it is clear that Cardinal's very conception of freedom derives directly from the comparatively recent "discoveries" of psychology and psychoanalysis. That Rorty takes for granted the sense of self understood by such "psy sciences," as Nikolas Rose refers to them, says much for the cultural prevalence of the "psy effect" and little for Rorty's narrowly focused philosophical historicism. In much the same way as Hacking has come to approach the history of statistics and probability, Nikolas Rose has provided a cultural history of the sciences of "psy."[53] Like Hacking, Rose has attempted to redescribe the history of psychiatry, psychology, and psychoanalysis, so as to understand how such linguistic innovation has enabled us to think and act in new ways, to fashion a new human existence, and thus to treat ourselves and others in new and historically particular ways. In this respect, Rose does not deny the freedom that Cardinal describes and Rorty takes for granted; rather, he hopes to increase the prospects of freedom not by endorsing the practices of psy but by attempting to describe the manner in which such practices have become central to the government of human conduct in advanced liberal democracies.[54] He suggests that

the subjectifying effects of psy are not simply a matter of the symbolic violence of a particular meaning system: language is structured
into variegated relations which grant powers to some and delimit the
powers of others, which enable some to judge and some to be judged,
some to cure and some to be cured, some to speak truth and others to
acknowledge its authority and embrace it, aspire to it or submit to it.
And if, in our vernacular speech, we think of ourselves in psy terms,
we do so only through the relations we have established with this truth
regime: for we each play our own part, as parents, teachers, partners,
lovers, consumers and sufferers, in these contemporary psychological
machinations of the self.[55]

From this historicist perspective, we might profitably view both
Rorty and Cardinal as principally concerned with the creative freedom
and individual agency possible within a psychological and thus self-
contained conception of the self, at the expense of the very public languages, practices, and techniques that have come to constitute such a
psychological understanding of personal agency in the first place. Freedom might therefore be redescribed in terms that neither privilege the
psychological agency of the modern self nor underestimate the political
relationships of power with which such selves are inextricably woven.
What is more, we should be sensitive to the employment of contemporary Western techniques of self-understanding and government when
we attempt to describe or approach non-Western subjects, such as the
Maya of Chiapas. International relations could therefore benefit from a
distinction already proposed in sociology — that is, a distinction between
"freedom as a formula of resistance and freedom as a formula of power."[56]
Thus, the ubiquity of freedom as presented in both the expansion of the
"free market" and the "free world" may come to be understood as con-
taining certain ethical and political costs. These costs might be better
approached from an internal and "untimely meditation" upon our contemporary practices of freedom — freedom understood as constituted
economically, psychologically, and therefore, inextricably socially.

Prescribing such an "untimely meditation" within the practices of liberal democracy thus recalls the philosopher Friedrich Nietzsche, who
first suggested that history might fulfill such a "political" task.[57] For
such histories, in their attempt to redescribe our contemporary practices of freedom, hope to create new opportunities for future understandings, understandings that might herald a time when women and
men may have greater freedom from the current truths within which

they often unhappily find themselves subject. The acknowledged inheritor of this philosophical and political approach to history is, of course, Michel Foucault. It was Foucault, after all, who not only refused to take for granted the liberal democratic culture from within which he too worked, but also sought to understand the nature of such a Western liberal culture in terms of a history of government, control, and freedom.

Identity — Governmentalized, not Stylized

Many of Michel Foucault's books can be read as historical stories about how different types of people were "made up." He can be viewed as providing genealogical accounts of how different historical practices led to the creation or construction of different historical subjectivities.[58] In his own words, "my objective . . . has been to create a history of the different modes by which, in our culture, human beings are made subjects."[59] Concentrating on the prison, the hospital, and the mental institution, much of Foucault's early work attempted to investigate or "interrogate" the workings of such locales from the perspective of how they objectivized their subjects. By focusing on the criminal, the sick, and the mentally ill, Foucault sought to reveal societies' implicit understandings of the legal, the healthy, and the sane. In this way, Foucault approached knowledge in a highly historicized and contextualized manner, and in particular, he attempted to underline the complicated relationship between knowledge and power. Like Nietzsche, Foucault sought to question the "will to truth," and he named his own brand of non-eschatological and non-edifying historiography "genealogy."[60]

Genealogy, he wrote, is best considered "a form of history which can account for the constitution of knowledges, discourse, domains of objects etc. . . . , without having to make reference to a subject which is either transcendental in relation to the field of events or runs in its empty sameness throughout the course of history."[61] Because Foucault is antiessentialist in his conception of "the subject," his project has not been concerned with finding out who we "really are"; rather, he has attempted to study the processes, both institutional and historical, that have both made us the way we are today and made it possible for us to conceive of ourselves in such historically and socially particular ways in the present. As Ian Hacking notes, "just as there was no pure madness, no thing-in-itself, so there is no pure subject, no 'I' or 'me' prior to the forms of description and action appropriate to a person."[62]

The Foucauldian genealogical method therefore propounds what

Hacking calls an "extreme nominalism: nothing, not even the ways I can describe myself, is either this or that but history made it so."[63] But this is not to revert to a historicized Kantian idealism whereby language alone constitutes human practice and social reality. Rather, the relationship between human thought and action is best understood as closer to Wittgenstein's reading of the self-language nexus. It was Wittgenstein who called attention to a way of acting, a form of life, that lies at the bottom of a language game, recalling the existence of a very concrete subjectivity within the discourses and practices that make its articulation possible. "By this he meant that although language games lack rational foundations they do have practical foundations: they are grounded by being woven into human activity and practices."[64] However, the historical process within which new language games or discourses constitute social beings is perhaps not best described as a process of "weaving," for as Foucault reminds us, such practices have historically emerged in something closer to the form of a war than that of a language: relations of power, not relations of meaning. Genealogy can therefore be construed as a strategy that engages with the political power of knowledge, not by "emancipating truth from every system of power, but by detaching the power of truth from the forms of hegemony, social, economic and cultural, within which it operates at the present time."[65]

In his later work, however, Foucault began to pay greater attention to a second aspect of subjectivity; as he explains, "there are two meanings of *subject*: subject to someone else by control and dependence, *and* tied to his own identity by a conscience or self-knowledge. Both meanings suggest a form of power which subjugates and makes subject to."[66] In addition to this, Foucault also began not only to outline a more general connection between the individual subject and particular instances of governmental power but to argue for a more comprehensive reunderstanding of the emergence and success of the modern Western state in its capacity to order and exercise power over whole populations and societies. In a series of lectures at the Collège de France between 1978 and 1979, he began to articulate these new analyses under the rubric of "governmental rationality" or, more often than not, under his own neologism, "governmentality."[67]

Foucault sought to chart a transformation in political thought during the Middle Ages that moved away from an often ill-defined domain of application traditionally linked to a monarch, the church, or a particular community, and toward a new modern domain of power, the governmental state. It was with reflection on reason of state — known in early modern Europe as Cameralism, or the "science of police," as Colin Gordon explains—that for the first time political thought consciously attempted to "postulate the rationality of government as something specific, intrinsic and autonomously proper to the state; reason of state is *par excellence* a reason different from the general divine and natural ordering of the cosmos."[68] As Foucault himself said, during his 1979 Tanner Lectures on the topic, "the doctrine of reason of state attempted to define how the principles and methods of state government differed, say, from the way God governed the world, the father his family, or a superior his community."[69]

Central to such a transformation in political thought, however, and key to its possible realization as a rationality of government, was of course the concomitant arrival of new practices. Foucault explains, "the art of governing, characteristic of reason of state, is intimately bound up with the development of what was then called either political *statistics*, or *arithmetic*; that is, the knowledge of different states' respective forces. Such knowledge was indispensable for correct government."[70] Later Foucault would connect up such new practices, alongside modern medicine and science, in the articulation of what he called a "biopolitics."[71] This new type of politics has been defined by Colin Gordon as "the phenomenon whereby the individual and collective life of human populations, or even the human species, becomes an explicit object of practices of government."[72] Clearly, such an analysis poses the question of whether there is, as Gordon puts it, "a latent eugenic totalitarianism or state racism" present within such a historical development.

When Foucault defines the aim of the modern art of government, or state rationality, as "to develop those elements constitutive of individuals' lives in such a way that their development also fosters that of the strength of the state," he suggests as much.[73] However, the principal contribution of Foucault is to identify not only a totalizing project at work in the modern art of government but also an individualizing aspect.[74] In this second vector of modern government, Foucault recalls his earlier identification of a dual conception of subjectivity as both power imposed upon a subject and power imposed upon oneself by oneself—this is what Foucault referred to as "techniques of the self." In his final works, Foucault would attempt to provide a history of such techniques, seeking to build an ethics of the self from a consideration of premodern concerns with "self-forming activity" (*practique de soi*) and early Greek notions of a "care of the self" (*epimeleia heautou*).[75]

Before promoting any new Foucauldian concept of ethics, however, it remains necessary to further explore Foucault's archaeology of modern governmental rule. New techniques of self-government could, after all, only be employed in light of an understanding of existing techniques and, in particular, how such techniques combine with political power. The uncovering of such self-knowledge is, Foucault admits, no easy task. "What makes the analysis of the techniques of the self difficult is two things. First, the techniques of the self do not require the same material apparatus as the production of objects; therefore they are often *invisible* techniques. Second, they are frequently linked to the techniques for the direction of others. For example, if we take educational institutions, we realise that one is managing others and teaching them to manage themselves."[76] Just as with the more sophisticated method of psychoanalysis to which I alluded earlier in respect of the claims of Rorty's feminist freedom, Foucault reminds us that the pursuit of a neutral, ahistorical or a-cultural language of freedom is a metaphysical one, and that even what we consider to be our current exercise of liberty is deeply enmeshed with our current exercise of power. Once again, though, Foucault recalls that "there is no power without potential refusal or revolt."[77]

Putting the Problem First

Governmentality as a concept that combines the micropolitics of individuals with the macropolitics of states would seem to suggest an alternative means of study that overcomes many of the state-centered and reductionist problems of the realist approach in international relations. Furthermore, as the process of governmentality is not necessarily linked to one particular state, but rather to the process of government that traverses the people and institutions of a particular territory, the benefits of adopting a Foucauldian methodology, even in the loose formation elaborated above, appear considerable in light of the current international dimension to national rule. In one of his last interviews, Foucault even suggests the possibility of extracting a method from his considerable body of work. In respect of my own preoccupation with the Zapatista conflict in Mexico, his words seem especially poignant. He suggests that a research project might move forward by "taking the forms of resistance against different forms of power as a starting point. To use another metaphor, it consists of using this resistance as a chemical catalyst so as to bring to light power relations, locate their position, find out their point of application and the methods used. Rather than analysing power from the point of view of its internal rationality, it consists of analysing power relations through the antagonism of strategies."[78]

The utility or otherwise of such a method depends, of course, upon what one is trying to study. However, assuming international relations (the subject) or international relations (the world of relations among states) to be one's basis must remain problematic. If we continue to hold to the antifoundational ethnocentrism of philosophers such as Richard Rorty, the "we" of international relations appears to refer to a community of liberal scholars. Michel Foucault was acutely aware of this issue, and, in what is thought to be his last interview prior to his death in 1984, he reacts directly to this missing Rortian element in what he then referred to as his problematization of politics.

> Richard Rorty points out that in these analyses I do not appeal to any "we"—to any of those "we's" whose consensus, whose values, whose traditions constitute the framework for a thought and define the conditions in which it can be validated. But the problem is, precisely, to decide if it is actually suitable to place oneself within a "we" in order to assert the principles one recognises and the values one accepts; or if it is not, rather, necessary to make the future formation of a "we" possible, by elaborating the question. Because it seems to me that the "we" must not be previous to the question; it can only be the result—the necessary temporary result—of the question as it is posed in the new terms in which one formulates it.[79]

Perhaps, then, in light of this theoretical introduction, it is now possible to recognize how in taking seriously both the challenge of anti-foundationalist thought and the difficulty of extracting a methodology from such thought, it became necessary to consider the constitution of knowledge in a discipline like international relations only to forego it in the end, or rather, to step beyond it. When seeking to excavate something of the lived realities that international relations as a discipline has for so long excluded, thinkers like Richard Rorty, while demonstrating compelling critiques of the creation and conduct of knowledge within the Western social sciences, prove disenabling when approaching human political subjects who to a very large extent live outside of such academic contexts.

Thus, the move to a Foucauldian method arises not simply out of any idiosyncratic choice but (with the help of Ian Hacking) because the later Foucault refuses the givens of disciplinary dictate and instead concerns himself with historically situated questions or problematiques that overflow the boundaries of anything we might neatly define as IR, sociology, politics, history, or philosophical inquiry. This study therefore takes inspiration from such a Foucauldian method and places the Maya Indian at the heart of a historical exegesis that seeks to provide a novel perspective from within which to consider the current "problem" of Indian rebellion in the modern Mexican nation-state.

Overview

The book will therefore commence with an excavation of the means by which the Maya Indian first became an object of Western political and cultural analysis, tracing a path from the first "discovery" through to the recognized establishment of a colonial system in the Americas. The second chapter will focus upon the transformation in colonial government that began under the Bourbon administration of the late eighteenth century and led to the eventual independence of Mexico and the creation of a liberal republic. The third chapter discusses and describes the implications in terms of policy and practice and recounts the rebellious reaction such governmental modernization provoked. Chapter 4 will lead us into the twentieth century, when Mexico first founded the corporatist and clientist system of government characteristic of the one-party state. At each step, I attempt to return to the historical experience of the Maya Indians of Chiapas to consider how transformations in governmentality effected transformations in political subjectivity at the local level. Chapter 5 will bring us up to the current neoliberal stage of governmental rule, and chapter 6 will describe the nature of the Indian rebellion that it currently confronts. Finally, in the conclusion, I will offer some implications for the future of Mexico and the nature of Indian-state politics in light of the historical account I have outlined. Throughout the narrative, I will tackle in a less explicit manner many of the points explicitly raised in this introduction, and once again in the conclusion, on the basis of such a historical analysis, I will return to theoretical issues.

ONE

Maps of the Mind

Spanish Conquest and the Indian Soul

*Victoria nulla est,
Quam quae confessos animo quoque subjugat
hostes.*
[There is no victory unless you subjugate
the minds of the enemy and make them
admit defeat.]

—CLAUDIAN, *DE SEXTO CONSULTA HONORII* [1]

Colonial Cartography

On March 4, 1493, the Genoan Christopher Columbus wrote to his royal Spanish sponsors announcing the discovery of the Americas:

> Most powerful sovereigns: all of Christendom should hold great celebrations, and especially God's Church, for the finding of such a multitude of friendly peoples, which with very little effort will be converted to our Holy Faith, and so many lands filled with so many goods very necessary to us in which all Christians will have comfort and profits, all of which was unknown nor did anyone speak of it except in fables.[2]

Columbus' characterization of the available knowledge concerning the possible existence of the Indies as "fables" was in actuality somewhat disingenuous. Believing, as he did, that he had in fact found a westward route to the Orient, Columbus had based many of his calculations on the freshly recovered second-century AD *Geography* of Claudius Ptolemy.[3] Unknown in the West during the Middle Ages, the work of Ptolemy was translated into Latin early in the fifteenth century by the humanist Jacopo d'Angelo. By the mid to late fifteenth century, editions of the *Geography* including colorful maps had become widespread throughout Renaissance Europe. It was a text that inspired Leonardo da Vinci in his attempts to provide a map of the human body as much as it did Columbus in his attempts to chart a westward passage to China.[4] While Ptolemy's maps, or rather their Byzantine renderings, were certainly considered authoritative, they were by no means considered beyond revision, for at their margins lay the two words most irresistible to the inquisitive explorer: terra incognita (see figure 1.3).[5]

What was to be found in such "unknown land" had been a favorite topic for many a fevered imagination since ancient Greece. It had been a tradition within Greek culture from the fifth century BC onward to write about the customs and institutions of neighboring peoples. These reports, best exemplified in the works of Herodotus and Ctesias, often moved from simple descriptions of barbarous non-Greek civilizations to more colorful tales of monsters and marvels that lurked at the known world's edge (see figures 1.1 and 1.2).[6] Later, the elder Pliny in his encyclopedic *Natural History* would list these monstrous beings who populated the marginal spaces unfamiliar to mankind: cyclopes, men with horns, men with heads of dogs, men with their heads beneath their shoulders, men with one large foot under whose shade they could rest in the desert sun. Although such classical sources of anthropomorphic surrealism found graphic pictorial illustration in the medieval era, it was their renewed and popular currency during the Renaissance that nurtured Columbus's already aroused and expectant disposition.[7]

It should come as no surprise, therefore, that while Columbus asserted that the islands he discovered were "densely populated with the best people under the sun," who "have neither ill-will nor treachery," his confidence in his capacity to understand the native language also allowed him to state that on other parts of the same islands there existed tribes in which "everyone is born with a tail." Furthermore, "he understood also that far from there there were men with one eye, and others with dogs' heads."[8] The power of expectation was so strong that it only allowed of minor adjustment, as exemplified in a recollection of one of Columbus's companions: "the day before, when the Admiral went to the Rio de Oro, he said that he saw three mermaids who rose very high from the sea, but they were not as beautiful as they are painted, for they had something masculine in the countenance."[9] And perhaps inevitably, Columbus also confirmed the existence of that being most other to the European imaginaire, the cannibal—for the admiral had "heard said" that the island of Quaris "was inhabited by a people who are regarded in all the islands as very fierce and who eat human flesh."[10] Nonetheless, while the *mentalité* of the explorer was clearly predisposed to encounter the marvelous and monstrous of classical cartography,

FIGURE 1.1 Illustration from the *Nuremberg Chronicle*, 1493. Copyright © University of Glasgow Library. Courtesy of Glasgow University Library, Department of Special Collections.

there were arguably other, more potent and durable desires that had an equal if not more prominent presence on the mental map with which Columbus navigated this "unknown land."[11]

The European Renaissance, after all, was a moment not simply of expanded knowledge but of competing knowledges. The very means of knowing, the very methods for encountering the "truth," had both multiplied and in many cases metamorphosed, as the combination of rediscovered Greek and Latin texts animated what often already lay dormant in the canonical tomes of the period. Figures such as the Dominican friar Savonarola, who took issue with the decadence of the new aesthetic of Botticelli, or fellow Dominican Giordano Bruno, who turned to occultist and hermetic texts, provide examples of an era that was marked more by its mystical, religious, and scholarly experimentation than by its epistemological orthodoxy. The belief in, and propagation of, such complex onto-theological cosmologies could by no means be reduced to the proliferation of "fables," a fact made only too patent by Savonarola and Bruno's executions. It is in this light, therefore, that we should interpret John Phelan's claim that "Columbus' frame of mind belonged to a Spiritual Franciscan tradition."[12] For while Columbus was most certainly a man of the Renaissance, an important product of the Renaissance was the desire to reform the church, a desire frequently informed and energized by the apocryphal writings of the Middle Ages. Columbus's invocation of the twelfth-century monk Joachim di Fiore, often regarded as the archprophet of the Apocalypse, should therefore be seen as revealing of a further and more primary motivation behind his desire to conquer the Indies. As history appeared to be nearing its climax, and as the discovery of the New World was thus seen to play an important role in the end of the old, "Columbus consciously sought to surround himself with the magic aura that over the centuries had enveloped the name of Joachim by proclaiming himself the Joachimite Messiah."[13]

It is with this sociohistorical context in mind that we might profitably return to Columbus's letter to the Spanish sovereigns and look beyond a seemingly rhetorical stance, toward a more profound location of discovery within an eschatological and spiritual narrative that can also provide us with some clues as to the essentially ambivalent relationship Columbus had toward the Indian. He writes, "Our Lord, who is the light and strength of all those who seek to do good and makes them victorious in deeds that seem impossible, wished to ordain that I should find, and was to find, gold and mines and spicery and innumerable peoples."[14] That discovery should be understood by Columbus as an act of divine providence, with himself chosen as the Lord's earthly receptacle, explains his apparent oscillation between an Indian only too unblemished by sin or vice and one whom the western European mind might even have difficulty including within its own species. Equipped with a mental matrix that included the necessity to encounter wealth (gold) and peoples (Indians), Columbus never viewed his mission as simply one of exploration. Terra incognita was, after all, approached with the burdensome desire of fulfillment rather than the always already questionable open-mindedness of discovery. Souls *had* to be saved, religious campaigns *had* to be financed, and Renaissance-nurtured intellects *had* to be accommodated — that is to say, the question of the "reality" discovered by Columbus had less to do with some fifteenth-century, communicated empiricism and more to do with the imposing of colonial limits upon what could convincingly be counted as the "real."

That Columbus's very first undertaking upon contact with the New World should consist in what Tzvetan Todorov calls "an act of extended nomination" is certainly revealing of the colonial mindset. Even though it may now seem preposterous to expect an ideal of free and open inquiry to have regulated the explorer's initial encounters, the juridical-textual pronouncement that accompanied Columbus's first footsteps on Indian soil nevertheless says much about the grounds of legitimacy under which the discoverer deemed himself subject. "Before the eyes of the doubtless perplexed Indians, and without paying them the least attention, Columbus ordered a deed of possession to be drawn up. 'He called upon them to bear faith and witness that he, before all men, was taking possession of the said island — as in fact he then took possession of it — in the name of the King and Queen, his Sovereigns. . . .'"[15] The islands did, of course, have their own indigenous names, yet as with the Indians themselves, the act of inquiry was never about the expansion of the knowable but about the act of nominal location within the realms of the already known. Even before the question of slavery had become an issue, "Columbus's behaviour implies that he does not grant the Indians the right to have their own will, that he judges them, in short, as living objects."[16]

While Columbus is in many ways representative of his era, and in other ways exceptional to it, we should be wary of assuming that his means of coming to terms with and locating the ambiguous Indian other within his own mental map were the same means and methods of appropriation and absorption adopted by his European Renaissance culture.

Insightful as they are, his letters and journals, rather than providing stable answers, in fact contributed to an already smoldering Renaissance anxiety, one that with the widespread circulation of colonial literature was to become increasingly pronounced.

Charting the Modern Mentality: Europe's Other Heading

"American natives were not usually regarded as true persons," writes Aldo Scaglione.[17] All the same, their discovery provoked disquiet rather than confidence within the European self because "in the contradictory and confused situation of the travelers' reports at the very beginning of literature on America, one finds a central underlying question: what is human nature?"[18]

It was a question that in Renaissance Europe no longer commanded a wholly orthodox response. While European culture was still dominantly Christian, within this culture already lay the seeds for a new conception of self whose conscious unfolding would necessarily lead to reform in politics, religion, and society. The pace of this reform, its content, and its consequences would vary as northern Europe came to embrace Lutheran Protestantism and the southern countries experienced the effects of an internal reform most commonly referred to as the Counter-Reformation. The two conflicting religious reformations, both spiritual and political in their nature, would in turn lead to the birth of an alternative conception of selfhood, one that is traditionally identified as the "modern self." The emergence of this modern self, the dualistic being of Cartesian design whose mind functions apart from its body, whose emotions run contrary to its rationale, whose soul will soon become the object of a new science, is, alongside that of its practical Galilean bedfellow, considered the founding moment in a standard modernist narrative that explains how we have come to arrive in the modern world we inhabit today.

In opposition to this standard account of modernity, Stephen Toulmin proposes a "revised narrative."[19] Rather than view the Renaissance simply as a transitional period between the medieval and the modern, Toulmin suggests that it is within this period itself that we can identify the birth of an antecedent modernist mentality, one that will later be overshadowed by the Cartesian creation, but one that nonetheless will remain present even if not dominant throughout our modern genesis. This is to suggest that modernity has what Toulmin calls "twin trajectories": the first beginning with the humanists of the Renaissance and the second emerging from the rationalist thought of the seventeenth century.[20] It is probably best to make clear at this stage that the humanism of sixteenth- and seventeenth-century Europe had little in common with the contemporary and predominantly North American idea of a "secular humanism." In contrast, Renaissance humanism — and its concomitant, the academic field of the humanities — first took hold within church-governed Catholic universities. So profound, in fact, was the amalgam between church and scholar that it would be more accurate, as for example Myron Gilmore suggests, to highlight the broadly theological nexus from within which humanism took form with the prefix "Christian." "The reality behind the term 'Christian humanist,'" writes Gilmore, "covers a wide range of accommodation between Christian and classical ideas, but even the broadest interpretation of the humanist position cannot obscure the basic assumption which distinguished the generation of which Erasmus was the leader."[21] It was an assumption, continues Gilmore, that came to express itself through the "most basic hope" that each humanist might witness "the more complete realization of the form of Christianity in which he believed."[22]

That humanist scholarship should provide the intellectual foundations upon which calls for church reform were based needs some explaining. While Europeans of the quattrocento were already familiar with the poetic scope of Dante's *Divine Comedy* and the autobiographical dogmatism of St. Augustine's *Confessions,* the novelty of these works' evocation of human life as lived history was curtailed by their more conscious invocation of an ailing medieval Christian order.[23] The real contribution of the recovered classical texts of the Renaissance was their multiplication of the possible orders within which man might exist. Whether the texts were Platonic or Epicurean, as in the case of Lucretius's poem, *De rerum natura,* their insertion within the broadly Christian schemata of the Renaissance did little to bolster the unity of the church and much to contest the dominance of any single religious interpretation. Although much of Greek and Latin learning had already been available to medieval scholars, the uniqueness of the Renaissance lay primarily in the rediscovery of ancient learning in *all* its variety and diversity of form.

While the foundations of modern political thought can be traced to the recovery of Aristotle's *Politics,*[24] it was only in combination with the later translation of both the *Ethics* and the *Rhetoric* that an Aristotelian sense of the "circumstantial" came to permeate Renaissance reflection.[25] In a cumulative manner, as the novelty of classical drama, poetry, and history began to be absorbed, the Renaissance came to experience the

Oe homib⁹ diuerſaꝛ formaꝛ dicit Pli.li.vij.
ca.ij.Et Aug.li.rvi.ꝺe ci.ꝺei.ca.viij.Et Iſi
ꝺorus Ethi.li.ri.ca.iij. oía q̃ ſequútur in in
dia. Cenocephali homines ſunt canina capita habé
tes cū latratu loquútur aucupio viuút. vt dicit Pli.
qui omnes veſtiútur pellibus animaliú.
Cicoples in India vnū oculum hñt in fronte ſup na
ſum bñ ſolas ferarū carnes comedūt. Ideo agnoſa
gite vocátur ſupꝛa naſomonas confineſqʒ illoꝛū ho
mines eſſe:vtriuſqʒ nature inter ſe viabus coeútes.
Calliphanes tradit Areſtotiles adijcit ꝺextram mā
mam ijs virilem leuam mulichꝛem eſſe quo herma
froꝺitas appellamus.
ferunt certi ab oꝛiétis pte intima eſſe homines ſine
naribus:facie plana eq̃li totius coꝛpis planicie. Ali
os ſupioꝛe labꝛo oꝛbas.alios ſine linguis ⁊ alijs cō
creta oꝛa eſſe modico foꝛamine calamis auenaꝛ po
tū hauriétes.
Item homines habentes labiū inferius.ita magnū
vt totam faciem contegant labio ꝺoꝛmientes.
Item alij ſine linguis nutu loq̃ntes ſiue motu vt mo
nachi.
Pannothi in ſcithia aures tam magnas hñt. vt con
tegant totum coꝛpus.
Artabatte in ethiopia pꝛni ambulát vt pecoꝛa. ⁊ ali
qui viuút p annos.rl.que̅ uullus ſupgreditur.
Satiri homúciones ſunt aduncis naribus coꝛnua i
fronhbus hñt ⁊ capꝛaꝛ pedibus ſimiles quale̅ in ſo
litudine ſanctus Antonius abbas vidit.
In ethiopia occidentali ſunt vnipedes vno pede la
tiſſimo tam veloces vt beſtias inſequantur.
In Scithia Ipopedes ſunt humanā foꝛmaꝛ eq̃nos
pedes habentes.
In affrica familias quaſdā effaſcinātiū Iſigonus ⁊
ꝑemphodoꝛus tradit quaꝛ laudatōne intereat p̃
bata.areſcāt arboꝛes: emoꝛiátur infantes. eſſe eiuſ
dem generis in tribalis et illirijs adijcit Iſogon⁹ q̃
viſu quoqʒ effaſtinent iratis pꝛapue oculis: quod eo
rū malū facilius ſentire puberes notabil⁹ eſſe ꝙ pu
pillas binas in oculis ſingulis habeant.
Item boies.v.cubitoꝛ nūqʒ infirmi vſqʒ ad moꝛtes
Hec ois ſcribit Pli.Aug.Iſi. Pꝛeterea legit i geſti
Alexādri ꝙ i india ſunt alij boies ſex man⁹ bñtes.
Ite̅ boies nudi ⁊ piloſi in flumine moꝛātes.
Ite̅ boies manib⁹ ⁊ pedib⁹ ſex ꝺigitos habentes.
ite̅ apothami i aq̃s moꝛantes medij boies ⁊ medij
caballi.
Item mulieres cū barbis vſqʒ ad pect⁹ ꝑ capite pla
no ſine crinibus.
In ethiopia occidẽtali ſūt ethiopeſ.iiij.oc̄los bñtes
In Eripia ſunt boies foꝛmoſi ⁊ collo gruino cā ro
ſtris aialium boimqʒ effigies mōſtriferas circa exire
unitates gigni mime̅ mirū. Artifici ad foꝛmāda coꝛ
poꝛa effigieſqʒ celandas mobilitate ignea.
Antipodes āt cꝭ.i.boies a 3ria pte terreui ſol oꝛit
qñ occidit nob aduerſa pedib⁹ ñris caleare veſtigia
nulla rōe crededū e vt ait Aug.16.ꝺe ci.ꝺei.c.9. In
gēs tñ ꝓ pug̃ lꝛaꝛ ꝓtraqʒ vulgi opioeꝛ circūfundi ter
re boies vndiqʒ coueriliſqʒ iter ſe pedib⁹ ſtare et cñet
ſilem ce̅ celi vtice. Ac ſili mō ꝓ q̃cūqʒ pte mediā cal
cari. Cur āt ñ ꝺecidāt:mureſ ⁊ illi nos ñ vecidere: nā
eſm repugnāte:⁊ quo cadat negatevt poſſint cadere.
Ñā ſic ignis ſedes nō e niſi i ignib⁹:aq̃ꝛū niſi i aq̃s.
ſpūs niſi in ſpū. Ita terre arcentibus cūctis niſi in ſe
locus non eſt.

FIGURE 1.2 Illustration from the *Nuremberg Chronicle*, 1493. Copyright ©
University of Glasgow Library. Courtesy of Glasgow University Library,
Department of Special Collections.

perhaps inevitable broadening of the image of man as he was presented in ancient literature. The humanists, as the principal promoters of this new literature, were no longer willing, nor able, to honestly restrict the interpretation of such texts to the limiting dynamic of a medieval moral casuistry. The fallibility of man, once described merely as a means to better contrast mortal beings with the divine, now became a realm of interest explored as revealing in its own right. As the human beings who populated these diverse texts could no longer be reduced to a saint/sinner duality, the constitution of humanity began to seem increasingly various, and the ambiguity of what might be considered a virtuous action or a vicious one, although most famously reflected upon in the writings of Machiavelli, also found itself manifest in narratives that were not so clearly "political."[26]

For the humanists, the textual "rebirth" of classical learning led to one enduring conclusion: that perfect human self-knowledge can never be realized.[27] "Human modesty alone (they argued) should teach reflective Christians how limited is their ability to reach unquestioned Truth or unqualified Certainty over all matters of doctrine."[28] Foremost among such humanists, and the undisputed intellectual leader in urging Christian reform, was Netherlander Desiderius Erasmus (ca. 1467–1536). In his satirical masterpiece *The Praise of Folly* (1511), Erasmus took issue with both the worldly corruption of theologians, monks, and prelates and the superstitious excesses they encouraged, in particular the cult of the saints. This entertaining and irreverent satire built upon a Christian humanist philosophy already partially elaborated in his earlier *Handbook of a Christian Knight* (usually known from its Latin title as the *Enchiridion*, 1501). In the *Enchiridion*, Erasmus argued "that the true essence of religion is an *inner* spiritual experience which then must be expressed in a life of constant struggle against worldliness in which the believer is sustained by God's gifts of prayer and knowledge."[29] His program for church reform embodied an opposition to what he viewed as spiritually vacuous and even harmful ceremonial acts of piety and an open disdain for the dogmatism of scholastic theologians, which stood in stark contrast to his own humanistic "Philosophy of Christ."[30] While Erasmus remained faithful to Catholicism throughout his life, his texts were soon to be placed on the *Index of Prohibited Books*, and his brand of humanistic reform came to be viewed as laying the preparatory steps for the more radical heresies being propagated in Germany by Martin Luther.

Although Erasmus made a public break with Luther in 1524, he could not help but oppose the condemnation of Luther outright, for in such a condemnation he also recognized the threat to a central tenet of humanist learning, one that valued education and religious instruction for their openness to reform and possible future interpretation. In this regard, and especially in light of the religious schism that resulted from the Protestant Reformation, it becomes clear that Luther is not the true intellectual heir of Erasmus. Rather, it is the work of the Frenchman Michel de Montaigne (1533–1592) that best represents the culmination of the humanist tradition. Furthermore, it is also through Montaigne that we can best recognize the contribution of the American Indian "other" to the creation of a truly modern European mentality.

The limits to the universal applicability of Christianity, or even its primary use as a means of judging or engaging with an alien culture, were all provocatively articulated in the *Essays* of Montaigne.[31] As a witness to the destruction wrought by the religious wars within his native France, Montaigne was able to recognize the dangers inherent in the universal application of any cultural or theological mindset that owed its political dominance simply to the contingencies and verities of a local and specific historical trajectory. Although he remained a Catholic until his death, Montaigne's faith was such that he did not shirk the logical implications of his intellectual stance. Thus, his brand of cultural relativism did not represent a spiritual abyss in need of metaphysical content so much as an acceptance of the natural limitations of context when making claims to certitude. To put it another way, Montaigne's modernism lay precisely in his capacity to confront the inherent and inescapable limits of knowledge, a position that holds great affinity with what, in more contemporary parlance, has come to be known as ethnocentrism.[32] Central to the construction of such a distinctly modern mentality was not only Montaigne's experience of the Thirty Years' War but also his particular experience of an often disdainful European reception of the discovery of the American Indian. His reaction to aristocratic and "educated" society's belittling of native culture was characteristic: "It is no lie to say that these men are indeed savages — by our standards; for either they must be or we must be: there is an amazing gulf between their souls and ours."[33]

As to the grounds upon which savagery and civilization might find their basis, Montaigne was unequivocal.

> I find (from what has been told me) that there is nothing savage or barbarous about those peoples, but that every man calls barbarous anything he is not accustomed to; it is indeed the case that we have no

other criterion of truth or right-reason than the example and form of the opinions and customs of our own country. There we always find the perfect religion, the perfect polity, the most developed and perfect way of doing anything! Those 'savages' are only wild in the sense that we call fruits wild when they are produced by Nature in her ordinary course: whereas it is fruit which we have artificially perverted and misled from the common order which we ought to call savage.[34]

Written in the final decades of the sixteenth century, Montaigne's essays resonate in a manner that is peculiarly modern. His approach to the reports emanating from the Americas is more akin to contemporary anthropological method than to Columbus's Renaissance medievalism.[35] Nonetheless, both Montaigne and Columbus did hold a shared belief in the value of experience. While I hope to have already shown the cultural limits present in Columbus's personal experience of discovery, this should not obscure the fact that Montaigne's far more self-reflective championing of experience as a means to knowledge set him, along with Columbus, in stark opposition to the methodology of abstract philosophical meditation that was to follow and outdo, in both political and intellectual terms, the significant merit of their own personal achievements.[36]

Why Europe could not accommodate the plurality of interpretation that was the logical conclusion of humanist thought and allow itself to explore the philosophical and ethical consequences of such beliefs is the subject of Toulmin's *Cosmopolis: The Hidden Agenda of Modernity.* For Toulmin, Europe's need for certainty, method, and objectivity over modesty, experience, and subjectivity rests upon the historical context of the religious conflict under which the Western polities of the sixteenth and seventeenth centuries labored. The dominance of scientific thought and the manner in which Descartes' quest for certainty and method was embraced represent for Toulmin the means by which Europe hoped to transcend its religious difficulties, investing its faith in rationality instead of religion, and constructing a modern Europe based on the nexus of science and politics rather than that of science and religion.[37] Such a transition to modernity has come to overshadow the ethical and philosophical gains present in Renaissance humanist thought and, to a large extent, has hidden the existence of an antecedent modernist mentality that was capable of living with uncertainty and difference.[38]

In light of this analysis, and in an effort to provide a historical basis for a claim that stands without one, we might turn our European ears to another European voice and agree that, yes, the discovery of the

Americas was a unique historical moment, one that, as Todorov writes, both "heralds and establishes our present identity; even if every date that permits us to separate any two periods is arbitrary, none is more suitable, in order to mark the beginning of the modern era, than the year 1492, the year Columbus crossed the Atlantic Ocean." This is so, Todorov continues, because

> we are all the direct descendants of Columbus, it is with him that our genealogy begins, insofar as the word beginning has a meaning. Since 1492 we live, as Las Casas would claim, in a time, "so new and like no other." Since that date the world has shrunk, "the world is small" as Columbus himself will peremptorily declare; men have discovered the totality of which they are a part, whereas hitherto they formed a part without a whole.[39]

New World Medievalism

While the literature surrounding the discovery of the American Indian can be seen to have had a salutary effect on the creation of a modern European mentality,[40] over in the actual, physical New World of the Americas, the Europe of the Middle Ages continued to sing what was to be quite a lengthy and often barbaric swan song.[41]

That this should have been the case was due in large part to the fact that the Americas were governed not by Europe in general but by Spain, and Spain, unlike many of its European neighbors, was still very much in the grip of a medieval system of theocratic monarchical rule. Despite the spreading influence of the Italian quattrocento Renaissance, Spain's colonial practice was more deeply colored by recent historical experience than by scholastic innovation. After all, the year 1492 saw not only Columbus's discovery of the Americas but also the final and comprehensive expulsion of the Moors from southern Spain, after nearly eight centuries of Islamic occupation. In light of the positive result of the economic and religious tactics employed during this campaign of reconquest, it should come as no surprise that when the Spanish conquistadors sought a model upon which to base their American colonial project, they looked little farther than Spain itself.[42]

Centuries of conflict with the Moors had somewhat inevitably led to a mental conflation of religious and racial superiority among Spanish Christians. Such an attitude, although most clearly evident in the symbolism and rhetoric surrounding the Spanish military campaigns, was also present throughout Spanish society as a consequence of the widespread practice of enslaving captured Moors and employing them in private service. Furthermore, in an attempt to consolidate recaptured land, the Spanish Crown permitted feudal concessions of estates, jurisdiction, and labor to those *señores* (local bosses) who could guarantee a workable degree of regional stability. As such areas were initially devoid of any rule of law, they also became popular refuges for bandits and fugitives, a state of affairs that led originally free peasants to entrust themselves to the protection of a local señor.[43] In this respect, therefore, and well before the discovery of the New World, fifteenth-century Spain had already shown that an individual with a combination of military prowess, paternalism, religious and racial arrogance, and most importantly, an adventurous and opportunistic disposition could reap large rewards. And while peninsular Spanish rule was never actually founded on a system of feuds/feudalities, the three pillars of early Spanish colonial practice — slavery, the *encomienda,* and the *repartimiento* — have all nonetheless been recognized as "vigorous offspring of the feudal system."[44]

From the very outset, therefore, it should be recognized that the techniques and strategies employed by the first colonists on their recently discovered subjects were by no means endorsed by royal decree. In fact, "it was quite unthinkable that the Spanish monarchs would tolerate in the New World an institution (like the *encomienda*) which would disperse their newly won authority"; but the feudal tradition was so deeply rooted in the conquistadors — including the buccaneering architect of conquest himself, Hernán Cortés — that they "tended to usurp all authority, grab land and treasure, to exploit Indian labor, and, in general, to conduct themselves like conquerors of all times."[45] The principal character of Spanish colonial rule was therefore marked more by conflict than by coherence. On one side lay the often naked ambitions of the original colonists; on the other, the spiritual zeal of the missionaries who accompanied them; and in between stood the Spanish Crown, which attempted to combine religious with economic concerns while at the same time maintaining a tight grip on the institutional tethers that constituted colonial control. Of course, at the center of all these competing forces was the real subject of colonial conflict: the Indian.

Spanish Theologians and the Indian Soul

It was a friar of the Dominican order (those charged with the care of the royal Spanish conscience) who, in 1511, incensed by the deplorable conditions and treatment of Indian slaves on the island of Hispaniola, first articulated the theological parameters of the Spanish sixteenth-century Indian problematique. Although he directed his sermon principally at the colonists within his own parish, Father Antonio de Montesino might as well have been addressing his royal monarchs when he beseeched his congregation to "tell me, by what right or justice do you keep these Indians in cruel servitude? On what authority have you waged a detestable war against these people, who dwelt quietly and peacefully on their own land? . . . Are these not men? Have they not rational souls?"[46]

As much as Father Montesino's inquiries may ring purely rhetorical to our modernist ears, the question of whether Indians did or did not, in fact, possess "rational souls" was paramount for establishing a legitimate basis on which Hispanic colonial actions and aspirations might be founded. The very conjunction of rationality with possession of a soul should also alert us to the continued and deep-seated entanglement of Christianity with societal and political understandings of selfhood, legitimacy, and conduct. In a pre-Cartesian configuration of the human "I," rationality found itself entwined with spirituality, or rather, the parameters of rationality were not to be dislocated from the innate divinity that was present within every one of God's human creatures. This presence of the divine within the self was the nature of the human soul, and thus, the recognition of what was necessary for the soul's nourishment was the nature of rationality. Suicide, madness, and self-abuse were therefore acts both against God and against nature. That such acts could happen at all was only explicable through the persistence of a medieval duality of good and evil, one that also allowed for demonic acts and spiritual possession. The Catholic clergy thus necessarily played an important role both as mediators and interpreters. Priests, and in particular confessors, were those who could make sense of the often torturous paths between the inner world of the human soul and the all-encompassing universe of the Christian transcendental.[47] If Indians did not in fact possess souls, and therefore were not actually men at all, they neither needed nor deserved priestly ministration. The nature of legitimate colonial conduct thus rested on the proof or refutation of the existence of an Indian soul.

While the dissemination of Father Montesino's sermon alone may very well have resulted in the creation of the 1512 Laws of Burgos, it was only after the conquest had fully penetrated mainland America, and regular reports of Indian culture and conquistador conduct began to filter back to Spain, that the issue of Indian status came to fully occupy royal attention. Thus it was in 1550 that King Charles V ordered the suspension of all expeditions to America while a junta of foremost theologians, jurists, and officials was convoked in the royal capital of Valladolid. The junta took the form of a debate, with Dominican friar Bartolomé de Las Casas and Italian-educated Juan Gines de Sepúlveda invited to argue the theological and juridical cases for and against Indian slavery in the Spanish colonial territories.

To a significant degree, the philosophical grounds on which such a debate was to be conducted, and thus the very terms within which the problematique of the Indian was itself to be phrased and interpreted, had already been dictated by the unquestionable historical predominance of Aristotle's *Politics* as *the* textual prism through which a society and its members could come to be judged. Employing what was known as John Mair's *via moderna* interpretation of the *Politics*, Sepúlveda was able to offer both a defense of the conquest as a "just war" and a defense of Indian slavery as "just by nature."[48] Clearly championing the cause of the colonists, Sepúlveda hoped to convince the council that American natives were in fact barbarians. For according to Aristotle, "among barbarians no distinction is made between women and slaves, because there is no natural ruler among them: they are a community of slaves, male and female."[49] Since they lacked knowledge of the Christian faith, Sepúlveda argued, Indian society could not be considered a genuine political society. Indian barbarity was, after all, a consequence of God's willing the Indians to "lack reason." Indians may have possessed souls, but they were not rational souls; and while they might well be considered perpetual minors needing instruction, they were certainly not men. Presenting a justification for colonial conduct that sanctioned both enslavement and evangelical instruction, Sepúlveda attempted to articulate nothing less than a new ethics of empire for Spain's sovereign rulers.

In contrast, and in language guaranteed to infuriate contemporary sensitivities, Bartolomé de Las Casas contended "that all the people of the world are men." Rejecting Sepúlveda's via moderna interpretation of Aristotle, Las Casas instead took up fellow Dominican Francisco de Vitoria's Thomist claim that there was an equal capacity in all men, whether or not they were Christian, to establish their own political societies.[50] This universal reasoning capacity (which allowed for the possible exception of a few extreme barbarians) negated Sepúlveda's claim that the Indians were in fact natural slaves, while still allowing

Las Casas to promote the legality of peacefully instructing the Indian in the word of God.[51] Illustrating his argument with descriptions of the impressive scale and organization of the Aztec and Mayan cities and temples still being discovered in the Americas, Las Casas made comparisons with the recognized achievements of Egyptian culture and even Greece itself. Although he could not claim that the Indians were Christians, Las Casas was still able to make a case for the rational coherence of Indian beliefs and societal structure that, while permitting peaceful evangelical instruction, in no way legitimized colonial enslavement and, more profoundly, even questioned the very right of Spanish sovereignty in the Americas.

The Valladolid conference, for Anthony Grafton, has come to represent "the most profound debate waged in modern times within a conquering power about the justice of its own actions."[52] J. A. Fernández-Santamaría however, suggests an interpretation that is altogether more refined. With the demise of Queen Isabel and the discovery of the Americas, sixteenth-century Spain experienced what he terms a "double constitutional crisis."[53] The fact that the Valladolid debate never resulted in a collective verdict should therefore be understood as reflective of Spanish uncertainty and fear in the face of the constitutional implications that the acceptance of any one interpretation would provoke. As Fernández-Santamaría writes, "torn between two versions of Empire, Castile was forced to depart from the straight road leading toward the modern state and steer an ambiguous middle course."[54]

The results of such equivocation and Castile's slow surrender to "the beckoning charm of the Imperial idea" were threefold. First, and thirty years prior to the Valladolid junta, Castile experienced the *comunero* revolt, an uprising that in its challenge to absolutist monarchical rule has been viewed by some as an early precursor to the modern revolutions that would later reinvent French sovereignty.[55] Second, the clarification of what might be considered legitimate colonial conduct was to be endlessly postponed, with debate and interpretation of the New Laws, post-Valladolid, being focused within the capricious corridors of the newly conceived colonial institution, the Council of the Indies. The third dimension of the Spanish sixteenth-century predicament was not so much a result as a result *and* a cause of the Iberian dilemma. It was what Fernández-Santamaría calls Spain's third crisis: "a crisis of the mind, of the spirit, and of the soul."[56]

Immediately following the Valladolid debate came the Council of

Trent. It was an event that finally put an end to the plasticity of an Erasmian Christian humanism, and in its place saw the institution of a rejuvenated and fiercely dogmatic Tridentine Catholicism. With the Inquisition as its key weapon, Trent sought to enforce an orthodoxy of Christian reason that could not otherwise be agreed upon.[57] Las Casas, in his confrontation with Sepúlveda, and through his application of what was known as the *via antiqua* as practiced by his Thomist allies and mentors, thus illustrated much that was central to the dynamics of the conflict between the Reformation and the orthodox Counter-Reformation that continued to trouble the hearts and souls of Europeans for some time.[58] In this respect, it is possible to regard the Indian problematique as an unsettling presence that came to illuminate rival theological and political positions in a manner unprecedented in both Hispanic and colonial history.

Thus, while the Europe of the fifteenth and sixteenth centuries buzzed with the dynamics of the new problematic of political governance, the Mexican subjects of the same period, experiencing the pioneering attempts of a foreign power to impose a semblance of imperial order, encountered institutions and modes of rule that, if anything, were even more medieval than those that were being practiced in peninsular Spain. This contrast was due in part to the simple fact of isolation, a fact that only accentuated what might be thought of as an already significant natural gulf between the concept of the modern state and the lived experience of the modern citizen. In the colonies Spain thus reverted to a system of rule that strongly embodied the medieval conjunction among subject, ruler, and Lord God Almighty. While this reversion was clearly a particular reaction to the Renaissance of classical scholarship that was to lay the foundations of modern political thought, the concept of the modern state, which was to be the end result of that historically peculiar period of intellectual intensity, was to be neither an idea nor a practical reality in the lives of Spain's newest subjects for some three hundred years to come.[59]

In the meantime, colonial conduct concerned itself with the creation of the ideal colonial subject form, that is, a royal subject who would be docile, God-fearing, and hard working. To achieve this aim, however, would involve an attempt to transplant and replicate the fragile marriage between the transcendental and the temporal that provided a questionable legitimacy for Spanish monarchical rule. It was a process that not only involved the re-creation of Spanish institutions in the New World but, more acutely, involved an attempt to enfold a Spanish

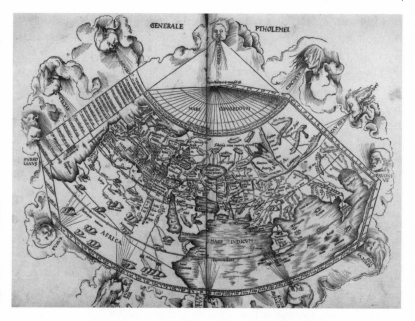

FIGURE 1.3 Mapamundi from Ptolemy, 1513. Copyright © University of Glasgow Library. Courtesy of Glasgow University Library, Department of Special Collections.

self-understanding into the opaque recesses of the newly discovered Indian soul.

Spanish Colonial Practice and the Indian Soul

The very first institution that made any attempt to mold the desired colonial subject was the *encomienda*. First established by Columbus and modified by Ovando on the Antilles, the encomienda gave individual Spaniards the right to demand labor and tribute from the Indians assigned to them and also turned them into de facto administrators, responsible for the control and welfare of these Indians.[60] The administration and exploitation of Indian labor was, however, principally conducted through the already-existing local Indian authorities, the *caciques*.[61] Relying in the main on the continuance of the local Indian economy and political structure, the encomienda system neverthe-less — and in this respect it was at least true to the Crown's "double purpose" — also entailed the position of *doctrinero*. This post was to be filled by a peninsular priest charged with ministering to and instructing the Indians. Being essentially under the encomendero's patronage, a doctrinero, unlike the mendicant orders, rarely found the liturgy to be in conflict with the materialistic demands of the encomendero.

The encomienda system was to be reformed many times throughout colonial history until eventually transforming completely into the highly productive *hacienda* of the eighteenth century. One major reason behind its early reform was the sheer number of Indian fatalities that resulted from the arrival of unknown diseases. It was a concomitant to Spanish conquest that is often overlooked: as exploration of the Americas became ever more comprehensive, the ferocious impact of alien illness reached epidemic proportions. Confronted with the enormity of Indian mortalities, and thus with the depletion of many Indian settlements and the geographical isolation of those that remained, the Spaniards decided to enact the *reducción*. This was a process whereby Indians were gathered into larger towns, "where conditions favoured the combination of Indian and Spanish patterns of behaviour and belief, thus making possible the development of a new 'Indian' society, which was not traditional but was still essentially indigenous."[62]

Resettling the Indian populace was not always easy. In one famous incident, the original Chiapaneco Indians, after putting up months of fierce resistance to the Spanish, eventually found themselves cornered in a sacred site high above the Sumidero canyon. Realizing that defeat was imminent, the Indians, women and children included, chose to throw themselves off the canyon's thousand-meter precipice rather than submit to the new colonial order.[63] While the encomienda no longer held the institutional primacy it had previously, the colonists' key concern with the control of Indian labor merely found itself manifest in the form of the *repartimiento* instead.[64] If an encomendero required manual labor, he would have to approach the government-sanctioned officers who now controlled the distribution of Indian labor. In the past it had at least been possible to pay encomenderos tribute with local products grown and harvested by the Indians themselves; under the repartimiento, however, the caciques were obligated under threat of severe sanction to supply laborers even at the times when the agricultural cycle necessitated their presence in the fields. Essentially forced, although at times paid a nominal fee, the indigenous workers constructed town buildings and private houses, worked fields, chopped wood, and looked after the colonists' livestock. As the obligation to pay tribute to the encomenderos was still applicable, the indigenous experience of the reducción and the repartimiento was one of an ever-increasing and ever-more-intrusive disruption of traditional life.

To describe this relationship between the Spaniard and the Indian as oppressive, although not incorrect, would be insufficient. Colonial institutions were never simply methods of exploitation. Urbanizing the Indians and employing them in tasks alien to the local indigenous economy always also involved an ancillary project of Hispanicization.[65] The external order of each settlement—with a central square or *zócalo*, dominated on one side by an impressively sized village church, on the other sides by council and official buildings, with side streets tailoring off in a symmetrical manner to produce a town of progressively smaller squares or blocks—represented not only a victory for the Spanish colonists but a lesson for the Indians in the superiority of the Spanish rationale. The obligatory labor that the Indian provided for the construction of these settlements was, in and of itself, meant to impart a sense of Hispanic civilization. The involvement in the creation of an external colonial order would, it was believed, instill an equally orderly, and Spanish, internal rationale in the native populace.[66]

Indigenous culture—admired for its textiles and pottery and little else—would simply have been dismissed by the colonists as inferior and savage were it not for the vital religious component within the Spanish colonial project. While the secular conquistadors restricted themselves to the strategies of brute force, implied threat, and sanction in their (never very successful) attempts to make peninsular peasants out of American Indians, the Catholic clergy, in contrast, arrived with a sophisticated array of techniques and methods designed to convert the natives to the "one true faith." Apart from the ineffectual preaching of the doctrinero of the encomienda, the religious fervor and spiritual zeal that manifested themselves throughout New Spain were the result of the additional presence of the religious orders—Franciscans, Dominicans, Augustinians, and later Jesuits. Armed with a combination of rituals, symbols, structures, doctrines, and pedagogical and proselytization techniques, the mendicant orders set about creating what they believed would be "the best Christians in the world."[67]

Conscious of the growing challenges to Christian orthodoxy in Europe, Catholic missionaries viewed the colonies as a unique and historic opportunity to realize the full potential within the Christian liturgy. Initially the Indians were looked upon as the ideal subjects to receive religious instruction and direction. In the eyes of Don Vasco de Quiroga, bishop of Michoacán, "such a people—so gentle, so new, so unspoiled and so like soft wax—were ready for whatever one might care to make of them."[68] Friar Gerónimo de Mendieta went further and even referred to the indigenous as *genus angelicum,* "of angelic descent," describing in his chronicles "the male and female Indians, especially old people and more women than men, who are so simple and have such pure souls that they do not know how to sin; so much so that confessors find themselves more embarrassed with some of them than with other great sinners, searching for some kind of sinful material for which they can give them the benefit of absolution."[69] For friars like Torbio de Benavente Motolinia, a member of the Franciscan order (one of the first mendicant orders to reach the New World, with one of the largest delegations there), there was no doubt that the Indians were literally "those poor and meek people with whom God wants to fill his house."[70]

It did not take very long, however, before the "innocent, pure and docile" Indian of the initial encounter was transformed into a far more ambiguous and untrustworthy being capable of all manner of evil and deviousness. In an extract from a pastoral letter dated 1698, the bishop of Chiapas, Don Fray Francisco Nuñez de La Vega, illustrates the nature of clerical concern:

> there are some bad Christians of both sexes who, bewildered in the darkness of error, have left the true light, and forgetting the solemn promise that they made to God when baptised, . . . are not ashamed to return to the school of the Devil that they had previously renounced, occupying themselves in trickery, divinations, witchcraft, curses, charms, spells, and sorcery and other superstitions to gain knowledge of the divine and the future. In all the provinces of New Spain these are the ones they call Nagualistas.[71]

A *nagual,* approximates La Vega, is like a guardian angel. It can take many forms: a star, an element, a bird, a fish, or a wild beast. The role of the *nagualista* is therefore one of divination: through invoking the Mayan ritual calendar, "these infernal teachers called the wise Indians of the villages, . . . some . . . without knowing how to read or write," can, from memory, identify the nagaul that corresponds to a person's date of birth.[72]

Nagualismo, for more contemporary students of Mayan culture, is considered "the system of practices and magic beliefs that are based upon the concept of the *nagual.*"[73] The nagual is in this instance described as being "naturally incorporeal or *invisible*, of 'pure air' as the natives say."[74] A nagual is thus generally understood as a spirit that, while not visible to the human eye, is capable of not only seeing but listening, protecting, or attacking, depending the situation, and its most feared power is its capacity to "eat" the souls of those who have seriously erred. According to Jacinto de La Serna, writing circa 1650, the significance of the term *nagual* or *nahual* stems from the Mexica Indian verb *nahualtin*, which means "to hide oneself," "to cover oneself," or "to disguise oneself."[75] In contrast to La Vega's interpretation, not everyone can possess a nagual. Only those who have reached a particular level within a group's politico-religious structure, or who have joined those referred to as the elders (*los ancianos*), have the capacity to become an "owner" of such a powerful spirit.[76]

Unlike Bernardino de Sahagún, La Vega has been accused of confusing the concept of a nagual with that of the *tona* or *tonalli*. It is the tona that is identified according to the date of birth, and following the ritual calendar, each person can be ascribed a particular spiritual guardian, what La Vega termed a "guardian angel." It is the tona that accompanies an individual for the whole of his or her life, and it is to those wise men who understand the ways of time that one appeals when there appears to be some disharmony between one's animal spirit or soul and one's human spirit or soul.[77] While belief in the nagual and the tona, although often described in different terms, is still widespread throughout Mexico and Guatemala, contemporary manifestations of these belief systems are most often considered remnants of the more complex and sophisticated Mayan politico-religious beliefs that permeated Mesoamerican culture from the first century AD onward.[78] In addition to Sahagún's account of tonalismo, as communicated to him by the Aztecs of the mid-sixteenth century, we are also able to consult two sacred Mayan texts of the same period that suggest that Indian beliefs in co-essences and calculable destiny were not only pervasive but profound.

The sixteenth-century *Popol Vuh*, also known as the Mayan book of the dawn of life, "tells the story of the emergence of light in the darkness, from primordial glimmers to brilliant dawns, and from rainstorms as black as night to days so clear the very ends of the earth can be seen."[79] The book itself was, and is, described by the Maya as an *ilb'al*, a "seeing instrument" or a "place to see."[80] While the *Popol Vuh* hails from the Quiche highlands of Guatemala, its textual contemporary, the *Chilam Balam*, comes from the Yucatan coast of Mexico.

Both texts survived as a consequence of an early process of translation. It was common practice for Franciscan missionaries to educate the young sons of Maya nobles in the European script, as a means not only to assist in the Christianization of the Indian populace but also to facilitate its regulation. The conquering clergy initially admired the fact that the Maya already possessed a hieroglyphic system of their own. Soon, however (but not before some of the Maya manuscripts had been translated into the European script—hence the survival of the *Popol Vuh* and the books of *Chilam Balam*), missionary curiosity metamorphosed into inquisitorial zeal. On one particularly tragic occasion in 1562, Diego de Landa, afterward bishop of Yucatan, burned twenty-seven hieroglyphic manuscripts at the now-famous auto-da-fé in Mani. Ralph Roys, anthropologist and translator of the books of *Chilam Balam*, explains that "although many Spaniards severely criticized him for this, there is little doubt that other missionaries followed his example whenever they had the opportunity."[81]

Pedro Sánchez de Aguilar, writing seventy years after the initial conquest, recalls the content of the destroyed Mayan manuscripts: "In these they painted in colors the count of their years, the wars, epidemics, hurricanes, inundations, famines and other events."[82] In fact, the Mayan obsession with the recording of events and their precise dating has led one contemporary ethno-archaeologist to consider the epithet *chronovision* as a more appropriate description of the Mayan world outlook than the more common anthropological term, *cosmovision*. Ever since the first "modern" explorations, Mayan specialists have been led to conclude that, as Eric Thompson puts it, "no other people in history has had such an absorbing interest for time as the Maya, and no other culture has ever developed a philosophy embracing such an unusual subject."[83] Miguel León-Portilla, in his classic account of Mayan culture, *Time and Reality in the Thought of the Maya*, attempts to summarize the ancient Mayan chronovision:

> Theirs was the desire for knowledge but also a concern for salvation, an attempt to discover the supreme order of things. Thus they conceived their myths, they created symbols, used the zero, invented new systems to adjust and correct their computations. They became worshippers of the primordial reality, omnipresent and limitless. To harmonize with that reality was the most precious aim in life. The wisdom of their priests and sages led them to discover their place on earth, and also to spy on the mysteries of the divine rhythms of the universe.[84]

Maya civilization, as it is most commonly called, reached its peak in what is known as the classic period, which runs from the second through the ninth century AD. During this period, around the third century, the Maya invented the concept of zero, a concept that would not become known in Europe until the eighth century AD—and even then only thanks to the mathematical sophistication of Hindustani scholars. It was during the classic period that the Maya constructed the majority of their most impressive large-scale civic-religious centers. The astounding grandeur and architectural confidence that draw hundreds of thousands of visitors each year to the sacred sites of Chichén Itzá, Palenque, Tikal, and Cobán, now spread among Mexico, Guatemala, Belize, and Honduras but once united under the single banner of Maya rule, bear potent testimony to the historical achievements of indigenous culture. The Maya were unable, for reasons that are still poorly understood, to sustain this level of imperial grandeur, and from the ninth century AD until the arrival of the Spaniards in the early sixteenth century, Mayan civilization was in decline. Although this postclassic period has been defined by its move away from the large politico-religious centers that have so enchanted foreign academics and tourists alike, the "collapse of Mayan civilization," as it is sometimes dramatically described, by no means resulted in a disappearance of Mayan culture. The fact that Spanish friars were still discovering Mayan manuscripts, and the "idolatrous practices" associated with them, as late as the close of the seventeenth century[85] should alert us to the continued existence of a Mayan culture. This culture, while no longer capable of the imposing triumphs of the classic period, was certainly a major component in the perpetuation of a Mayan self-understanding whose dogged persistence was exactly the concern of Spanish clerics of the unsavory character of Bishop La Vega.

It was not long, therefore, before the religious passions excited by the virgin territory of the colonies were doused by ecclesiastical suspicions as to the sincerity of indigenous conversion. Soon the idolatrous practices of the Indians were to be found everywhere. La Vega's opinion as to the widespread nature of nagualismo was itself widely shared: "there is not one village in which it has not been introduced and their simple souls infected with the contagious pestilence of their diabolic superstition, and they are rare or very few those that have a faith with the purity of true believers, sons of the Church."[86] The bishop of Chiapas was, however, willing to forgive those lost sheep who had strayed from the path. Before one could benefit from the church's forgiveness, though, it was necessary to recognize the sinfulness of one's actions and to repent. The concept of the confessional, which Mendieta had previously found almost redundant in light of the "angelic" conduct of his own chosen flock, was soon to take on a more overtly instrumental function.

Confession, writes Serge Gruzinski, can become "an instrument for expressing Church-approved forms of individualization and guilt, eroding the traditional ties and interpersonal relations of colonized societies."[87] Through a study of manuals written specifically to facilitate the confession of Indians in New Spain, Gruzinski recognizes that confession imposes a series of fixed categories on the indigenous penitents, within which they must learn to evaluate their acts and thoughts. "These categories form a system of values that claim to be universal and leave no margin for the most minimal improvisation, since they are supported by written texts and thus protected from the hazards of oral transmission."[88] The confessional insisted that the Indian

> put aside his surroundings, his social group, the weight of his tradition, and the external forces that used to influence his behavior, such as the power of god's ire, the incantations of a witch, the envy of a neighbor or a relative, the ill-omened emanations of a sexual deviant or a transgressor of prohibitions. . . . In other words by centering on the "subject" — in the Western meaning of the word — the interrogation of the confession breaks down the ancient solidarity and social networks, as well as the physical and supernatural ties.[89]

Probing in a way that strategies such as the reducción, with their emphasis on the physical environment, could never have achieved on their own, the process of the confessional created a psychological "deterritorialization" of the Indian that should be recognized as the most radical break from the traditional indigenous context that Spanish colonialism introduced.

Advancing a conception of selfhood that involved the idea of a free will and a specifically Christian understanding of a soul, clerics instructed that the Indian, to be penitent, had to follow the ancient dictum of the Greeks: "It is very necessary first to learn what is inside your soul, which is not what it seems outwardly; know thyself. . . . The right knowledge is the knowledge of yourself."[90] This exercise of introspection cannot, however, be conducted without prior memorization. It was thus vital to first "know and remember all the sins" and then to "put your sins in order."[91] What was fundamental about such psychological operations was that they should produce the correct feelings of guilt. Confessors would therefore emphasize to the Indian the necessity "to know thyself as sinner, to cry for your sins," and to "tell your sins with feelings and crying; declare them with an abundance of tears and deep sighs."[92]

Gruzinski, better than anyone else, summarizes the profound nature of acculturation that is intrinsic to the psychological process of the Catholic confessional:

> This exercise comprehends the entire course of life, concerning itself with actions as well as "thoughts, desires, intentions." It is an attempt to master new categories, to read into past actions through the individualistic filter of the Christian ethic. That is to say, to organize such material according to a concept of "Western" time, perceived as a concatenation of causes and personalized consequences that shape the singular and irreducible trajectory of the biographical self.[93]

At the conclusion of one Indian confessional, the penitent of Juan de la Anunciación succinctly communicates the desired outcome, confiding, "I am not the one I used to be."[94]

The Indian Soul as a Smoking Mirror

Although the confessional should certainly be recognized as among the most invasive, if not *the* most invasive, of Hispanic colonial practices, it was to a very large extent atypical in terms of the degree of subject observation entailed. The majority of transplanted Catholic rituals neither involved nor permitted anything near a comparable level of clerical interference. Whether as a result of overconfidence, ambivalence, or perceived necessity, the indigenous population was often left, after an initial period of instruction, to regulate the style and to some extent the content of religious worship conducted within their own communities. In the highland villages of Chiapas, one enduring example of the creative cultural and psychic possibilities afforded by a low level of religious monitoring can be witnessed in the unorthodox manner in which the Spanish *cofradía* was absorbed.

Perhaps it should have come as no surprise to the ecclesiastical authorities that the adoption of the cofradía, or confraternity, as a means of Indian worship should have been problematic. After all, the cofradía, essentially a cooperative association of lay believers whose principal objective is the maintenance and financing of the worship of a patron saint, had been a practice of contention even within the twelfth- and thirteenth-century European society from which it hailed. It is arguable, however, that any reservations concerning the appropriateness of the brotherhoods for the Indian population were overridden by the financial requirements confronted by an economically depressed colonial church at the end of the sixteenth century.[95] The structure of the confraternities was standard: each village, with its appointed patron saint (usually the same as the community's designated Spanish name, e.g., Santa Marta), would appoint a group of men among whom the roles of *mayordomo, alférez,* and *fiscal* would be apportioned. After the *alcalde* (the village mayor), the fiscal held the most important role in the community, since it was he who, in addition to recording the number of masses, baptisms, confessions, and weddings conducted by the local parish priest, also shouldered the responsibility for recording the amounts and regularity of the community's cofradía contributions. While the economic aspect of colonial religious practice should not be underplayed, it was the opportunity afforded by even this limited degree of religious autonomy — though undoubtedly accentuated by the financial pressures associated with it — that gave the celebrations of the village patron saint an increasingly indigenous dimension.

In much the same way as the cofradías had previously been criticized in medieval Europe, it did not take long before the colonial administration and high clergy of the Spanish Audiencia of Guatemala became openly critical of this particular form of worship. Decried as an extravagance, with overly elaborate processions that created a carnival atmosphere conducive to excessive drinking and dancing, and including flags, standards, and rituals whose origins were unknown, the cofradías soon resulted in the rearticulation of the never-fully-silenced charge of idolatry.[96] During a period when the competition for the control of Indian tribute and labor was intense, the discourse of idolatry had a double function whereby it not only suggested the need for even greater religious supervision and instruction but, in doing so, also reinforced the local Dominican friars' position of power and further fortified their already considerable claim to royal support.[97] While the diversions from accepted Catholic practice remained limited — or rather, as long as the cost of their disruption was considered less troubling than the financial gain associated with their continuance — the religious and cultural space presented by the cofradía celebrations greatly contributed to the creation of what Murdo MacLeod has called "Catholicisms of the people."[98] Soon, however, this limited taste for the autonomy, and exclusiveness, of Christian worship was to grow into a desire for complete autonomy.

Early signs appeared in the preaching of a *ladino* (white) hermit who exhorted the Indians to recognize an image of the Virgin that was giving off rays of light near Zinacantán. This incident was closely followed by the appearance of the Virgin to a woman in the village of Santa Marta, and later by the "miraculous" sweating and illumination of the patron saints of Chenalhó. All of these events were dismissed as hoaxes or further examples of nagualismo by the colonial authorities. Then the appearance of the Blessed Virgin[99] to a young Indian woman in May 1712 in Cancuc heralded the start of the largest coordinated Indian resistance to colonial rule that Chiapas ever witnessed.[100]

María de la Candelaria, as the witness soon became known, was only thirteen or fourteen years old when the Virgin appeared to her in the form of a "very beautiful and very white lady." The heavenly apparition spoke to the young girl, and, as in previous instances, asked that a cross and a candle be placed in the hamlet near where she had appeared. She instructed that the villagers should first cense the site and afterwards build a chapel there so that she (the Virgin) could live among the Indians. Some time later, the local parish priest, Fray Simón de Lara, was informed of the incident. Incensed by the "dangerous" and "diabolic inventions" being promoted by the young woman, Father Lara immediately removed the cross from the now-sacred location and had María, her father, and another Indian woman whipped for their blasphemous tales. His exemplary castigations were to no avail, however, and as soon as he left the village, to which he would not be permitted to return, the Indians set about constructing the chapel exactly as divinely requested. Upon completion, as later recounted to the Spanish judiciary by a young Indian villager,

> María López [de la Candelaria] entered the chapel accompanied by the other Indian woman called Magdelena Díaz with a bundle covered with their clothing and put it behind the [hanging] mat; and they announced that Our Lady had been placed there, that she had appeared to them; and then the whole town entered the Chapel and worshipped [before] the mat counting the Rosary and crossing themselves. . . . And having proclaimed the miracle in the towns of the province, their inhabitants came to this [town], some carrying pine needles, others candles, and others alms that they gave to that Indian girl María

López, who before all the collected villagers declared, "Believe me and follow me, because now there is no tribute, nor King, nor Bishop, nor village Mayor, and now you need do no more than follow and believe this Virgin that I have behind the mat."[101]

The Virgin cult of Cancuc might well have amounted to little more than a minor lapse in colonial order were it not for the arrival of an Indian from Chenalhó who introduced himself as Sebastian Gómez de la Gloria. Gómez, armed with an image of Saint Peter, told the people of Cancuc that he had gone to heaven, where he had spoken with the Holy Trinity—the Virgin Mary, Christ, and the apostle Saint Peter—who had given him the authority to appoint literate Indians to serve as priests in all the towns of the province.[102] Furthermore, he had been advised that "there was no longer King, tributes, *alcalde mayor*, nor officials of Ciudad Real [now San Cristóbal] because they had come to free them from all this; and that there was no longer Bishop nor priest because all this was now ended; and that they should now enjoy their ancient liberty; and that they should have only *vicarios* [vicars] and parish priests of their own who would administer all sacraments."[103]

Not only was Gómez's peculiar story embraced as further proof of the divine legitimation of the Virgin cult, but in addition, his intimate knowledge of the structure and practice of the Spanish colonial church provided the movement with a novel yet familiar means with which to organize and sustain an already heightened climate of indigenous resistance. Soon the majority of villages in the highland districts of Chiapas received the following summons:

> Jesus, Mary and Joseph—Honorable alcaldes of . . . (such and such a town)—I, the Virgin, who has descended to this sinful world call you in the name of Our Lady of the Rosary and order you to come to this town of Cancuc and to bring with you all the silver of your churches, and the ornaments and bells, with all the coffers and drums and all the cofradía books and funds because there is no longer God, nor King, and thus come at once, because otherwise you will be punished if you do not respond to my summons and God's, Ciudad Real of Cancuc.— The Blessed Virgin María de la Cruz.[104]

In the end, some thirty-two villages responded, or were forced to respond,[105] and although the result was the creation of what some have referred to as a "Tzeltal Republic," there were in fact a near-equal number of Tzotzil and Chol Indian villages involved in the rebellion.[106] In a revealing display of symbolic and rhetorical appropriation, the rebel center of Cancuc was renamed Ciudad Real Cancuc de Nueva España; Hueytiupán became Guatemala; the Spaniards themselves were denigrated as "Jews"; and the actual Ciudad Real (Royal City, now San Cristóbal) became Jerusalem (see figure 3.2).[107] The rebel Indian forces also adopted a consciously Spanish model of military organization, with ranks of *capitanes generales* (captains general), *capitanes* (captains), *sargentos* (sergeants), *cabos* (corporals), and *soldados* (soldiers); and the soldiers considered themselves, in their own words, "soldiers of the Virgin."[108] This reversal of the colonial nomenclature took on a more chilling aspect when, after the first attack on a Spanish settlement, the rebels disposed of all the non-Indian adult males and took the captured women and children to Cancuc, where they were called "Indians" and compelled to serve the native authorities as domestics.[109] However, it is the ordination of an indigenous clergy (including priests, vicars, and bishops), the plans to crown an Indian king,[110] and ultimately the mimicry and promotion of an indigenized version of a Spanish theocracy that bear most potent testimony to the deep-seated and persistent Indian desire to maintain an active role between the realms of the supernatural and the temporal, whose recent Spanish colonization provoked such an unusual form of violent contestation.[111]

Although the rebellion was eventually suppressed after some four months of fighting, the memory of its occurrence remained strong in the minds of colonists and their historical successors. But rather than a reassessment of the nature of colonial conduct, the longest-lasting effect of the Cancuc rebellion was a suspicion that the Indian mind and soul might not be as transparent as once imagined, a preoccupation that even today strikes fear into the hearts of the non-Indian population of Chiapas.

Conclusion

So who, or what, in fact was the colonial Indian? In this chapter, I hope to have at least outlined some of the contours of a colonial Indian subjectivity. I have shown that at various moments, and often simultaneously, the Indian has been understood as a monster, a noble savage, a natural slave, the possessor of a rational soul, a tribute payer, the best Christian in the world, a nagualista, an idolater, and finally a rebel. The question of identity thus becomes a far more difficult question to answer; in fact,

I hope that at every moment when *the* Indian has been defined in this chapter, it has been an instance more revealing of the different matrices of power in which the colonized Indian subject found himself, or herself, enmeshed, than of any "true" identity per se. This attempt to locate the Indian subject within the maps of the colonial mind has thus been an attempt to uncover the relationship between colonial identifications and colonial practice. It has been an endeavor to show that the idea of a Spanish colonial oppressor — and equally, that of a completely defeated Indian colonial subject — is not only insufficient as a description of the colonial encounter but also conceals the more slippery element that lies at the heart of any human subjectivity: freedom.[112]

To suggest that the colonial Indian subject was essentially free might sound peculiar, even ridiculous. However, only if we insist on an understanding of freedom that is entirely untrammeled by circumstance, that reifies the freedom to act over and above the freedom to think, and fails to interrogate the unpredictable relationship between the two, shall we wish to deny that the colonial Indian subject was free in some sense. Freedom in this understanding is therefore a relationship enmeshed within society, culture, and the self. As such, it is inevitably a deeply contextualized relationship, both personal and public, to such an extent that it is highly questionable whether it can even be usefully articulated outside of the concrete parameters from which it draws content. It is for this reason that I have approached the question of Indian subjectivity historically, for in doing so it hopefully becomes possible to at least discern the sociocultural limits imposed upon the Indian subject. A historical narrative that attempts to describe this nexus of power, while never being totally transparent, nonetheless affords us the opportunity to consider the limits of freedom inscribed upon the Indian subject and to question the nature and rationale of such a peculiarly circumscribed freedom, as well as the subsequent ethics that it provokes.

Anthropologists, for their own disciplinary reasons, have often wished to impose a fixed definition on the nature of Indian subjectivity as it was at the end of the colonial period and even as it is now. Most commonly, they have referred to it as a case of religious syncretism.[113] The Indian in these analyses created a new culture — a meaning system or, as it is most often called, a cosmology — by merging or meshing the traditional Maya culture and the conquering Hispanic culture.[114] While this type of analysis is not particularly wrong, it is particularly facile. To say that the Indians adopted some aspects of Spanish culture and rejected others, maintained some pre-Hispanic beliefs and lost others, is in fact not to say a great deal. What's more, in concluding that the end result of the colonial encounter was the creation of a syncretic indigenous culture, many anthropologists sidestep the more demanding and interesting questions of how such syncretisms came about. They fail to tackle difficult questions like, in whose name or upon whose authority were culture, village life, and individual relations with the self and others legitimized or, at minimum, made possible? In fact to be satisfied with the description "religious syncretism" is to depoliticize and decontextualize the complex power relations, both Indian and non-Indian, that infused the creation of "new" indigenous identities.[115]

Since Chiapas is currently home to some nine different Indian ethnic groups, and the category Maya itself refers to a further seventeen different ethnic groups spread throughout southern Mexico, Guatemala, Belize, and Honduras,[116] we might even wonder what purpose such a broadly encompassing term as *Indian* or (in this case) *Maya Indian* performs. The purpose is, of course, political, both within the disciplines of anthropology, Maya studies, and history,[117] and within the practices, rationales, and mindsets of those who govern the Maya Indians of colonial and modern-day Mexico. As we will see later, the two realms are by no means distinct, and the politics of representation should never be considered confined solely to the domain of public policy. To speak and write of the Indian is therefore to engage in this politics of representation, and thus to involve oneself in the intercultural, intersubjective, and international relations of the political subject. This study thus hopes to intervene in the most contemporary and violent manifestation of the politics of identity, as raised by the Zapatista Army of National Liberation (EZLN) and their continued contestation of the latest modern Mexican governmentality. But before doing so, it must first ask the difficult question, in what exactly does modernity consist? And in particular, in what way has a Mexican modernity impacted upon the limited freedom of the Indian subject?

In this chapter, I hope to have made some initial steps toward answering such questions. I hope to have demonstrated that (1) Europe and the Spanish colonies had different modernist historical trajectories; (2) European modernity has within its own dynamic humanist traditions worth recovering, which in some way are indebted to the discovery of the American Indian "other"; and (3) the Indians experienced the govern-mentality of an ailing (Counter-Reformation) Spanish medievalism rather than a modern European governmentality. The governmentality that the Indians experienced can best be understood not simply through a specific medieval genealogy of colonial economic and religious practice but through a particular relationship with the transcendental that, if not classically medieval, was certainly premodern. In fact, it is probably important to remind the reader that the Spanish never completely dismissed the Indians' beliefs as primitive or ineffectual. It has been shown that throughout the colonial period, the colonists took the Indian capacity to commune with the transcendental very seriously, even while viewing such practices as demonic and idolatrous rather than merely as those of another, alternative religious and spiritual culture. But the existence and power of the supernatural was never itself doubted.[118] Finally, I hope to have shown that the colonial Indian as a subject of study presented neither a tabula rasa awaiting colonial inscription nor a cultural entity predetermined by traditional pre-Hispanic practice. Rather, the Indian soul, so precious to clerical desire, seems to be that very intangible absence upon which the various historical masks of Indian identity have come to be placed. Ambiguous until the end, Indian identity has only ever been fixed when caught in the powerful nexus of discourse and authority. And as long as the Christian dynamic was part of Spanish rule, the unpredictable nature of the colonial encounter, probably best understood as a process of mimesis and alterity, at least allowed for the conscious acknowledgement of the spiritual realm as something active and pertinent to the government of the temporal. However, as we shall soon see, this was an understanding fast declining as the new modernist visions of a postcolonial government began to impose themselves on a less-than-malleable Mexican Indian subject.

TWO

Enlightenment Legacies

Colonial Reform, Independence, and the Invisible Indian of the Liberal State

How shall we judge, then, from these miserable remains of a powerful people, of the degree of cultivation to which it had risen from the twelfth to the sixteenth century and of the intellectual development of which it is susceptible? If all that remained of the French or German nation were a few poor agriculturists, could we read in their features that they belonged to nations which had produced a Descartes and Clairaut, a Kepler and a Leibniz?

—ALEXANDER VON HUMBOLDT, *POLITICAL ESSAY ON THE KINGDOM OF NEW SPAIN*

With these words, written in 1808, some three hundred years after the initial discovery, the famous scientific explorer Alexander von Humboldt conveys the profound sense of loss and mortification that his encounter with the American Indian provoked. Although dedicated, like the writings of Columbus before him, to His Catholic Majesty of mainland Spain, Humboldt's *Political Essay on the Kingdom of New Spain* makes no secret of the reason behind the native population's current condition of degradation. But although he attributes blame directly to the "European ferocity" and "Christian fanaticism" that characterized much of early colonial rule, Humboldt's humane recognition of the Indian plight should nevertheless be recognized as more reflective of the significant transformations in European intellectual life than revealing of any true arrival at an understanding of the colonial Indian predicament per se. As the epigraph to this chapter reveals, Humboldt's rhetorical references to "intellectual development," Descartes, Kepler, and other Enlightenment luminaries epitomize the early modern European gaze with which he, as one of Europe's greatest scientific minds, came to rediscover the elusive marvels of a once-more-new world.[1]

Landing first at Cumana, on July 16, 1799, Humboldt and his erstwhile companion, French botanist Aime Bonpland, began what was to be a five-year scientific adventure that would take them through Venezuela, Ecuador, Cuba, Columbia, Peru, and Mexico. Looking today at the multivolume product of their research, one cannot fail to be impressed by the painstaking descriptions and delicate illustrations of the thousands of exotic specimens of flora and fauna that the two men took such care to record. Neither can one dismiss that theirs was at times an arduous and perilous journey, one that saw the adventurers flee pirates, brave the snake-, alligator-, and mosquito-infested rivers of the Orinoco, scale the heights of Chimborazo (at 6,310 m, then thought to be the highest peak in the world), while all the time engaging in the meticulous measurement, mapping, and classification of the foreign environment that surrounded them. Their motivation, however, was unique. Even three centuries after the conquest, both Humboldt and Bonpland understood that they would be the first to objectively *know* the true nature of America. They were, after all, the self-conscious ambassadors of the European Enlightenment, which in its thirst for knowledge had literally begun to remap the contours of the known universe.

Like Columbus before him, Humboldt set about making his new world fit with the knowledge he had already embraced from the old. Unlike Columbus, however, Humboldt was armed with an impressive array of some thirty-six scientific instruments, including eudomitors, hygrometers, barometers, chronometers, inclinometers, sextants, quadrants, achromatic and reflective telescopes, a cyanometer, and a Ramsden graphometer. Emboldened this time with the certitude of scientific method, Humboldt, like his Renaissance predecessor, confronted the strange and made it familiar: he forced unknown flowers and plants into classical botanical and biological categories; he likened peculiar rock formations to those in his native Prussia; he even understood the altitude and air pressure through comparison with data from his previous European expeditions.[2] With these novel scientific acts of naming and recording, Humboldt took what Anthony Pagden has called "cognitive possession" of his surroundings. His charting of isotherms and isolines allowed him to "dissolve in the imagination" the huge physical and cultural distances that lay between the Americas and his enlightened Europe.[3] Whereas the world had once been expanded by the discoveries of the inspired navigator, now the planet could be shrunk thanks to the detailed study of the scientist and his microscope.

Viewed by many as an early predecessor of our current understanding of the world as an ecosystem, Humboldt possessed a singular drive to achieve total scientific comprehension that spurred on his American expedition. In the words of one commentator, "he went because the entire world must be made to yield up its common laws, and Spanish America had not been adequately studied toward that end; it was part of the 'Globe as a great whole' whose relationship to the rest was unknown, and which might give new insight into the laws of the universe."[4] Nowhere can Humboldt's belief in such universal laws be more clearly witnessed than in his unfinished project, *Kosmos*. An undertaking that he himself described as that "mad fancy," *Kosmos* sought no less than to represent "in a single work the whole material world."[5] However, as systematic and focused as his lifetime quest for knowledge might now appear, Humboldt was no cold rationalist. As a contemporary and friend of both Goethe and Schiller, Humboldt was deeply influenced by the harmonious and sublime understanding of nature characteristic of early German romanticism, and it is to this aspect of his intellectual formation that we must look in order to better comprehend his approach to the American Indian.[6]

Perhaps best demonstrated by the frontispiece to his 1814 *Atlas géographique et physique des régions équinoxiales du nouveau continent* (see figure 2.1), Humboldt's romantic empathy with the American native contributed to an already well-established European tradition of the noble savage.[7] The illustration, in which a fallen Aztec warrior, surrounded by the toppled gods and ruins of the once-great Tenochtitlán, is helped up by the twin figures of Greece and Rome, represented by Minerva and Mercury, vividly captures the neoclassical values to which Humboldt subscribed. So as not to leave the reader in any doubt, below this picture he placed the caption "HUMANITAS, LITERAE, FRUGES" (Liberal Arts, Science, Agriculture). With these three words, Humboldt answered his own rhetorical question as to how Indian culture could best be judged. Since the living Indians who surrounded him showed, in his opinion, little evidence of these basic tenets of civilization, Humboldt paid them scant attention, instead preferring to investigate the already mythical achievements of the fallen Aztec past.[8]

Nonetheless, while limited in ethnographic detail, Humboldt's published volumes on Mexico remain obligatory reading for their startlingly modern style of analysis. Purposely contrasted with the mainly historical theses previously published on America, Humboldt's *Political Essay on the Kingdom of New Spain* was written in a style revealing of the new relationship between Western science and government. Guided by the Enlightenment benchmarks of utility and progress, Humboldt's essay provides not only an accurate map of the kingdom but detailed statistical data on population, health, manufacturing, commerce, agriculture, Crown revenue, and mining. Viewing New Spain as a working whole, and in a manner not at all dissimilar to contemporary World Bank

HUMANITAS. LITERÆ. FRUGES.

Plin. jun. L. VIII. Ep. 24.

FIGURE 2.1 Frontispiece of the *Atlas géographique,* from Alexander Humboldt and Aime Bonpland's *Voyage aux régions équinoxales du nouveau continent, fait dans les années 1799 à 1804,* 1813. Copyright © University of Glasgow Library. Courtesy of Glasgow University Library, Department of Special Collections.

country reports on Mexico, Humboldt was able to make science-based assessments of the progress and efficiency of the Spanish colony that were both unthought of by, and unavailable to, his intellectual precursors. Although Humboldt himself should in this regard be recognized as a unique individual representative of both a European culture and its novel modern means of encounter with America, his personal contribution was only possible with the sanction and assistance of the Hispanic colonial authorities, a body that, as we shall soon see, had already undergone what some refer to as a revolution in government.

Enlightened Despotism

While the seeds of a European modernity first began to flourish within the historically novel environment of artistic, textual, and scientific experimentation that characterized the Italian Renaissance, it is generally agreed that it was not until the advent of the Enlightenment that the European states began to undergo institutional and governmental transformations that laid the societal and practical foundations for that paradoxical entity we now call the modern European nation-state. Although the seventeenth century may well boast the 1648 Treaty of Westphalia, an undeniably pivotal moment in the creation of a Europe of "nations," the consequence and logic of this agreement centered on the institutional resolution of Reformation religious differences. Seeking to provide sovereign boundaries within which the vexed question of religion would at last remain contained, Westphalia renegotiated the relationship between church and state, finding in favor of a European peace temporarily provided by a seemingly transcendent international judicial process. For many international relations scholars, Westphalia marks *the* foundational moment of a modern international state system.

Irrespective of the dubious nature of any such historical assertion of an international system or society, our principal focus is the Mexican Indian, and it is with some confidence that we can say that the Westphalian moment had little direct effect on the Mexican experience of modernity with which we are concerned. The influence of the Enlightenment, however, was significant. With the accession of Louis XIV's grandson, Felipe V, to the Spanish throne in 1700, Spain and her colonies began to experience a transformation in the style of governance that was to be a harbinger of more radical change. Throughout the eighteenth century, beginning with Felipe V and then continued by his sons, Fernando VI and Carlos III, the Bourbon dynasty introduced a program of reform often described as a period of enlightened despotism.

Although on first reading such a description may appear to be something of a contradiction in terms, the political reality to which it applies was, in fact, just such an unusual conjunction of intellectual desire with royal necessity. On the one hand, during the early stages of the eighteenth century, the authority of the king was still seen by most as indispensable to the realization of an enlightened new world. "What was essential," writes Georges Lefebvre, "was that the despot listen to the physiocrats and philosophes, that he follow the natural laws they had discovered, that he accept the rationalist conclusions they had formulated — in short, that despotism became *enlightened*."[9] On the other hand, as monarchs throughout Europe became increasingly absolutist in reign, in large part to curb the internal conflicts provoked by the Reformation, the royal courts came increasingly to be populated by nonreligious advisors. What propelled such advice to the realm of practice, however, was the vital imperative for fiscal reform, "which may be expressed very simply as the inadequacy of traditional sources of revenue to meet the staggering costs of 'modern' warfare in the eighteenth century."[10]

The Spanish empire that Felipe V inherited at the beginning of the eighteenth century was very much an entity laboring under a financial burden — so much so that most historians refer to the seventeenth century in Spain as a period of depression, a result of the costly wars and internal rebellions faced by the Hapsburg dynasty. After the royal splendor of the sixteenth century, usually considered Spain's golden age, the seventeenth can be regarded as a "text book example of Imperial over extension."[11] Within this context, it is perhaps not surprising that the advice of the Physiocrats, considered the founders of modern political economy, and a major influence on the work of Adam Smith, should find a receptive audience among the Bourbons.[12] Finding its strongest expression in the philosophe commitment to science as the proper tool to redefine the laws of society, the predominantly secular nature of Bourbon reform should therefore be seen as broadly in keeping with the continent-wide influence of the Enlightenment on royal governance.

In this particular case, however, we find that the nature of governance undergoes a transformation, resulting in the equation, for the first time, of good government with "economic government." Michel Foucault explains the significance of this transformation:

> To govern a state will therefore mean to apply economy, to set up
> an economy at the level of the entire state, which means exercising
> towards its inhabitants, and the wealth and behaviour of each and all,
> a form of surveillance and control as attentive as that of the head of a
> family over his household and his goods.[13]

To this end the Bourbon reign defined itself by its administrative priorities rather than its judicial principles. It thus marks a clear departure from Hapsburg Spain in its practices of centralization, uniformity, and distinctive "governmentality."[14]

While in the Spanish peninsula itself such new policies were both created and introduced by a new breed of government ministers and royal bureaucrats, led by the likes of Campomanes and Floridablanca, the process of governmental transformation in the American colonies rested principally on the shoulders of one man, José de Gálvez. Although spared the obstacle of aristocratic privilege, unlike his peninsular counterparts, Gálvez confronted an administrative structure far more deeply entrenched in a modus operandi resistant to change than anything encountered in Europe. For centuries colonial bureaucrats had adopted a flexible approach, often referred to as the Hapsburg consensus, to reform and policy changes emanating from the metropolitan center that they viewed as disruptive to the colonial status quo. In a practice encapsulated in the much-employed bureaucratic expression "obedezco pero no cumplo" (I obey but do not execute), previous attempts at centralization and uniformity had inevitably found themselves reduced to the dictate and whim of a long-established hierarchy of influence and vested interest.[15] In an attempt to break such local intransigence and ensure reform, Gálvez himself embarked upon a visitation to New Spain that lasted some six years.[16]

Predictably enough, Gálvez was not well received. Ignoring Viceroy Bucareli's advice not to tinker with the delicate balance of local power elites, he set about undoing the twin strands of lay and ecclesiastical privilege that operated throughout the colony. Although long since settled in the unique manner of a colonial accommodation, the moral dispute between friar and encomendero, once so symptomatic of sixteenth-century colonial rule, now found itself displaced by a singular bureaucratic force that sought to outflank instances of both corporate and private intervention. More precisely, with the extinction of tax *fueros* and the termination of the sale of public offices, Gálvez sought to remove local Mexicans from the decision-making process and, by doing so, achieve his primary goal: the increase of royal revenue.[17]

Early in his *visita*, Gálvez encountered the ingrained corruption of the colonial office of alcalde mayor, the very agency created by the Crown in the sixteenth century to collect Indian tribute and oversee Indian labor. Even though it was prohibited by royal decrees as recently as 1687 and 1716, and explicitly attacked by the previous *visitador-general* in 1721, the abuse of the system of repartimiento had persisted, effectively functioning as a private trading monopoly benefiting both the individual alcalde mayor and the merchant financiers of Mexico City, at the expense of the native population and the Crown. While the level of exploitation varied with the level of greed and avarice particular to each alcalde mayor, the role of middleman — through whom wages, tools, seeds, and basic commodities were distributed to the Indian populace in exchange for labor, dyes, cotton, and textiles — had become a prime example of the institutionalized corruption that Gálvez sought to eradicate.[18] His plan was simple but radical: he proposed the introduction of the intendancy system.[19]

Following a system already at work in Spain, Gálvez established twelve intendancies in New Spain with the aim of completely overhauling the colonial administration, remapping the spheres of responsibility and the nature of office at district, provincial, and metropolitan levels. Alcaldes mayores would be replaced by intendants, who were to be paid on a commission basis, thus providing the foundation and incentive for a more professional approach to the task of tribute collection. So as to ensure a clean break from past practices, Gálvez also promoted the appointment of "new" men from the peninsula, effectively bypassing local creole aspirations and strengthening Crown control. With such a structure in place, Gálvez hoped to increase bureaucratic efficiency and thus generate extra revenue. First, though, tobacco, playing cards, and gunpowder were all made Crown monopolies; new taxes were introduced to extract profit from the colony's richest resource, silver mining; and with the establishment of the *comercio libre* in 1778, a new era of free trade began to challenge the dominance of the Mexico City trading houses, which in turn increased the proportion of customs and excise duties collected by the Crown's newly salaried civil servants. In all these measures Gálvez was eventually successful; his appointment as minister of the Indies on his return to Spain permitted the full realization of his reform program.[20] However, the degree of disruption to New Spanish society, both elite and Indian, should not be underestimated. Perhaps best exemplified by the Bourbon attack on the role of the church, the comprehensive nature of enlightened despotism led to the breakdown of a long-standing social accommodation that, although blatantly unequal, had nevertheless maintained a relatively high level of colonial stability for hundreds of years.

La segunda aculturación

No single act expresses more clearly the Bourbon administration's demand for absolute loyalty than the expulsion of the Jesuits from New Spain in 1767.[21] That the order for their arrest and exile was greeted by the Indians and mine workers with violent revolts in both Michoacán and the Bajío region should also tell us something of the popular religious sentiment with which Enlightenment reform took issue. Gálvez himself left little doubt about the determination of the Bourbon government when, with a cruelty rarely witnessed in the colony, he hanged 85 people, flogged 73, banished 117, and condemned 674 to prison, all for their participation in the uprisings.[22] Since the Jesuits had long been the principal educators of the American-born Spanish (or creole) elite, their expulsion could also not fail to be seen as another attack on the growth and autonomy of an educated and increasingly independent New Spanish society.

The special attention accorded to the Jesuit order should not, however, overshadow the broader renegotiation of the role of the Catholic Church as part of a more general reassessment of the potential of the colonies based solely on the new materialistic and economic governmentality of the Bourbons. For the Indians in particular, after a sustained period of recovery in both demographic and cultural terms, this new onslaught of external intervention heralded nothing less than a second wave of colonial acculturation.[23] The priest, long since accepted by the indigenous population as the sole legitimate colonial mediator between the spiritual realm and the distant yet acknowledged presence of the Spanish king, now found his role increasingly redefined to include greater control, surveillance, and discipline of his Indian parish.[24] Along with the new tax inspector, the priest was now expected to advise the Indian population to "avoid extravagant practices and the inefficient spending occasioned by their celebrations, worship of images, and cofradía" and to promote the use of "their limited resources to the improvement of their manner of dress, their diet, and their education."[25] In this last respect, the priest encountered administrative pressure to fulfill the role of teacher in a renewed campaign of "linguistic unification" that involved swapping his classes of catechism for lessons in Castilian Spanish.[26]

The Bourbon emphasis on education reflected a general Enlightenment belief in the role of schooling in the creation of a "civilized republic." However, the complicity of the hierarchy of the Catholic Church in such a project must also be recognized as an attempt to move away from popular displays of devotion and worship, and evidence of a greater emphasis on the interiorization of piety and the privatization of religious experience.[27] In Althusserian and Foucauldian terms, the weakness of the European Catholic Church at this time, after sustained challenges from science, Protestantism, and internal factions, resulted in a subversion of doctrinal purity in favor of an increased role in the normalization and discipline of the populace, as the church became, unwittingly or helplessly, an apparatus of state control. In New Spain, this combination of governmental edict with ecclesiastical conservatism created an environment within which the church-inspired practice of the Indian confraternity, or cofradía (whereby an image of the Virgin or a local saint is worshipped with a procession, music, and community celebration, as discussed in the previous chapter), once more found itself subject to colonial censure. Instead of the charges of idolatry previously raised against perceived indigenous adulteration of the ceremony, criticism of this now well-established act of Indian religiosity and sociability now revolved around questions of decency and, of course, economy.[28]

The new utilitarian and paternal sentiment of colonial rule was well expressed in a document of the time:

> It is not just, nor must we permit in a civilized republic that whatever person with the title of mayordomo of a [sacred] image . . . can seek contributions, because in that way each saint or each advance upon [a saint's] behalf will lead to the suffering of the [Indian] people of grievous extortions.[29]

In this way then the "civilized republic" of the eighteenth century replaced the Christian republic of previous centuries, and the early evolution of the modern state made its numerable interventions on the life of the Indian under the guise of guarding against communal and individual excess, exorbitance, and ignorance.[30] So entwined, in fact, had Indian cultural life become with the practices of an earlier baroque and Tridentine Catholic Church, that the Indians' defense of the cofradía was based on the grounds that it was a ceremony conducted since "time immemorial."[31] While some parish priests became little more than civil servants, others became increasingly disaffected, and when they had the support of a "loyal" indigenous parish behind them, the combination would soon prove incendiary.

Nascent Creole Nationalism

While the experience of Bourbon enlightened despotism had created feelings of resentment and bitterness among the creole elite, their displeasure stemmed more from the manner in which reform was introduced than from the premises on which it was based. The American-born colonial elite had, after all, fully embraced the new world of science and philosophy that the European Enlightenment had to offer. The warm reception accorded to Alexander von Humboldt and the assistance and respect given to his methodical collection of data, although supported in large part by the new peninsular bureaucrats, were principally due to the creole elite's shared belief in the advancement and progress that such an intellectual project embodied. The Crown itself had actively facilitated the diffusion of Enlightenment ideas and methods through the foundation and support of several centers of elite learning. Thus it was that the eighteenth century saw the creation of the Royal School of Mines, the School of Textiles, the School of Fine Arts, and the Botanical Garden of Mexico City. Like their European counterparts (and many of the heads of these schools were European), the New Spaniards eagerly adopted the rigors of scientific study, altering their knowledge and understanding of the colony, and in so doing, transforming not only their relationship with the geographical, historical, and scientific constitution of New Spain but their relationship with themselves.

While the continuing influence of the church can by no means be completely dismissed, we may well view this period as the founding moment of creole nationalism and identity. As already mentioned, with the belief in the practices and transparency of Enlightenment knowledge, the relationship toward the self, and self-knowledge, became dichotomized; that is to say, the understanding of the relationship between an individual and the church began to be seen as something appropriate to the private domain, while the new sciences of the Enlightenment and the self-understanding and practices they engendered became increasingly public.[32] One result of this transformation was the publication in New Spain of a wide array of new, and often short-lived, journals; at the same time, the essay, preferably including statistics, became the favored means of intellectual expression and exchange within a freshly developed public intellectual domain.[33] Even though the Americas had not yet experienced what Ian Hacking refers to as "an avalanche of numbers" on the same scale as Europe had, statistics as an illustration of the new science of state became almost obligatory as a means of analyzing the colonial kingdom.[34] It is no coincidence that it was at this time that the first census of New Spain was conducted. However, what was distinctive about the American experience of Enlightenment ideas was the role of the Jesuit order in the creation of a historical imaginary upon which the colonial-born Spaniards could soon base their claim to independence.[35]

The Spanish monarchy was indeed correct to regard the Jesuit order as a challenge to its power in the colonies. The Jesuits had been, after all, the main educators of the higher echelons of New Spanish society for some time.[36] Just as in Spain the Jesuits held a near monopoly on the instruction of the administrative and bureaucratic elite, nearly all the creole members of the New Spanish ruling council (the *audencia*) were graduates of Mexico City's Jesuit university, San Ildefonso. Although the expulsion of the Jesuits in Mexico mirrored the *manteistas'* attack on the *colegios mayores* in Spain, it also differed in that it left no alternative educational structure with which to ensure creole appointment to high office.[37] This frustration of ambition only made the creoles reflect longer on their old teachers, and in particular created an ever-more-receptive audience for the continuing scholarship of the Jesuits in exile.

Displaying a loyalty to the colony and a familiarity with the great books and debates that occupied European intellectual life, several Jesuits continued their project of creating a historical genealogy that situated the colony as a separate, and culturally legitimate, polity from that of its peninsular overlords. Building on the work of the seventeenth-century savant Carlos de Sigüenza y Góngora, one particular Jesuit, Francisco Javier Clavigero, made the greatest impact with his Italian publication of the *Storia antica del Messico* (The Ancient History of Mexico) in 1780. With his novel interpretation of pre- and post-conquest New Spanish history—which, owing to the employment of a wholly secular explanation of the causation of human affairs, was in itself heavily indebted to Enlightenment thinking — Clavigero managed to present a convincing basis upon which an independent cultural identity for the New Spanish creole could be argued.[38]

Like his predecessor, Sigüenza y Góngora, he exalted the high civilization of the central Mexican Indian past, even renaming this culture the Aztec to emphasize the cultural and historical distance between the contemporary Indian populace and their geographical progenitors.[39] The Aztec "civic life" was thus robustly reclaimed as a means of rewriting an indigenous past that could supply a burgeoning New Spanish identity with an antiquity equal, and on occasion superior, to that of the Greeks. It was in effect a history that employed the noble savages of the Amerindian past as the basis for creole claims to a political and civic culture independent from that of Europe. There was, of course, the inescapable question of the plight of the contemporary Mexican Indian, but even while blaming their depressed condition on the cruelty of the early colonists, Clavigero made no attempt to argue for a return to their sophisticated, and now deeply mythologized, former glory.[40] The future clearly lay with the American-born Spaniards, and although Humboldt most certainly shares with Clavigero a romantic attachment to the "Aztec past," as a commentator who had witnessed the French Revolution of 1789, he at least could recognize that within the huge divide between Indian and colonist lay the worrying potential for the "explosion of social conflict," a potential that, as we shall see, was soon to be realized.

The Wars of Independence

As all Mexican schoolchildren know, not least because it is still honored with an annual public holiday, the key historical moment upon which independence was founded came on September 16, 1810, with the *Grito de Dolores* (the Cry of Dolores). With the words "Long live Ferdinand VII! Long live Our Lady of Guadalupe! Death to the *gachupines!* Death to the rotten government!" the parish priest of Dolores, Miguel Hidalgo, started a rebellion that would become a civil war and eventually — ten years later — would result in an independent Mexico.[41] It was undoubtedly an incendiary moment, and although the details of an alternative government had been given little thought, the widespread feelings of resentment and anger against the ruling peninsular Spaniards, contemptuously referred to as *los gachupines*, ensured that Hidalgo's call to arms was swiftly answered. Furthermore, as his rebel forces began to march, and with an inspired feeling for popular instinct, Hidalgo seized from the church of Atotoniclo a standard with the effigy of the Virgin of Guadalupe, thus providing the rebel movement with a uniquely Mexican image behind which the revolutionary force of Indians and creoles could unite.

Our Lady of Guadalupe, the dark-skinned Virgin who had appeared to an Indian, Juan Diego, on the site of the principal shrine to the Mexica mother goddess Tonantzin some centuries earlier, had long been the object of official and public devotion. More recently, however, the "cult" had come under attack from the Bourbon and church hierarchy. For Jacques Lafaye, her invocation as a revolutionary icon symbolized a final step in the spiritual emancipation of the Mexican people, which he believes was the "necessary prelude" to the creation of a popular national consciousness, to which Hidalgo's revolt gave violent expression.[42] However, Eric Van Young, among others, has done much to explore the subjugated history of the Indian beliefs and motivations that have come to be written out of a still-popular narrative, or foundational myth, of Mexican nationhood.[43] He concludes,

> In the plentiful primary documentation of the era there is virtually no evidence to suggest that Indian soldiers, rebels, and rioters subscribed, except in the vaguest and most passive fashion, to the tenets of proto-liberal elite ideology, and indeed there is abundant indication that they held very different beliefs and goals from those of the elite directorate of the movement.[44]

In particular, the Indians appear to have been inspired by a mixture of millenarian and messianic notions, often with King Ferdinand VII in the role of the messiah figure. An example of such beliefs can be found in the popularity of rumors surrounding the existence of a mysterious person who was always hidden behind a silver mask or obscured from view in a curtained carriage, and who was most often assumed to be the king of Spain.[45] Before laying claim to the birth of a Mexican national consciousness, then, we might well consider how a mixture of clergy, Indians, *castas* (blacks and mulattoes), mine workers, artisans, and creole men of a distinctively New Spanish managerial and commercial class found common cause in a revolt against the Spanish. While by no means dismissing the spiritual, transcendental, or psychological elements of the Hidalgo revolt, we should also recognize that the Bajío region, from which the rebellion hailed, had suffered particularly grievously under what David Brading calls "the concluding act in the Bourbon revolution in government . . . the amortisation decree of 1804."[46]

With this act, the Crown ordered that all ecclesiastical funds should be paid into the royal treasury. As the majority of the church's funds took the form of mortgages and loans, over the next couple of years the new law threatened the very economic basis of a good many agrarian, commercial, and mining interests in the region. Combined with this financial assault came the added hardship of poor harvests and a disastrous drought. However, above and beyond these local conditions came the dramatic transformations in the fortunes of the Bourbon dynasty itself. In 1808, as part of the expansionist policy of Napoleon Bonaparte, Charles IV and his recently proclaimed heir, Ferdinand VII, found themselves forced to abdicate in the name of Bonaparte's brother, Joseph, who was proclaimed the new king of Spain. The coup d'etat resulted in a widespread insurrection, and rebel juntas were quickly established throughout the peninsula. It was not long, though, before French troops regained control of the majority of Spanish cities, leading the Central Junta to withdraw to Seville. Faced with a constitutional crisis, in 1810 the Junta called a general council in Cádiz, inviting deputies from the Americas as well as from the loyal provinces of the peninsula, in an attempt to reconstitute Spanish rule.

Wary of the American-born elite, the European-born Spaniards in the colony reacted to the Napoleonic invasion by overthrowing the vacillating viceroy, José de Iturrigaray, in 1808. Witnessing the political turmoil in Spain, and ever resentful of a now illegitimate Spanish-born minority, the creole community began to plot. It was in one such conspiracy that the parish priest of Dolores, Miguel Hidalgo, was involved. Already active in the promotion of self-reliance and cottage industries among his Indian flock, Hidalgo was a victim both of Bourbon reform and of church hierarchy displeasure, but on hearing the news of the discovery of the Querétaro conspiracy, he became the historical catalyst for the dissolution of colonial rule. The rebellion Hidalgo began — and in particular the manner in which it was embraced — was thus the result of a combination of factors, all of which coalesced around a hatred and distrust of Spanish rule. However, the murder and pillage that followed in the wake of Hidalgo's army soon lost it creole support. By 1811, Hidalgo had been captured and was executed; his army was dispersed and no longer controlled the areas north of Mexico City. But the forces of rebellion Hidalgo had unleashed could not be quelled as easily, and immediately another priest and onetime student of Hidalgo's, José

María Morelos, led a far more strategic and better-organized revolutionary army, this time from the south.[47]

With Morelos came a far more conscious articulation of the demands of the rebels, and at the Congress of Chilpancingo in 1813, the rebel leader presented two documents, the "Reglamento" (concerning the form of government) and his "Sentiments of the Nation, or Guiding Principles." With these two documents, Morelos laid the clearest foundations for a Mexican constitution, and in his opening address he boldly stated the republican aspirations that have inspired Mexican patriots ever since:

> Our enemies have been obliged to reveal to us certain important truths. . . . They are: that sovereignty resides basically in the people, but is transmitted to monarchs; that by their absence, death, or captivity, it devolves once again on the people; that they are free to reorganize their political institutions in any way agreeable to them; and that no people have the right to subjugate another. You, who govern this august assembly, accept the most solemn pledge that we shall die or save this nation. . . . We are going to re-establish the Mexican empire and improve the government; we are going to be the spectacle of the cultured nations that will respect us; finally, we are going to be free and independent.[48]

The "we" to whom Morelos referred was one irrespective of social gradation; it included Indian, mulatto, and mestizo (into which category Morelos himself fell), "for all native-born were to be designated Americans."[49] He called for the end of Indian tribute, the abolition of slavery, the institution of Catholicism as the state religion, and the exclusion of Europeans from government. His southern movement was, however, to suffer some heavy defeats, and two years after the congress, he was captured and executed.

With the return of Ferdinand VII from captivity in France, events in Spain rapidly transformed. The liberal constitutionalists of the Council of Cádiz found themselves imprisoned, and suddenly a force of some fifteen thousand Spanish regular troops was made available to the New Spanish viceroy. Large parts of the colony soon fell under the heavy-handed rule of military law, and the entry of the Spanish troops into the colonial conflict has been widely recognized as the final blow to the possibility of a recovered relationship between the Spanish Crown and its American subjects. Instead, "what gripped New Spain was one of the greatest guerrilla insurgencies in modern history."[50] The fighting continued for another six years, causing the colonial kingdom to break down along increasingly regional lines, and when in 1820 the Spanish liberals rebelled and restored the constitution, the subjects of New Spain were war weary and nearly bankrupt. Under these circumstances, when a previously royalist officer, Augustín de Iturbide, proposed a compromise, known as the Plan of Iguala, the proposal received widespread support.[51] The eleven years of war eventually ended with the Declaration of Independence signed on September 28, 1821.

Liberalism and the Invisible Indian

Rather than as the arrival of peace, independence might better be seen as just one (albeit structurally the most important) of the many political options available to a group of creole individuals who for some three decades to come would continue to be engaged in a war of ideas. Although primarily nourished in the late eighteenth century, the questions of "how to govern oneself, how to be governed, how to govern others" — all the problems that Michel Foucault has identified as being characteristic of sixteenth-century Europe — seem to have first appeared in Mexico in all their full and complex intensity during this early independence period.[52] However, to suggest that New Spain — now Mexico — was awash with a multitude of diverse political ideas in response to such questions would be a mistake. The central problematique of government that had in Europe been given such impetus by the colonies themselves, the Reformation, and the Counter-Reformation found itself expressed in the debates of the creole elite in the singular, if often expansive, vocabulary of liberalism.[53]

Apart from the obvious liberal implications of a Mexican constitution (to which we shall return), the central tenets to which nearly all the postindependence creole elite could agree surrounded the economic project of liberalism rather than its political management. As in peninsular Spain, the doctrines of economic liberalism were discussed both in public forums, such as the Sociedades Económicas de Amigos del País, and in secretive societies, such as the Masonic lodges.[54] Most of these societies had first made their appearance during the Enlightenment, and their existence constituted the beginnings of a newly secularized and public space, what the liberals themselves recognized as the formative stages of a "civil society." That the parameters of this nascent civil society only encompassed a few thousand individuals of the creole elite was a reality not lost on its members, not least because of the constant reminders of social fragmentation that characterized the postindependence period. Undoubtedly, it was this realization of the limited appreciation of their economic vision that brought the first contradiction of the liberal doctrine to light.

Based on the Physiocratic thought of the late eighteenth century, and developed by Adam Smith and David Ricardo, classical liberalism was premised on the idea of the self-interested individual in society. In Smith's *The Wealth of Nations*, the logic and equivalence of this self-interested individual with an industrious individual were set out. Smith believed that the mechanism of the market operated independently of its participants. Both massive and socially complex, it made possible the exchange of the work of individuals and allowed the egotistical interests of all to be served. What he called the "natural harmonisation of interests" was due to the work of "an invisible hand" that directed each and every individual to achieve an end that had not entered into his original intentions. In following their own self-interest, individuals would increase the prosperity of a nation more effectively than if they entered into its design. Now that Mexico was independent, such a conception held radical implications for the scope of government. On the one hand, it suggested that the wealth of a nation was best achieved through the non-interference of the state; and on the other, it implied that "the work of an individual — and consequently his idleness and lack of a productive occupation — was an issue of public interest that exceeded the limits of the private sphere."[55]

Clearly, the existence of a market economy could not be taken for granted, and as shall be witnessed throughout the history of Mexico, rather than the mythical "invisible hand" of classical liberalism, the creation of a "free" market would require the near-constant intervention of the state. Soon the debate turned to questions concerning the conduct of individuals, and just as quickly, in recognition of Mexico's difference from nations like France or England, where such doctrines originated, a distinction was made between the "industrious individual" and his "idle and needy" compatriots.[56] The "absolute freedom" to choose the nature of one's employment soon became the demand of those with property. Those creoles who already had commercial interests thus called for the abolition of a variety of rules and regulations that they viewed as impediments to the accumulation of wealth. To a large extent, there was among the educated elite a shared view that industrialization was necessary. After the destruction and near bankruptcy wrought by eleven years of war, however, the financial stimulus to engender such a process was little in evidence. Lucas Alamán, later to be recognized as Mexico's foremost conservative, sought to combat this lack of private capital with the foundation of a national bank, the Banco de Avío.[57]

Alamán recognized the need for investment to create an industrialized nation, and in doing so he also recognized another of liberalism's contradictions. To promote a technologically advanced industry such as the production of textiles, it would become necessary to defend and protect such domestic industries from the influence of an international market. He realized that countries such as Britain would rather maintain Mexico in a position of only producing primary materials, such as cotton, which could then be manufactured back in Europe. Defending budding domestic industries from the perils of international free trade was only one aspect of Alamán's policy. He also soon recognized that for independence to have any meaning, greater intervention on the part of the government would be necessary in the planning of large-scale agriculture and industry. However, when liberals such as Esteban de Antunano extended this logic, as the Bourbons had done before them, to suggest that an unexploited source of capital lay in the wealth and land holdings of the Catholic Church, the latent conservative and corporatist limits of Alamán's liberalism were revealed.[58]

There was at least one question upon which agreement was broadly reached: the question of legitimacy. It was an issue that had long troubled Spanish jurists in regard to their colonial kingdoms, and following the French and American examples, it now found itself resolved in the adoption of a modern liberal constitution. However, while a constitution took on the theoretical task of creating a social contract with the people, it was in fact the first step in the juridical erasure of the indigenous subject.[59] For in the newly envisioned liberal republic, the question of the Indian came to be subsumed in the wider question of the citizen and his economic counterpart, the industrious individual. In liberal eyes, therefore — apart from the first tentative steps toward a liberal understanding of the individual undertaken by the Bourbon reformers — the Spanish regime, in particular its ecclesiastical missions, was considered both negligent and oppressive for its failure to develop a sense of personal independence among the Indians.

From this perspective, the principal means by which Catholic missions maintained the Indians in such a "condition of stationary infancy" was through "perpetuating the notion of common property" among them.[60] For it was in the institution of private property that the squab-

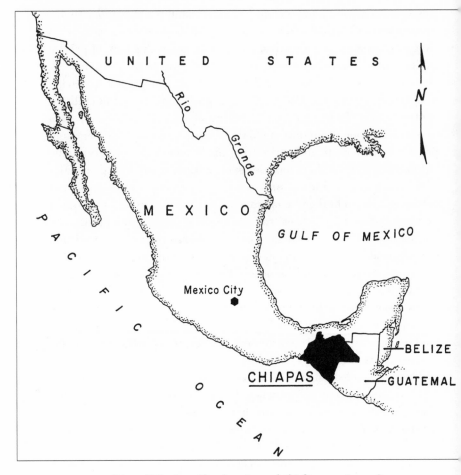

FIGURE 2.2 Map of Mexico. *Akwe:kon, Journal of Indigenous Issues,* Summer 1994.

bling Mexican liberals sought the individual and constitutional stability that the creole elite so dearly desired. Thus it was that "the communal property of the village was threatened by liberal theory as well as by the traditional encroachment of the large landowner."[61] In attacking the special juridical and societal privileges awarded the Indians by both church and colonial Crown, the liberals were adamant. "We must insist," said José Luis Mora, the leading liberal of the era, "that by law Indians no longer exist."[62]

While church wealth and the relationship between church and state would be one of the principal dividing issues between liberals and conservatives in the future, the truth of Mexico during the postindependence era was that even if a single coherent government policy could have been agreed upon, the conditions of stability necessary for its fulfillment did not exist. In the twenty years that followed independence, the Mexican republic endured three constitutions, twenty governments, and more than one hundred cabinets. The era was dominated by generals who wanted to be presidents if not emperors and local bosses who wanted to be regional rulers. Debates surrounding federalism versus centralism were thus often more of the pragmatic sort, as Mexico sought to consolidate itself as a nation. In the words of José Luis Mora,

> In Mexico there is no established order; neither that of the ancien regime because its principles are now nullified and the interests that supported them practically destroyed; nor that of the new, although the doctrines upon which it is founded and the desires which they excite are already common throughout the country, still we have not hit upon the means to combine them with the remains of the old order, or to make such (remains) disappear; in sum, one cannot go back nor go forward without great difficulty.[63]

Conclusion

Finally, attempts to forge a liberal nation, with their concomitant attempts to create the private subject of liberal national loyalty, were to face fresh internal and external threats. The first serious external challenge came with the United States' invasion of the northern Mexican states in 1847. Mexico lost half of its land mass during this war, and the trauma of defeat was compounded by the fact that the enemy had embodied the very model of liberal nationalism that the Mexicans themselves had been hoping to emulate. Just one year after the U.S. act of aggression, the shallowness and sociological myopia of postindependence Mexico were further laid bare by Indian uprisings in both the Yucatan and the Sierra Gorda regions.[64] These rebellions became known as the caste wars, and they ignited latent fears of social dissolution and ethnic division that liberal constitutionalism, after the violent excesses of the independence struggle, was meant to prevent. Now that the liberals could no longer ignore the rebellious Indian base of Mexican society, their reaction made explicit the nature of their Mexican vision. They proposed concerted colonization of the troubled areas by European settlers with the aim of the complete fusion of the Indians with whites and thus "the total extinction of the castes."[65] The Indian himself was seen as obstinate and resigned to clinging to former customs, leaving all the hope for Mexico's future to reside in its white race.[66]

The issue of the caste wars, their genesis, and their means of settlement also provided one of the clearest moments of political rupture within the creole elite. In a series of articles published in Mexico City's *El Universal*, it is possible to see the articulate elucidation of the new conservative position. It was a position that defended the system of colonial paternalism, the Catholic Church, and by extension, the monarchy.[67] In so doing, it laid the foundations for the short period of monarchical rule presided over by the Austrian archduke Maximilian. And in another sense, the caste wars and conservative reactions to them also led the liberals to resolve the inherent tension within their thinking, a resolution that led them to the seemingly contradictory conclusion of authoritarian rule.[68]

THREE

The Governmental State

Indian Labor, Liberal-Authoritarianism, and Revolt

While some commentators have interpreted the Mexican postwar compromise of the early independence years as a triumph of reactionary thinking, others have considered the period a paradigmatic example of political chaos.[1] The first interpretation is certainly correct in that the initial uprising of the masses triggered by Hidalgo concluded with the deal making of a creole elite, a scenario that, although dressed in liberal rhetoric, led to little significant change for Mexico's millions of indigenous peoples. Nevertheless, and despite the common attachment to the legality of a constitution and other more pervasive ideas about liberal economics, the remaining vestiges of Hapsburg colonial privilege and vested interest effectively placed two powerful elite groups in opposition to each other, a predicament that in its vigor rendered any attempt at the creation of a unified nation-state unworkable. In fact, in the view of Mexican historians like Daniel Cosío Villegas, it was not until the years 1867–1910 that the semblances of a modern Mexican nation-state could be clearly discerned.[2] For it was only then, it is argued, "that the bases of the modern administrative state were formulated, that the work of economic modernization began, and, lamentably, that a tradition for the abridgement of constitutional liberties became established."[3]

That the creation of this modern Mexican governmental state, as we shall call it, would involve the powerful meshing of science with politics, a process much like the earlier governmentality of the European Bourbon administration, is not mere coincidence. Neither, perhaps, is the fact that the establishment of a Mexican governmental state would require the *mano duro* (hard hand) of a presidential dictator innocently unrelated to the eighteenth-century understanding of an enlightened despot. However, to appreciate just what becoming modern in name and structure meant for the indigenous of Mexico, we shall first turn our attention to the more localized politics of Mexico's newest province: Chiapas. In doing so, we will hopefully better understand how government and independence came to impinge on the life and culture of the Maya Indians of the region, an experience that continues to be negotiated to this day.

A Brief Moment of Indian Florescence

On December 22, 1867, a young Indian girl, Agustina Gómez Checheb, was looking after her father's sheep near the hamlet of Tzajahemel, when three stones fell from the sky.[4] Collecting them up, she rushed back to her home and placed them on the small family altar. She claimed that as soon as she had done so, the stones began to communicate with her. Since the community had no reason to doubt this otherwise unexceptional little girl, word of the miraculous "talking stones" of Tzajahemel soon spread. As worship at this new shrine began to attract Indians from throughout the highlands of Chiapas, one visitor in particular, Pedro Díaz Cuzcat, also declared his ability to "talk" with the stones, and soon, with the aid of his intimate knowledge of Christian rituals, he became the self-appointed Indian "priest" of this now-sacred place.

With Cuzcat leading the rituals, the ceremonies and the local market that sprung up around them began to flourish, and for a brief moment, Tzajahemel represented a unique and peaceful expression of Indian spirituality and cultural autonomy. By June, however, the success of this cult had become too much for the local ladino (non-Indian) community to bear. Finding their social and economic position of superiority challenged, they issued condemnations against the "barbarous" Indians and the threat they posed to "civilization." Quickly the rhetoric was followed by intervention, and as the Indians sought to protect Cuzcat and their holy relics, the ensuing clashes eventually led to what has become misleadingly known as the Chiapas "caste war."[5]

Unlike the caste war of Yucatan (although both regions faced similar pressures), the 1869 Indian conflict with the ladinos of Chiapas was in fact a tragic consequence of a temporary period of Indian autonomy that arose during a lull in the incessant and divisive struggles of a regional elite that characterized the first fifty postindependence years in Chiapas. To make matters worse, over time the story surrounding the conflict has become embellished to include the crucifixion of a young Indian boy, seemingly representative of an Indian Christ—an untrue detail that was meant to further emphasize the Indians' propensity for cruelty and inhumanity.[6] In light of the 1994 Zapatista uprising, such stories have received renewed currency. Propagated by both supporters and detractors of the Zapatistas, talk of the "caste war" has sadly only served to further encourage a belief in the inherent divide between Indian society and non-Indian society, a distinction that, just as the nineteenth-century ladino provocateurs had hoped, only obscures a more detailed consideration of the skewered nature of the relations between the two groups. After all, the cynical manipulation of the Tzajahemel "talking stones" was originally a means to unite a divided non-Indian elite and subsequently to reinforce its position of dominance over an emboldened Indian populace. It is thus to an analysis of these elite divisions and their relations with the Chiapan Indian that we shall now turn.

Chiapas: National Conflict on a Local Level

In the confused moments between the end of colonial rule and the establishment of independent republics, a group of influential merchants and ranchers from Chiapas sought temporary refuge in the establishment of the Free State of Chiapas. Recognizing the convergence of their economic and real estate interests, the group became known as *la familia chiapaneca* (the Chiapas family).[7] Such unity, however, did not endure, and soon the familia began to fracture along geographical lines, with a group from the lowlands, *tierra caliente*, preferring inclusion among the new republics of Central America and a group from the highlands, *tierra fría*, preferring annexation to Mexico. When the issue was eventually formalized with the annexation of Chiapas by Mexico on September 14, 1824, the settlement was viewed as an arrangement engineered by the oligarchy of the highland capital of Ciudad Real, a group whose interests very much mirrored those of the pre-independence Hapsburg colonial elite.[8]

To a certain extent, the lowland members of the familia chiapaneca of the central valley owed their fortunes to the tax reforms of the Bourbon colonial administration. In reality, though, the 1797 abolition of tax on trade between Mexico and Guatemala was only the beginning for an entrepreneurial group that sought to avoid all taxation in their smuggling of cotton, cattle, and sugarcane (for rum) in exchange for cloth and wine from international trading partners like Britain and France.[9] In the early years of Mexican rule, the investments of this group, who clearly had embraced the logic of liberal economics, expanded considerably, and by 1838 no less than ninety-six plantations were established in the zone. "Ironically, however, although they soon laid claim to vast amounts of unused lands, they nonetheless faced one serious, indeed insurmountable, problem: a critical shortage of labor."[10] It is at this juncture that the Chiapan Indian as the principal source of regional labor enters the uncomfortable dynamic between the spheres of influence and control that divide the non-Indian lowland and highland elites.

Although affected by the Bourbon reforms, Ciudad Real (renamed San Cristóbal in 1829) had, ever since the arrival of the first Spaniards, been the undisputed bastion of corporate colonial privilege in Chiapas. Church and Crown had ruled side by side, as both groups sought to promote their interests among the extensive indigenous populace that inhabited the highland zone. With annexation by Mexico, this clearly conservative group found itself in an ironically advantageous position: the liberal agrarian laws of 1826 and 1832, which defined the maximum legal extension of village *ejidos* (communal lands) according to population size, made it possible for highland ladinos to increase their land holdings and consequently their control over the Indians themselves. This was because the laws "opened up the *terrenos baldíos* (the "vacant lands" that surrounded Indian communities and had been held in trust by the Crown to protect Indian land-holdings) to entitlement by private citizens."[11] The stripping of land from Indian communities was, however, only one aspect of what was effectively a three-pronged assault that resulted from liberal reform — or rather, from the use to which it was put.

The second and most reprehensible aspect of land reform was that very soon the Indians found that the parcels of land they had previously used for farming and sustenance were now the property of ladino landlords, a fact that led either to their migration in search of a new means of subsistence or to their effective enslavement to the new proprietors. Called *baldíos*, the Indians who remained on their land in return for the "permission" to continue cultivating it were required to provide between three and five days of labor per week for their landlords without any payment whatsoever.[12] In addition to this, the landlord could also periodically demand seven days' further labor, usually as a servant in his household, an added indignity that led many to seek a living elsewhere.[13]

FIGURE 3.1 Group of Mexican Indians, circa 1890. Photo by Gustavo Scheibe.

Those who left their communities were usually referred to as *mozos* and considered free workers. Often these Indians sought work as seasonal laborers on the lowland farms. Tragically, those who had hoped to escape the servitude of highland peonage soon found themselves entrapped in an equally exploitative relationship with their tierra caliente employers. Payment for labor, although officially meant to consist of cash, most often came in the form of food and other basic necessities that were supplied exclusively from the farm shop. Through the supply of more goods than the wage supposedly could cover, the patron gradually became the creditor of his seasonal worker. Soon "fines" for lack of productivity were also added to such debts, and in this way, the farmer ensured himself a permanent and cheap supply of labor.[14] Since these Indians could no longer return to their villages, and since their debts were hereditary, their suffering was doubly tragic, for it not only led to the loss of the limited freedom they had once known but also resulted in a painful severing of the cultural and community bonds that had once given meaning to their lives as Indians.

For the indigenous who had remained in the highlands — either those lucky enough to still have some land or those now known as baldíos — the third aspect of the liberal assault was cultural. In colonial times, apart from a priest, Indians had lived in separate communities from ladinos. Little by little, though, during the early independence years, as ladinos were able to claim or buy Indian lands, the communities began to experience the slow invasion of their villages by non-Indians. Usually men of modest resources, these newcomers set up stores or small land holdings, nearly always taking the best lands for themselves. An indication of how the Indians felt about these legal incursions on their communities can be seen in the discovery of a plot among a group of Tzeltal Indians in February 1848 to take the lives of the new mestizo settlers in their midst.[15] Apart from the preemptive discovery of the Tzeltal conspiracy and the emigration of large numbers of male Indians from their native communities, another reason that more Indians did not rise up against their oppressors may well have been what Jan de Vos has described as "the arrival of the most injurious agent of exploitation that the Indians have had to endure until recent times," the seller of *aguardiente*.[16]

Although alcohol had long formed an integral part of Indian ceremonies (above all when petitions were being made or when healing rituals were being conducted), with the establishment of a community salesman, consumption began to take on the characteristics of a vice in which many Indians lamentably sought refuge from the deprivations that surrounded them. Tragically, though, the temporary relief afforded by aguardiente usually only led to an increase in debts to non-Indian settlers, and consequently, the amount of work the Indians would have to supply in repayment also grew.[17] In sum, as Jan Rus writes, "through land denunciations, usurious loan practices, and sales of alcohol and over-priced commodities, such 'homesteaders' were able in the barely twenty five years from 1826 to the 1850's to transform more than a quarter of Chiapas' Indians from 'free' villagers into permanently — and legally — obligated peons and laborers."[18] By midcentury, then, if one were to ask the Indians how they had benefited from independence, the question would most likely have seemed perverse.

The questions that divided the familia chiapaneca, however, were for whom and for how long the Indians were obligated to work. Obviously, if a large body of Indians were tied to the baldiaje practices in the highlands, there would be insufficient numbers to work on the ever-expanding farms of the lowlands. Recognizing a similar conflict on the national stage between an old order and a new, the familia chiapaneca soon found itself split into lowland liberals, keen for further reform, and highland conservatives, wary of further attacks on the church and still-existing colonial and administrative privilege. "Conflict between these two factions," writes Rus, "whatever the appearances, was never so much over ideals or future models of society as over division of the spoils left by the Spaniards."[19]

The key to the power of the conservatives was their control over the state capital, San Cristóbal. Located in the highlands, San Cristóbal served as the administrative center for the region, a situation that gave the conservatives a large degree of control over the tax revenues of the state, and as a consequence, over its Indian populace. In addition to these official bureaucratic functions, San Cristóbal also served as the religious center for the Catholic Church in Chiapas, which, since the sixteenth century, had built up significant land holdings throughout the highlands and especially the Grijalva valley. Local priests also collected a religious tax, from which they drew salaries and maintained their church. For extra masses, christenings, marriages, registration of births and deaths, cofradía celebrations, and wedding certificates, the priest also made additional charges. Just like the Bourbons before them, the liberals objected to this second tier of government that the Catholic Church effectively constituted. On the national level, it was precisely this issue of church wealth and power that brought the country to arms.

Since independence Mexico had been unable to consolidate itself as a nation. It had experimented with several piecemeal attempts at rule, usually presided over by a military figure, the most famous of whom was General Santa Anna, who assumed the office of president on no fewer than five separate occasions.[20] At each juncture, cabinets both liberal and conservative had been unable to overcome internal and external opposition to their policies. The country was split along regional lines, with each local elite maneuvering for a liberal federal arrangement or a conservative centralist government according to their individual concerns. Then in 1848, after a two-year war, Mexicans suffered the indignity of witnessing U.S. troops enter their capital. In the treaty that followed, Mexico signed away nearly half its land mass, and six years later, with the Gadsden Purchase, it would sell more. In light of the Indian uprisings of the Yucatan Maya, the Apaches of Sonora, and the Indians of the Sierra Gorda region, claims by any government to represent a "Mexican nation" were illusionary to say the least.

So in 1855, when the liberals seized power, they did so with a greater conviction to push through the reforms that they believed would eventually lead to the creation of a "modern" Mexican nation. Central to this conviction was a belief that the constitutional and legal protection under which the Catholic Church had been able to operate would have to go. They achieved this reform with the creation of a new constitution in 1857. Catholicism then ceased to be the official state religion, marriages could be granted through a civil authority, and the clergy were subject to the censure of civil courts. With the Lerdo Law, the liberals also sought to undermine the influence, wealth, and income that made the church such a powerful force within Mexico. These reforms started a process of nationalization of church property and also aimed to remove the civil enforcement of religious taxes — thus, liberals hoped, creating a new class of propertied citizens with an interest in the continuance of liberal rule.[21]

Predictably, such reform was too much for the conservatives, and the country once again went to war during the years 1860–1861. Although the liberals won, their victory was short lived, for in 1862, under the pretence of collecting on unpaid debts, the French troops of Napoleon III intervened in Mexican politics. Welcomed by the defeated conservatives, the French provided the force under which the Austrian archduke Maximilian Hapsburg was installed as emperor of Mexico. Liberal troops, financed by the U.S., fought a guerrilla war for the next four years, and after the retreat of the French, hunted down and executed an unrepentant Maximilian in 1867.[22] In Chiapas, all these convulsions within the central government of Mexico City found themselves played out in armed confrontations between the two embittered local factions. For the Indians, in contrast, the short period during the liberal reforms was arguably the best years since independence. With commerce interrupted and taxes left uncollected, the indigenous savored a rare moment of peace. However, with the rise of the French imperialist government, Indians once again found themselves drawn into a conflict to which they were expected to contribute not only finances but also, on many occasions, their own lives.

Unpleasant though the postindependence years were, the Indians at least felt relatively certain as to where power lay in their relations with ladinos. What the liberal reforms and the subsequent wars also brought was a traumatic uncertainty surrounding just where and how the lines of power and authority were drawn. The structure of Indian communities seems to have suffered as a consequence, with village schoolmasters and municipal secretaries competing with priests and

local landlords for the loyalty and support of the indigenous community. In 1863, in the highland village of San Juan Chamula, this tension
boiled over into interethnic violence, leading to the deaths of twenty-
three people in one day.[23]

With the defeat of the conservatives in 1867, the Indian communities once again enjoyed a moment of peace. However, it was at this very
time that the defeated highland conservatives played their last cynical
card in the hope of recovering at least some of the control over Indian
labor that had for so long been the primary source of their wealth — and,
in doing so, perhaps even restoring themselves to a position of influence
in the soon-to-be-reunited familia chiapaneca.

The Chiapas "Caste War"

In 1864, Pantaleón Domínguez was appointed military governor of the
all-but-tamed state of Chiapas by the commander of liberal forces at the
time, General Porfirio Díaz. Three years later, when the liberal victory
was complete, Domínguez retained his post, becoming the constitutional governor of the state. Having removed the capital from San Cristóbal to Tuxtla during the war, Domínguez and his liberal compatriots
were both disappointed and concerned when the federal government
announced that not only were all state capitals to be returned to their
prewar locales but all except the highest-ranking conservatives were
to be granted an amnesty that left them free to reenter elected office.
In local terms, such national conciliatory gestures once again raised
the specter of a conservative elite gaining control over the temporarily
untapped Indian labor force whose presence was soon to be required
on the plantations of the lowland farmers.[24]

Recognizing this threat, Domínguez only moved the capital halfway
from Tuxtla, to Chiapa, a town on the edge of the central lowland plain,
and using all the liberal reform laws available to him, he set about undoing whatever remaining ties the conservatives had with the Indian communities of the highlands. His first act was to impress upon the Indians
the claim to religious toleration included in the 1857 constitution. The
main implication of this legislation for the Indian communities was the
removal of any legal obligation to pay religious taxes to their priests.
To ensure this reform would penetrate, he took the further step of abol-
ishing the two key native religious offices of mayordomo and alférez,
effectively removing the means by which contributions were collected
from the Indian congregations and further ensuring the collapse of
an already declining cofradía system.[25] Central to the governor's strat-

egy were the roles of the municipal secretary and the village school-master, or *maestro*, whose task it was to inform the Indians of their new rights and even to go so far as to encourage them to "abandon the churches altogether" and to "practice Catholicism without the priests and temples!"[26]

It seems likely that the Indians, who had always given transplanted Spanish Catholicism its own distinctive Indian interpretation, had already taken advantage of earlier periods of clerical neglect to reintroduce customs that had previously been prohibited. With the addition of the legal backing of the liberal government, it is not surprising, therefore, to find that native religiosity and culture enjoyed a brief period of florescence. Consequently, at this time, "the water sources, caves, forests, and maize fields [*las milpas*], that had always been privileged sites at which to make petitions and bring offerings, underwent a welcome renaissance."[27] "It is important to highlight," writes Jan de Vos, "that we are dealing with a world that is truly rural, where the concern for the tenancy and the cultivation of the land never stopped holding a central position."[28] It is for this reason that de Vos believes the Indians have always maintained a devotion to deities that are pre-Hispanic, revering objects and sites that have a deeper link to the forces of nature than that of the Christian god of European conception.

Within this context, the animism granted to the three "miraculous" stones that fell before a young Indian girl in Tzajahemel, and the manner in which this apparition was embraced by the surrounding communities and converted into an organized cult, becomes less fantastic and more understandable. In fact, the ceremonies that took place and were sometimes attended by thousands were similar to those conducted in the other traditional Indian centers, the only principle difference being that in Tzajahemel everything was presided over by a native clergy. Bells were rung, trumpets were blown, candles and incense were burned, masses were conducted, and sacristans and acolytes led and organized the rituals. In the opinion of anthropologist Jan Rus, "having been mistreated by ladinos of all parties, especially during the preceding civil wars, many Indians seemed to find in the isolated shrine a kind of sanctuary, a place where they could not only pray in peace but could meet and trade with their neighbours without fear of ladino interference."[29]

Perhaps unable to grasp the peaceful nature of the Indian cult, and after seeing their initial attempts to break up the shrine rebuffed by liberals and Indians alike, the conservative highland elite, financially and socially challenged by Indian separatism, played the one card they had left: race. They began by circulating rumors that the Indians were planning to attack San Cristóbal and that the long-feared outbreak of a caste war was imminent. In what was supposedly a preemptive strike, in December 1868, the leaders of San Cristóbal sent a force of some fifty armed men to arrest Agustina Checheb and the leader of the newly formed native clergy, Pedro Díaz Cuzcat. Faced with this small but well-armed force, the Indians were unable to prevent the capture of their leaders. However, in the temporary state capital of Chiapa, such a clear example of Cristobalense repression was not greeted with the immediate condemnation of earlier months. In fact, the liberals themselves had begun to realize that in seeking to deny conservatives control over the Indians, they had failed to replace the bonds of servitude that they had been so keen to break.

Indian separatism thus began to appear threatening not only to the highland elite but to the commercial interests of the lowland farmers as well. What brought the issue into sharper focus was the attempt in early 1869 to enforce a state tax code among the Indian communities. Although the collectors were given generous financial incentives and extrajudicial powers with which to enforce collection, it soon became clear that the Indians had begun to avoid their official village centers and had once again taken to the forests and the smaller hamlets like Tzajahemel to conduct their affairs away from government control. As their actions were to greatly affect commerce not only in San Cristóbal but also in the lowlands, the Indians' return to their separatist ways even after the arrest of their leaders quickly led to calls for another armed intervention, this time one that would teach them a serious lesson. However, on learning of these plans, Ignacio Fernández de Galindo, a liberal teacher who had only recently moved to San Cristóbal, set off with his wife and a student to warn the Indians of the impending danger.[30]

Perhaps deterred by the knowledge that the Indians had been forewarned, on the morning of June 13 the citizens of San Cristóbal sent, rather than an armed force, a small group of local officials led by Father Martínez, the parish priest of Chamula, to speak with the Indians. At Tzajahemel the group found only a few pilgrims at the shrine, and so compliant were they that without any violence the group was able to take possession of the cult's remaining holy relics. Before the priest and his companions could return, though, they were caught by another group of Indians who, on hearing of the removal of the sacred objects, had pursued them. Apparently Martínez and his fellow ladinos refused to give back the sacred possessions, and in the struggle that followed all

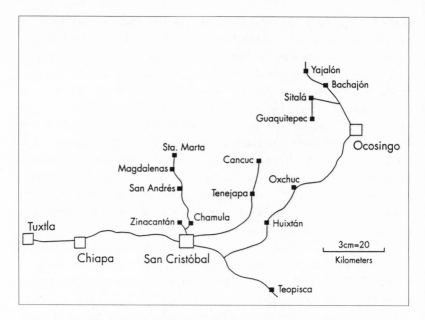

FIGURE 3.2 Map of areas of rebellion in 1712 and 1867. From Jan Rus, "The 'Comunidad Revolucionario Institucional': The Subversion of Native Government in Highland Chiapas, 1936–1968," in *Everyday Forms of State Formation*, eds. Joseph and Nugent (Duke University Press, Durham, 1994), p. 226.

four were killed. The news of the ladinos' murder sent panic throughout the zone, and in the days that followed other ladinos were also killed. Rus claims that the killings were not indiscriminate, that "apparently most of the Indians' rage was directly at those with whom they had old scores to settle or who had in some way threatened them."[31]

Nevertheless, the terror that must have engulfed the ladinos of San Cristóbal when, on June 17, a force of several thousand Indians appeared on the outskirts of the city can only be imagined. But the Indians had not come to attack. Rather, they came under a white flag offering Galindo, his wife, and the student in exchange for the jailed Cuzcat, Checheb, and other Indians. The swap was duly made, and leaving a small force of some six hundred Indians on the hills around San Cristóbal, the rest returned to Tzajahemel to celebrate the release of their leaders. All the same, the continued vigilance of the Indian lookouts led the local newspapers to the conclusion that was perhaps inevitable all along. They wrote that "there could 'no longer be any doubt that the Indians were sworn enemies of the whites,' that their most fervent desire was to 'ravish and kill San Cristóbal's tender wives and sisters, to mutilate the corpses of its children.' The only solution, they wrote, was a 'war to the death between barbarism and civilization,' a war in which — and here was the key — Chiapas's ladinos would for the first time in decades recognise their essential unity."[32]

It appears Domínguez was motivated to respond to the call of the whites of San Cristóbal less from any belief in the dangers of a caste war than from a recognition of the personal political ambitions such a campaign could serve. Either way, he arrived in the highland city with a force of three hundred heavily armed men. The Indians who had remained on the outskirts of the city, armed only with sticks and machetes, were quickly cut down, leaving some three hundred dead. As more reinforcements arrived, the ladino ranks eventually numbered over a thousand men. It was with this force behind him that Domínguez set out for Chamula on June 30 to put down the Indian unrest once and for all. What followed is best explained in the words of a lowland foot soldier present on the day:

> When we first spied the Chamulas, hundreds of them were scattered in disordered groups on the hillsides, and before we were within rifle distance all, women and children as well as men, knelt on their bare knees to beg forgiveness. In spite of the humble position they took to show submission, however, the government forces continued to advance, and they, undoubtedly hoping they would be granted the mercy they begged with tears of sorrow, remained on their knees. At a little less than 200 meters, the soldiers opened fire on their compact masses — and despite the carnage done to them by the bullets, despite their cries for mercy, continued firing for some time.
>
> When the government forces finally reached the Chamulas, their thirst for the blood of that poor, abject race still not slaked, there were suddenly such strident yells that even knowing nothing of what they said one knew their meaning: with those shouts they threw themselves against the government forces with an almost inhuman valor. These poor men, unable to secure the clemency they implored with tears and prostration, charged with a barbaric bravery.[33]

As the campaign continued throughout the region, the final death toll came to around one thousand Indians and two hundred ladinos; but perhaps the most tragic aspect was that in the weeks and months that followed the Chamula attack, Indians were forced to join the ladino forces and hunt down their own people. By July 1870, all the final pockets of resistance had been suppressed, and business, at least in ladino terms, began to return to normal. Distinctions between conservative and liberal soon lost their meaning, and while the church never fully regained the position it had once held, the organization of Indian labor once more fell under the control of a ladino highland elite. After the wars of reform and the French intervention, a certain stability was also beginning to reshape the structure of the Mexican state on a national level, initiating a process of modernization that would affect the Indians of Chiapas perhaps even more severely than the experience of independence.

Porfirio Díaz and the Governmental State

With the victory over Maximilian in 1867 and the imposition of the Laws of Reform by Benito Juárez, what appeared to be the triumph of liberalism was in fact its transformation "from an ideology in combat with an inherited set of institutions, social arrangements, and values into a unifying political myth."[34] Although classical or doctrinaire liberalism had begun as the dominant political vision in postindependence Mexico, faced with the vested colonial interests championed by an opposition conservative party, a country divided along regional lines and loyalties, and the humiliation of foreign military and monarchical intervention, liberalism could claim only the successful drafting of the constitution of 1857 as its highest achievement. Among the postwar liberal establishment, the constitution thus took on an almost inviolate status. However, when confronted with the pressing problem of how to create a strong and peaceful nation, the new generation of liberals adopted policies and practices that took their inspiration from ideas and theories that were anything but liberal.[35]

Viewing Europe as a disorganized shambles, a mess mostly due to the dogmas of the French Revolution and those "metaphysicians and legists" who tried to make them a reality, Henri de Saint-Simon was the first to seek out a strong principle of order to rescue the beleaguered European state. Although they were still wrapped in the rhetoric of the postindependence liberal state, the correctness of such a vision also struck deep and lasting chords among the new Mexican intellectual and political elite. Saint-Simon's idea that society should be administered and not governed soon became the foundation of a style of Mexican politics that proudly called itself scientific.[36] "Managers and administrators, experts performing their functions, were to replace rulers and governors. Individual liberty, the social goal of the liberals, was to be put aside in favor of association, based on functional specialization."[37] After his death, the theories of Saint-Simon were to find their most persuasive and articulate continuation in the work of Auguste Comte, and it was familiarity with Comte's ideas and with the man himself that gave the greatest impetus to Mexico's new style of governmental thought.

Centered on the Mexico City daily newspaper *La Libertad*, and headed by the figure of Justo Sierra, a group of young intellectuals began to consciously express the principal concepts of scientific politics. At heart, the new politics contained the basic conviction that the methods of science could be applied to national problems. However, the growing support for the applicability of scientific methods to the Mexican predicament was also due to a new understanding of the Mexican nation. This understanding owed its acceptance as much to the influence of the historical school of law made popular by Edouard Laboulaye, and of the evolutionary theories of Charles Darwin and Herbert Spencer, as it did to the positivist philosophy of Auguste Comte.[38] What all these theorists had in common was the central belief that society changed and developed over time and thus that, rather than a static object, society was best understood as a living, growing, and developing organism. While each theorist drew his own conclusions from this perspective, it was also generally agreed that history was the principal method by which such changes could be perceived and therefore either partially influenced or more overtly directed. Nonetheless, while the historical school in particular can be seen as having a direct influence over the creation of a Mexican senate, it was principally the work of Comte that led to such a move being welcomed as one more step toward the centralization of power in the Mexican state.

Comte believed that the human mind naturally passes through three successive stages of development. First comes the theological, which is understood as a type of imaginary stage, then the metaphysical, which is understood as principally abstract, and finally the scientific or positive stage.[39] This Law of Three Stages, as it is known, is also applicable by extension to the development of society in general. Even in light of the limited and necessarily schematic picture of Mexican pre- and postcolonial history that has been presented in the preceding chapters, it is possible to recognize the appeal of a Comtean periodization for analyzing the development of Mexican society as viewed from the closing decades of the nineteenth century. Coming after the earlier struggles, and combined with the deep-rooted desire to create a modern Mexican state, Cometean thought struck many in the political elite with a near-millennial intensity.[40] For if Mexico had passed through the theological (colonial) stage and the metaphysical (liberal) stage, it was now ready to realize the positive, or what I shall term the governmental, stage.

The so-called prophet of positivism in Mexico was Gabino Barreda, who had actually attended Comte's lectures in mid-nineteenth-century Paris. Barreda supported the creation of an intellectual and governmental elite through his founding of the Escuela Nacional Preparatoria (national preparatory school).[41] The positivist-inspired curriculum was later to make its mark on the more widespread, yet not necessarily more influential, national curriculum, which would become the backbone for a campaign of obligatory schooling throughout Mexico. Arguably, however, the school's main achievement was to supply the state with a generation of administrators convinced of the secular character of a modern state. It thus fell upon this new generation of bureaucrats to ensure that vital statistics, fiscal processes, judicial procedures, education, and even the calendar, births, marriages, and deaths were all removed from remaining church control. Citizens were no longer seen merely as the holders of rights but rather as important parts of a civil organism requiring both regulation and administration. This sentiment was expressed dramatically and revealingly by Francisco Cosmes when he stated that society now rejected "rights" for "bread . . . , security, order and peace." Rights, after all, had only produced distress, in Cosmes's view. "Now let us try a little tyranny, but honourable tyranny," he suggested, "and see what results it brings."[42]

The "honourable tyranny" to which Cosmes referred, and for which the científicos came to provide both intellectual and political support, was embodied in the thirty-five-year dictatorship of President Don Emilio Porfirio Díaz. In their keenness to bring strength, peace, stability, and order to Mexico, the advocates of scientific politics thus found themselves taking on the role of intellectual apologists for dictatorial government in much the same way that Comte had himself welcomed the "republican dictatorship" of Louis Napoleon's coup in 1851, and the Physiocrats before him had rationalized the need for an "enlightened despot." Probably the most extensive defense of the necessity for such an obviously anticonstitutionalist measure can be found in Emilio Rabasa's *La constitución y la dictadura*.[43] Rabasa's argument had a clearly Comtean genesis in that his criticism of the existing constitution was

centered on its failure to concur with sociological laws. While the implications of this constitutional disjuncture legitimized the strong authoritarian rule of Don Porfirio, the dictatorship was nonetheless considered
a temporary step toward the day when society might have developed
sufficiently to truly fulfill the liberal vision expressed in the 1857 constitution.[44] Exactly what this was to mean for Mexico's indigenous
population was made patently clear when the selfsame Emilio Rabasa
was made governor of Chiapas in 1892, making him, at thirty-five, the
youngest governor in the history of Mexico.[45]

At the core of this new order—and it was a belief that stood above
all others—was the unquestioned view that the political future of the
country depended entirely on the development of the economy. The
whole nature of the Díaz system was based on a deep understanding
that stability was necessary first and foremost for economic reasons, in
particular for the attraction of foreign investment. Dismissing as unre-
alistic the liberal idealism of the earlier reform period, with its emphasis on democratic institutions and individual equality, the government
instead channeled revenue toward mechanisms of control and security.
It has been claimed that Díaz in fact invested 55 percent of Mexico's
revenue in military and police services, and another 30 percent to maintain his state bureaucracy.[46] The main instrument of the new Mexican
governmental state was therefore a loyal and obedient urban and, more
importantly, rural police force. *Los rurales*, as they were known, were
equipped with smart uniforms, good horses, and a plentiful supply of
arms and ammunition. As Díaz began to invest in railroads and telegraph systems, their effectiveness as a mobile and responsive arm of
political power invited both internal fear and external admiration.

With Mexico no longer a country of bandits or feuding regions, Díaz
sought to woo investors from the United States and Europe with generous concessions and legislative reforms. In 1884 he changed the old
Spanish code concerning mineral rights, making ownership of the land
sufficient to claim extraction of what lay below. Even this considerable
concession was deemed insufficient by some científicos, leading to a
further amendment in 1892, whose objective in many ways summed
up the aims of the Díaz reforms: "facility to acquire, liberty to exploit,
and security to retain."[47] This new Mexican governmentality did not go
unnoticed, and soon some of the biggest names in U.S. industry began
to extract ores from Mexico. With the importation of U.S. managers
and technology and the railroads built specifically for the purpose, the
extraction of copper, zinc, and lead, as well as traditional silver mining,

became profitable. They were so profitable, in fact, that "by 1908, the *Wall Street Summary* could report that three-fourths of the dividend-paying mines in Mexico were owned by U.S. interests and that these 'paid a sum 24 percent in excess of the aggregate net earnings of all the National Banks in the United States, or about $95,000,000.'"[48]

When oil was first discovered in 1901, it was by a U.S. company, Doheny and Associates. By this time, though, Díaz and the científicos were already feeling the pressure of so much U.S. investment, and the administration attempted to counterbalance this influence with capital from Europe.[49] Hoping to achieve some kind of neutrality among the major powers, the government gave a large part of the oil drilling in Mexico to a British company, El Aguila (Mexican Eagle, controlled by Weetman Pearson and Sons of London). German finance was also initially sought for assistance with loans, banking, and most controversially, arms sales. The French, too, were approached for loans, and their expertise helped establish the Mexican National Bank. Citizens from all these countries came and lived in Mexico, often to manage and oversee their investments, but often also to seek out further opportunities in textiles (the French), agriculture (the Germans), public works (the British), and heavy industry (the Americans). The time of Díaz, as much of the architecture and many of the trading houses of Mexico City can still attest, was a time of opulence and European-inspired refinement.[50]

Far removed from the decadent lifestyle of the Mexico City elite, however, were the millions of peasants who found themselves subject to the mano duro (heavy hand) of the Díaz regime. After suffering under the midcentury liberal land reforms, whose stated intention was to create a class of small landholders or yeoman farmers, peasants and the indigenous once again found themselves confronted with legislation and corrupt business practices aimed at removing what little land they had managed to keep. This time, though, there was no social ideal behind the land grab. The question of society, particularly the place of the lower working classes, was approached in an instrumental manner. Just as all other natural resources in Mexico had come to transcend in importance the people and communities that surrounded them, land was to be distributed in what was adjudged the most productive manner. In line with such a rationale, large estates or haciendas were created, and throughout the country considerable investment, often foreign, was put into the establishment of henequen (sisal), rubber, guayule, cochineal, and coffee plantations. Often, however, land was purchased for purely speculative reasons, either for its mineral rights or in view of possible future railroad construction. By 1911 only 5 percent remained in the hands of communal—that is, Indian—villages, and over 90 percent of Mexico's peasants had become landless.[51]

Nowhere was this governmentality more apparent than in the north of the country. Having more or less wiped out the Apache Indians, the states of Chihuahua and Sonora still boasted significant populations of Tarahumara and Yaqui Indians. Considered the most modern region of Mexico, the zone near the northern border with the United States had witnessed the greatest influx of people both from the U.S. and from other, more impoverished regions of Mexico. With the establishment of iron smelters, mines, cattle ranches, networks of communication, and transport links, the landscape of the north and its people were transformed. Progress, if that's what it was, came at a price. As the government attempted to confiscate the best agricultural land of the Yaqui to hand over to the American Richardson Company, the Indians fought back. For years the Yaquis bravely resisted the onslaught of a modernity that wanted to remove from them the communal land that was their means of subsistence and, perhaps more importantly, the basis upon which their indigenous communal life had managed to survive up to that point. However, when the full force of the governmental state came to bear down upon the Yaqui, it was relentless in its adherence to the logic of positivist economics. Between 1903 and 1907, thousands of rebellious Yaquis were deported to the henequen plantations of the Yucatan and sold into virtual slavery.[52]

Apart from the wealth of Mexico's natural resources, foreign investors were also attracted by the plentiful supply of cheap and obedient labor. Obedience in this instance usually resulted from the conditions of peonage that the Díaz reforms created, if not from the more overt interventionist tactics that led to the Yaquis' enslavement in the south. Estimates of the number of workers effectively existing in conditions of bondage have ranged anywhere from 750,000 to 5 million.[53] Even those workers who might be more reasonably considered to have entered into a voluntary labor contract found that when they raised any objections to their working conditions, they were met with a harsh response. Unions were banned, as were strikes, and those that did occur were broken up either by the rurales or, on occasion, by U.S. officers who crossed the border to protect the interests of their fellow countrymen. With a mixture of repression and co-optation, Díaz managed to keep a relative peace in Mexico for some thirty years. Opposition newspapers were censored, as were opposition parties; infiltrators and spies were used in both international business practices and domestic affairs. Those who refused the opportunity to join the system were often shot as they supposedly attempted to escape, a practice that famously became known as the *ley fuga.*

"Enlightened Caciquismo" in Chiapas

The arrival of the new governmental regime in Chiapas was no less radical than in other parts of the country, and in many respects it was perhaps even more so. In the figure of Emilio Rabasa, the young dictatorial apologist and científico, the theory of the governmental state found a zealous and committed practitioner, who, although he was officially governor of the region for only three years, introduced the reforms that would determine the state's development for decades to come. His modernization program for local government centered on three interrelated spheres: finance, administration, and police. One of his first decisions was to remove the state capital from highland San Cristóbal to lowland Tuxtla, where it currently remains. Although in many ways a symbolic gesture in recognition of the earlier liberal victory, it was also a move that heralded what most Mexican observers have come to interpret as the foundational period of modern Chiapas. Following a rationale nearly identical to that applied in the national capital, Tuxtla was to be the stronghold of a centralizing governmental tendency considered vital to ensuring the local changes conducive to state and national development.

The system of local government that Rabasa had inherited was one dominated by local political bosses, or caciques, as they continue to be known. These men, like Sebastian Escobar of Soconusco, Julian Grajales of Chiapa de Corzo, and Miguel Utrilla of the central highlands, had effectively divided the state into private fiefdoms within which local bureaucratic appointments and questions of law and order fell under their control. Rabasa sought to undermine such institutionalized relationships by first founding a state rural police force, the Seguridad Pública, and then transforming the structure and means of tax collection.[54] In a move not at all unlike that of his Bourbon predecessors, Rabasa attempted to break the influence of local loyalties and vested interests through the imposition of men from Oaxaca, a neighboring state, in decisive administrative and security positions. Furthermore, he reformed the position of *jefe político*, a departmental-level bureaucrat whose task it was to collect taxes, removing the post from "democratic" election and instead making it subject to governmental appointment—that is, his own. He then founded the post of *visitador de jefaturas*, or inspector general, as a means to better monitor the conduct and efficiency of these more localized *jefes políticos*.[55] In this way, Rabasa, in a manner very reminiscent of the "enlightened despotism" of the Bourbons before him, began to bring local finances and community expenditures under greater governmental control and administrative surveillance. In fact, even at the time, the transformations in local government became known as examples of a *caciquismo ilustrado*, an "enlightened caciquismo."[56]

Rabasa also believed in the civilizing tendencies of modernization, introducing several public works programs, including a telegraph network, a (limited) public education system, sanitation work, and his favorite project, road construction. There were no roads in Chiapas when Rabasa first arrived, but with Díaz's approval, the Mexican army was mobilized to help construct a route that ran from San Cristóbal, via Tuxtla, to Oaxaca. As Thomas Benjamin notes, "since the road favored the Central Valley more than the highlands, it became part of a discriminatory pattern of development, whose effect is apparent even today."[57] With a combination of land privatization, improved communication, and transport networks, including modernized port facilities at Tonala, the commercial agriculture of the lowlands experienced a boom. As in other parts of Mexico, the commodity that fueled such local expansion was the warm governmental reception given to foreign capital. According to Robert Wasserstrom, "between 1880 and 1910, British, French, American, German, and Spanish businessmen invested 4.3 million pesos in Chiapas' burgeoning coffee industry, concentrated in Soconusco."[58]

Coffee was not the only crop that attracted international interest. Both rubber and tropical hardwoods also witnessed large-scale investment from U.S. companies during the period, and on a smaller scale, local creole *hacendados* (hacienda owners) turned their attention to cotton, cattle, and cacao. Common to all these endeavors, however, was the need for cheap and regular labor. Unsurprisingly, therefore, whereas the postindependence vision of the liberals had erased the Chiapan Indian in the attempt to create the juridical construct of the private citizen, the científicos opted for a more sectorial understanding of the native population. In keeping with their understanding of the state as a developing organism, the científicos ignored individual liberty, the professed telos of earlier liberal elites, as they took the imperative of functional specialization to its logical conclusion. Blind to the significance of cultural heritage and communal traditions (unless as bothersome obstacles), the governmental vision reduced the Chiapan Indians to the monolithic category of "worker."[59] As a human resource rather than a human being, Chiapan Indians once again began to fall prey to tactics and legislation designed to ensure a mobile yet consistent native workforce (see figure 3.1).

If not already tied to a particular *finca* (farm) under the baldiaje system—which, if anything, only expanded under the *reparto* (privatization) of lands initiated by the Rabasa administration, a policy that led to the end of village *ejidos* (communal lands), and one he would later regret—most Indians found themselves forced by economic necessity into migrant wage labor. "Economic necessity," however, was often merely a more polite euphemism for describing the system of labor entrapment called the *enganche*, a recruitment strategy described, in less ambiguous terms, by one contemporary as "the commerce in human flesh."[60] The *enganchadores* (approximate translation: trappers) employed a variety of tactics to ensnare their victims, most common among which was the creation of a debt, either through the lending of money (usually before or during an Indian feast day or celebration) or via the supply of large amounts of aguardiente liquor.[61] Some types of labor were considerably worse than others, however, and the *monterías* (mahogany lumber camps) held such an unsavory notoriety that the enganchadores actually had to kidnap highland Indians to form labor gangs.[62] Conditions were in fact so dire that many of the workers had to be culled from the ranks of criminals or deported rebellious Indians from Sonora and the Yucatan. Whether convicts or not, all were chained up at night and watched over by armed guards during the day.[63]

One other aspect of Chiapan commerce that reveals the limited extent of the Díaz modernization project was the continued use of Indians as human porters, known as *tamanes*. It was a practice increasingly at odds with governmental ideas of progress, yet nonetheless the savage logic of the economic rationale that underpinned the work permitted its continuation. In an 1898 letter to President Díaz from Francisco León, then governor of Chiapas, we can read, in tones of muted outrage, the advantages for the local merchant of using Indian carriers rather than mules:

> He makes a contract that places all the responsibility on the carrier;
> he thus has faith that all the merchandise will be treated with care,
> needing no one else to supervise its transport; he need not worry about
> feeding the carrier, nor paying him in advance; he pays the carrier one
> peso per journey and charges three or four, gaining two or three pesos
> on every journey; if a mule dies or becomes useless, it monopolizes the

business, impeding competition, because it prevents the timely transport of the merchandise. . . .

The opening of paved roads does not suit, nor can it suit, these merchants, even less the opening of railways, which would lead to the disappearance of this type of exploitation that leaves wounds on the bodies of many indigenous, the same as those which the beasts of burden bear on their backs.[64]

Perhaps one of the most tragic aspects of these years of modernity for the Indians of Chiapas was that they saw the initiation of a new structure of civil and religious hierarchy within the communities themselves. By taking advantage of the new administrative roles within the communities, such as that of the jefe político, it was possible for the non-Indian authorities to force native leaders to provide reluctant workers. Since these administrators also had control over the sale of land and could call upon the Seguridad Pública to enforce their decisions, initially resistant Indian leaders often found themselves corrupted. Thus it appears that it was during this period that native cofradías and religious *cargos* (responsibilities) first began to take on the early characteristics of the civil-religious hierarchies that anthropologists would later suggest were characteristic of an indigenous response to social stratification.[65]

Conclusion

The governmental vision and the drive for modernization that characterized both Chiapas and Mexico in the late nineteenth and early twentieth centuries led in many ways toward a revolutionary change in conditions for the majority of the Indians of the region. The paper rights that had been so much a part of the liberal rhetoric of the postindependence era gave way to the interventionist tactics of a new scientific politics, a politics that merely gave intellectual credibility to a widespread restriction of social freedom. As one American who lived in Chiapas at the time noted, "as long as a man owed money to his patron, his freedom was only a meaningless technicality."[66] As the Porfiriato wore on, the chasm that divided old liberals from new would eventually lead to a ten-year social revolution whose battles, although momentous in other parts of Mexico, would not greatly affect the Indians of Chiapas, but whose later political and social results would be significant.

FOUR

Institutionaliz-ing the Indian

Corporatismo, Indigenismo, *and the* Creation of an Authoritarian Regime

Initially born of a legitimate campaign against the reelection of Porfirio Díaz, the Mexican Revolution became a combustible mixture of elite dissatisfaction, popular resentment, foreign interest, and political ideology. Its greatest achievement was probably the 1917 constitution, with the inclusion of the all-important article 27, a legislative measure that restricted the ownership of Mexican land to Mexican nationals and in so doing provided for the redistribution of property so central to the agrarian demands of the rural masses. In the end, though, the revolution was won by the members of an elite regional faction that had first sought to replace Díaz within his own system. Hailing mainly from the state of Sonora, in the northwest of Mexico, the group fought under the Carrancista or constitutionalist banner.[1] By 1920 they had all but secured their victory, having already orchestrated the assassination of Emiliano Zapata, the popular leader of the rebel army of the south. In 1923 Pancho Villa, the charismatic general of the northern forces, was also murdered. So violent, in fact, was the new government's response to perceived threat that by 1929, the year Diego Rivera was commissioned to paint an allegorical history of Mexico on the walls of the Palacio Nacional, nearly all the heroes of the ten-year rebellion were dead, and the revolution itself was already well on the way to becoming that peculiar Mexican political creation, *la revolución institucionalizada*, the "institutionalized revolution."

Even after writing what is considered by many the definitive account of Emiliano Zapata, one of the revolution's greatest heroes and the figure most representative of the populist interests that came to be enshrined in article 27 of the 1917 constitution,[2] John Womack still believes that the real nature of the historical transformations of those ten years of violence "is not so much social revolution as political management."[3] It is a view also shared by Kevin Middlebrook, although for Middlebrook the resolution of the revolution embodies a more puzzling paradox. Thinking not only of the Mexican experience, he explains, "the paradox of social revolution is that popular mobilization and socio-economic transformation most commonly eventuate in a new form of authoritarian rule."[4] Irrespective of whether such a broad generalization is valid or not, in the case of Mexico it certainly appears to be true. Nevertheless, while agreeing with Middlebrook's characterization of the outcome of the revolution, we may well wish to question his description of this process as paradoxical.[5]

This is because it is entirely possible to view the conclusion of the Mexican Revolution as a continuation of, or a fulfillment of, rather than a radical departure from, the new governmentality that came into being at the end of the nineteenth century. It could be argued that the policy reforms and classifications that exemplified the application of scientific methods to a "social organism" in the time of Porfirio Díaz also paradoxically resulted in the creation of an agrarian and labor consciousness. The revolution can therefore be interpreted as a struggle to close the political gap between the industrial or agrarian worker and his or her political representation. Embracing the revolutionary potential inherent in their new governmental classifications, the diverse regional and agrarian insurgent groups can be seen as rising up to contest the policies and practices that had come to alter their lives so radically, while nevertheless leaving the very governmental understandings that made such policies thinkable uncontested. For although the Mexican Revolution undeniably represents a dramatic moment in Mexican history, it does not represent a significant transformation in governmental understanding. Giving rise to the corporatism that has come to characterize the Mexican political system, the revolution can be viewed as securing the institutionalization of historically contingent classifications, which have determined the limits of legitimate political representation ever since.

Pursuing the idea of continuity, we would do well to recall that key to the political thought of that late-nineteenth-century Mexican governmental period was, of course, the philosophy of positivism, and in particular the work of Auguste Comte. It is revealing, therefore, to think that "Comte's ideal was a hierarchically organised non-competitive collectivism in which state and society were one."[6] Some ten years after the revolution, this ideal appeared to be close to fulfillment: Mexico had made the transition from the personalist rule of Díaz to the institutional rule of the official party, at that time known as the Partido Nacional Revolucionario (PNR), later to become the Partido Revolucionario Mexicano (PRM), and eventually to become what was to be the sole ruling party for seventy-one years, the Partido Revolucionario Institucional (PRI). The Mexican system of corporatismo seemed to embody the very method of which Comte had dreamt, because corporatism, as Charles Hale writes, "is defined as a system of interest representation by hierarchically organised and non-competitive groups, recognised and regulated (if not created) by the state."[7]

In fact, it is Hale's opinion that this political continuity is only possible because the proponents of scientific politics in the Díaz era were in reality also a breed of liberal constitutionalists — not, of course, constitutionalists of an absolutist, doctrinaire, or metaphysical nature but rather constitutionalists of a historical and sociological taint.[8] Hale's interpretation is supported by the response of Andrés Molina Enríquez, one of the architects of the postrevolution constitution of 1917, when facing criticism that the inclusion of article 27 concerning property was "radically communistic" and that the constitution itself gave too much power to the executive. While Molina "acknowledged that the 'spirit' of the Constitution was 'collectivist' as opposed to the 'individualist' spirit of 1857, he claimed this change merely reflected the Comtean concept (unknown in 1857) that societies were 'living organisms.'"[9]

Hale is not the first to recognize the continuity of positivist thought both during the revolution itself and throughout the postrevolutionary period,[10] but his originality lies in his suggestion that just as the liberal triumph of the 1870s came to take on the role of a unifying myth for the political community of the late nineteenth century, so too has the revolution come to play a similar role in the political configuration of Mexican politics post-1920.[11] In both cases, the consequences of concrete historical experience have led to the creation of a consensus — a consensus that leaves little political space for real opposition or discord. Positivism, therefore, could claim to underpin a strong centralized political system, one that could support dictatorial rule in the short term and constitutional fulfillment in the long term.[12] Nonetheless, the particular contingent historical experience of the Mexican nation provided the broad legitimization for the creation of a political Leviathan that such a governmental rationale first theoretically advocated. This is not to deny the potential for radical social reform that can be introduced under such a system; it is, however, to highlight another possibility, one that whiggish retrospective history seems to uphold: that such unity, in its negation of the necessity for any plural, critical, and oppositional political discourse, lays the seeds for an oppressive and authoritarian political system.

Mestizaje: The Revolutionary Ideal

After ten years of fighting, with a death toll somewhere between 1.5 and 2 million, postrevolutionary Mexico was a country in need of reconstruction and reunification. While the vision that held sway among the new northern rulers was one of unremitting modernism, the realignment of social forces and the burden of expectation that the revolution had unleashed often threatened to unravel and return the country to the widespread violence of the *decena trágica,* the "tragic decade." The priority of those early years, dominated in the main by the presidency of Plutarco Elías Calles (1924–1928), was one of national integration combined with governmental control. As far as ideology was concerned, apart from the rhetoric surrounding presidential claims of a "revolutionary nationalism," perhaps the most original moment of revolutionary reform was realized under the influence of José Vasconcelos, the idealistic minister of education from 1921 to 1924.

The novelty of the Vasconcelos vision lay in his conception of the modern Mexican nation as a cultural entity that went far beyond the narrow power politics and economics of his fellow ministers. Along with Antonio Caso and Pedro Henríquez Urena, Vasconcelos was a product of the Ateneo de la Juventud, a study and lecture society created in 1909 in open opposition to the positivist-dominated curriculum of the Escuela Nacional Preparatoria (ENP).[13] The Ateneistas sought inspiration in the aesthetic and philosophical texts of Kant, Schopenhauer, Nietzsche, and above all, Bergson. Their conception of modernity differed from the determinist views of the Díaz científicos insofar as they allowed for an element of contingency to temper their own evolutionist beliefs and, in so doing, placed greater emphasis on the creative force and vital impetus (*elán vital*) that they argued is present in all nature. Their attempt to marry a version of metaphysics with positivism was not in itself new—we need look no further than Comte's own positivist spiritualism for evidence of this—but what made the Ateneistas distinctive was their self-conscious sense of Latin Americanism.

Influenced largely by the then-famous essay *Ariel,* penned by the Uruguayan José Rodó, Vasconcelos and his companions refused to accept the racial determinism and European superiority of writers such as Herbert Spencer and Comte.[14] A reinterpretation of Shakespeare's *Tempest* and Ernest Renan's *Caliban, Ariel* told the story of a wise teacher, Prospero, who calls upon the youth of America to reembrace the ideals of spirituality, grace, and intelligence that Ariel embodies. The threat to Ariel's ascendancy was Caliban, the symbol of materialism, "sensuality and torpor" that in Rodó's text was openly identified with the United States.[15] In their journal, *Revista Moderna,* the Ateneistas discussed Rodó's work and, like their intellectual contemporaries in Argentina, Peru, and Brazil, contributed to the articulation of an optimistic and consciously Latin American idealism. "Our America," Vasconcelos once proclaimed, "is the creation of *mestizos,* of two or three races by blood and of all cultures by spirit."[16] His philosophical and cultural beliefs would eventually lead him to write *La raza cósmica* (The Cosmic Race), a philosophical rather than a biological justification for the superiority of the Latin American mestizaje.[17] In those early years of postrevolutionary Mexico, it was thus Vasconcelos who strove hardest to raise from the ashes of a war-torn land a being whom he believed worthy of the sacrifice that had been endured. This being he called *el hombre nuevo,* the "new man" of the revolution.

Vasconcelos began, as it were, at the bottom, dispatching thousands of *maestros rurales* (rural teachers) to some of the most remote parts of the republic.[18] His teachers were imbued with a missionary zeal, and their objective to create a basic library and school in every Mexican village, although never achieved, was embarked upon with a true revolutionary vocation. In their own disciplinary journal, *El Maestro Rural,* it is possible to read of the incomprehension and, on occasion, the outright hostility with which these rural teachers were often met. In their promotion of a secular state and their sincere belief in a revolutionary nation, the teachers confronted the entrenched loyalties and beliefs of a still predominantly regional and provincially focused populace. With their keenness to replace the social and educational role of the church, it was perhaps inevitable that the new state-backed rural schools would soon inflame the Catholic congregations of the countryside. The Cristero Rebellion of 1926–1929 was the most significant result of this conflict, and although it was limited to the states of the midwest, the relationship between church and state nationwide remained fraught for decades to come.[19]

While Vasconcelos's rural schools laid the foundations for the later socialist educational programs of the state, he will probably be better remembered internationally for his instrumental role in employing art in the service of the revolution. Through his belief in the monumental and didactic nature of art, Vasconcelos managed to excite the imaginations of muralists such as Diego Rivera, José Clemente Orozco, David Alfaro Siqueiros, and Rufino Tamayo. He financed artists' trips to rural and indigenous parts of Mexico, constantly recalling the triumphs of pre-Columbian Indian heritage, and urged the artists to paint the walls and entrances of major public buildings. In the 1923 *Manifesto of the Union of Workers, Technicians, Painters and Sculptors*, it is possible to hear the influence of the Vasconcelos vision on the artists of the day:

> The popular art of Mexico is the most important and healthiest of spiritual manifestations and its native tradition is the best of all traditions. . . . We repudiate the so-called studio art and all the art-forms of ultra intellectual coteries for their aristocratic elements and we extol the manifestations of monumental art as a public amenity. We proclaim that all forms of aesthetic expression which are foreign or contrary to popular feeling are bourgeois and should be eliminated, in as much as they contribute to the corruption of the taste of our race, which has already been almost completely corrupted in the towns.[20]

Apart from Vasconcelos himself, nobody represents the successes and failures of the early metaphysical idealism of the revolution better than Diego Rivera. Ambitious and iconoclastic in equal measure, Rivera at one point sought no less than to paint the whole of Mexican history. This aim (best exemplified by the mural at the National Palace in Mexico City) should give an insight into the tenacity and confidence of the man, but it should also remind us of the very pliability of art, a quality that human beings do not so easily embody. In his mural *Man, Controller of the Universe*, we see a fair-skinned male seated at the center of the composition. In his hands he holds the control levers for a universe that surrounds him. The painting, in all its historical and political complexity (not least of which was the cancellation of its original commission for the Rockefeller Center in New York), portrays better than any philosophical tract the central belief that the new man of the early twentieth century stood at the crossroads of science and history and was, unlike his superstitious and oppressed predecessors, uniquely poised to direct these mechanisms of progress. It offers all the excitement and awe that such an idealized universal humanism commands, and in light of the Soviet revolution, with which Mexican intellectuals increasingly sought solidarity, it also transformed Mexican mural art into international revolutionary art.

After the exile of Vasconcelos in 1924, this transformation of an always-tentative revolutionary Mexican philosophy into an international revolutionary philosophy was, in the opinion of Octavio Paz, all but inevitable. He writes, "the inexistence of a large proletariat or a socialist movement of significance — that is to say, the lack of relation between the social and historical reality and the painting that attempted to represent it — gave the murals of Rivera, Siqueiros, and others a tragically inauthentic character."[21] Nowhere is this charge of inauthenticity more compelling than in Rivera's depiction of the indigenous of Mexico. While his glorification of the pre-Columbian Indian past should be recognized as a loosely understood pro-Indian interpretation of Mexican history, in general his adoption of Indian cultural motifs should be seen as highly selective and subject to his own aesthetic and cultural biases. In the words of one commentator, "he presented a casually eclectic view of pre-Columbian history, often deriving his images from Colonial sources that manifest demonstrable European influence, and his strong preference for the exotically sophisticated culture of the Aztecs gave a skewed view of the Indian populace."[22]

Like the *indigenistas* before him, in particular those who employed images and histories of the Aztec past as a means to legitimize a postcolonial identity and political independence, Rivera had difficulty equating the contemporary Indian with that of his pre-Hispanic past.[23] In fact, during those postrevolutionary years, toward what became officially termed "the indigenous problem," Rivera had a surprisingly orthodox Marxist approach. In his own contribution to what was then surfacing as a significant debate, he wrote, "the 'indigenous problem' has been employed by the aristocratic-bourgeois politicians, or petite bourgeoisie, to cover up by means of an ethnological denomination that which is in reality nothing more than a question of class."[24] The "Indian problem" was therefore no different from the problem of the poor *campesino* (field worker/peasant). The question of culture, which was increasingly becoming the central question in the new social science of anthropology, was thus dismissed by Rivera. He argued instead that poverty and oppression were the issues of priority and that the notion of culture was best restricted to the domain of a new, national, modern, and revolutionary Mexican society that he hoped to encourage through his art. However, Rivera's opinions, although popular in certain quarters and later echoed in the policies of Cárdenas, would not become "official" for long.

Official Indigenismo, or The Story of Cultural Anthropology and the State

Arguably, the story of official indigenismo does not begin in Mexico at all, but in Germany. From Germany it progressed to the United States, and from there, like so much that is assumed to be modern, to Mexico. The reason for this geographic complexity lies in the personal and intellectual trajectory of the individual considered "the most important single force in shaping American anthropology in the first half of the twentieth century" — Franz Boas.[25]

The singularity of Boas's achievement was to steer U.S. anthropology away from the evolutionist theories of Spencer and Darwin, spurning the concept of race, with all the perilous implications of hierarchy and superiority that it suggested, and instead proposing the "new" concept of culture.[26] Having experienced and escaped the increasingly chauvinistic and nationalist tendencies of late-nineteenth-century Germany, Boas was nonetheless keen to bring what he considered the progressive aspects of the German scientific tradition to his adopted America. That this personal experience gave his "cultural anthropology" an added political and ethical dimension has not gone unnoticed. Likened at times to both the *Nationalcharakter* of Alexander von Humboldt and the *Volksgeist* of the romantic Johann Gottfried Herder, the Boasian culture concept attempted to engender an academic respect for the value of the "primitive societies" that lay outside the U.S. and European sphere.[27] Believing that in these primitive societies, culture was located in the myths and folklore of the people, Boas promoted detailed ethnographic fieldwork in an attempt to "establish the facts" and ultimately to "find the eternal truth."[28] In this regard, however, Boas's seemingly relativized culture concept embodied a central tension between the ethnographic particular and the scientific universal. That ultimately this tension would resolve itself in the creation of an enduring research methodology for the social science of anthropology reveals the inescapable influence of enlightenment thinking on the Boasian project.

George Stocking, the most attentive interpreter of the Boasian legacy, explains further:

> On the one hand, in defending the mental capacities of non-European peoples, he was defending their capacity to participate fully in "modern

civilization"; on the other, in defending their cultural values, he was establishing a kind of Archimedian leverage point for the criticism of that civilization. The need for such an external reference point was one of the leitmotifs of Boas' career, and it tended to carry with it a double standard of cultural evaluation: a universalistic one in terms of which he criticised the society in which he lived and a relativistic one in terms of which he defended the cultural alternative. Whatever the emotional roots of this need, the external cultural alternative was for Boas an essential precondition for the achievement both of scientific knowledge in the social sphere and of the freedom of the individual in society. Just as the "scientific study of generalised social forms" required that the student "free himself from all valuations based on our [own] culture," so also did true freedom require that we be "able to rise above the fetters that the past imposes upon us." Without an external cultural reference point by which to bring these valuations to the level of consciousness, both scientific knowledge and true freedom would be impossible. This then was the ultimate meaning of Boas' lifelong fight for culture.[29]

The enmeshing of the Boasian reification of science and academic study within the *official* revolutionary nationalism of America's southern neighbor can be traced in the main to the institutional and intellectual influence of Manuel Gamio, the first Mexican to receive a doctorate in anthropology outside of Mexico. Gamio first went to Columbia University in New York to study for a master's degree in 1909. There he became a protégé of Boas, eventually receiving his doctorate under Boas's tutelage in 1921.[30] As early as 1916, however, Gamio had already published *Forjando Patria* (Forging the Nation), the book for which he is best known, and where he first set out his belief in the instrumental utility of anthropology for the creation of a revolutionary Mexican nation. Arguing that the Mexican population around the time of the revolution was at least two-thirds Indian, Gamio, unlike Vasconcelos, believed that the future of the *patria* rested with the country's indigenous population. Where Vasconcelos sought to realize his revolutionary future through the patriotic ministrations of his maestros rurales, Gamio, much like their more inquisitive and sensitive missionary forefathers, sought first to understand indigenous culture before "forging" it into the new nationalist ideal of mestizaje.

Mestizaje was therefore not simply a case of racial intermixing, as at times it was articulated by Vasconcelos, but rather a process of social and, especially, cultural amalgamation. The "Indian problem" and the

Mexican postrevolutionary policies of indigenismo to which it gave birth were therefore a problematique born of white/mestizo elite intellectual analysis rather than the product of direct Indian pressure. As Alan Knight writes, "the Indians themselves were the objects, not the authors, of indigenismo," and, as he dryly notes, "perhaps for that very reason it could be safely adopted."[31] As early as 1917, such a culturalist approach to the "Indian problem" found a place in the official bureaucracy with the founding of the Dirección de Antropología.[32] Over the next twenty years, Gamio, alongside Lucio Mendieta y Nuñez, Carlos Basuri, and Moises Saenz, to name but a few, occupied the most prominent positions in a series of institutions created specifically to address the indigenous issue, including the Misiones Culturales (1922), the Casa del Estudiante Indígena (1926), Educación Socialista (1934), the Departamento Autónomo de Asuntos Indígenas (1936), and the Instituto Nacional de Antropología e Historia (1938).

In strictly academic terms, Gamio was best known for his direction of a group of scholars working on the archaeological and anthropological reconstruction of the Aztec site of Teotihuacán. Apart from the physical excavations themselves, the result of this work was a two-volume survey entitled *The Population of Teotihuacán* (1922). Gamio's attempts to link archaeology and ethnography, previously the domain of U.S. academics, were novel if not wholly successful. Although he was an adherent of the Boasian culture concept, Gamio's style of analysis tended more toward the positivistic collection of data than the social-scientific method of ethnographic fieldwork.[33] For this reason, in academic terms at least, the work of the American Robert Redfield perhaps made a more lasting contribution to the understanding of contemporary Indian communities. His own version of culturalism, in recognition of the significant historical upset presented by the Spanish conquest to the somewhat ahistorical theory of environmental adaptation as first adopted by researchers, came to consider the Mexican Indian as a special instance that he named "folk culture."[34]

Folk culture was defined as "the unwritten, verbally-transmitted knowledge and world-view that exists in small, relatively isolated societies like the provincial societies of Mesoamerica."[35] "Folk" was to be contrasted with "urban," and the relative isolation of folk societies was to lead Redfield to make the further step toward a recognition of a process of acculturation, one that varied in degree depending on the proximity of folk societies to urban centers. It was a conceptual outline that was to have great influence and longevity among Anglo American and

Mexican anthropologists. Its effect on Mexican Indian policy, however, was due in the main to its claim that traditional native sociopolitical structures were at the heart of the difference between Indian communities and the wider national community.

The very concept of acculturation nonetheless suggested that this difference of worldview could be altered, and thus that the Indian could become more fully integrated into the Mexican national way of life. The idea of development thus presented itself as the means by which all the positive aspects of the urban centers could be brought to the Indian communities, while avoiding all the undesirable effects of having the Indians move to the cities. While this may have been the logical conclusion of the culturalist theory, it was only through the inclusion of Mexican anthropologists in the domain of political policy that such an approach came to have significant human consequences. As one contemporary anthropologist laments,

> From initially suggesting that the process of development be humanised and the Indian's point of view be taken into account, anthropology had strayed into becoming the ideological justification for a policy that proposed to solve the Indian problem by gradually eliminating the Indian as such.[36]

While the implicit aim of mestizaje was only rarely publicly articulated, at least to the indigenous themselves, this new institutional and academic concentration on Indian culture became increasingly widespread throughout Latin America. In Mexico, though, and in particular during the presidency of Lázaro Cárdenas, indigenismo took on its most politically intrusive form, moving from culturalism to corporatism, as a means of state control.

Cardenismo

Despite the intellectual and institutional efforts of individuals such as Gamio and Vasconcelos, the majority of postrevolutionary Mexico remained governed by a style of politics that, while not autocratic to the same degree as the Porfirian regime, was nevertheless highly personalistic at local, regional, and national levels. Admittedly, the relations of power were under constant renegotiation after the "revolutionary awakening" that had occurred among the masses, but nevertheless, although bosses changed, governmental style did not radically alter until the ascension of Lázaro Cárdenas to the presidency in 1934.

Although Cárdenas is rarely credited with an intellectual master plan, his rule, known as Cardenismo, has come to be recognized as a politico-symbolic phenomenon in its own right. The six-year period of his presidency (1934–1940) marks a moment when revolutionary politics took on a utopian air. Through his presidential tours of the country, Cárdenas sought out the rural populace of Mexico, making a point of listening, eating, and promising reforms to his humble hosts. That many of these peasants did in fact receive that for which they had petitioned explains in large part the respect and political capital that the name "Cardenismo" can still command today.[37] However, Cardenas's role as rural benefactor cannot obscure his more openly nationalist and administrative political strategy. It was, after all, during his presidency that the political tentacles of the soon-to-be-formed PRI were most deeply implanted among the working masses. Though unions had been organized prior to his rule, and the official party was itself founded by Calles in 1929, it was nonetheless under Cárdenas that the adoption of corporatism as the state's principal system of interest representation created the mechanisms of control and surveillance that would become integral to the next fifty years of PRI rule.

In many ways, Cárdenas was the revolution. He took the piecemeal reforms of his predecessors and combined them in a manner that allowed him to transform the nation while at the same time indelibly combining the future of that nation with the future of the new official party. This double-edged nature of the postrevolutionary Mexican political system would hold major implications for the indigenous populace.[38]

> Whatever the ratio of idealism to considerations of practical political gain in the actions of the government between 1934 and 1940, the facts remain that during this period the agrarian reform affected one third of all the lands it would touch from the adoption of the Constitution of 1917 until 1970, that there were more workers organised and strikes called than in any similar period of Mexican history, and that for the first time ever a Mexican government had actually attempted to introduce Indians into local and national politics as an organised force.[39]

Initially within the Cardenista political vision, however, the Indian was not seen in terms of his or her particular ethnic specificity; rather, the Indian was to be subsumed under the more general conception of the proletarian class.

Breaking the Mexican nation down into four key sectors — the labor sector, the peasant and agrarian sector, the popular sector, and the military — Cárdenas sought to govern through the creation of mammoth centralized associations. In adopting this sectorial approach, the Cárdenas political strategy, described by one commentator as a "politics of the masses," realized to a very large degree the Comtean ideal of corporate rule.[40] First, in 1938, in an attempt to harness the political power of the campesinos, the Confederación Nacional Campesina (CNC) was created. Then, under the positivist-influenced tutelage of Vicente Lombardo Toledano, the Confederación de Trabajadores de México (CTM) was formed to direct the might of the labor sector.[41] The Indians, although certainly considered part of the nation's work force, were also recognized as a special case. Although the creation of the new organizations can fairly be viewed as a politics of the masses, it was nevertheless always vital during the Cárdenas regime, and ever since, that the peasants' and workers' unions be kept apart, ensuring that the process of social reform remained under the control of the state and avoiding the creation of any single proletariat mass movement.[42] In Arnaldo Cordova's opinion, under Cárdenas, "the party thus resurged as an *administrator* of corporations, more than as an administrator of masses."[43]

Alongside this governmental desire for administrative totalism came other aspects of Cardenismo's view of revolutionary nationalism (including such controversial policies as the expropriation of oil and railways) that came closer to altering the country's external relations of power than the policies of any other period. Furthermore, while sharing with his Sonorense predecessors a distrust of the Catholic Church, Cárdenas went further, identifying hacendados (large landowners) and caciques (local bosses) as among the most significant obstacles to revolutionary change. Following Vasconcelos, he thus gave increased financial and institutional support to rural education, heralding a period of "socialist education" that differed from previous educational missions in that rural schools were also viewed as useful locales for educating peasants about their rights as workers and teaching the skills and habits necessary to create productive agricultural units. As Mary Kay Vaughan has noted, "whereas the pre-revolutionary school had etched itself into a restricted place in daily life, the revolutionary school presumed to overflow customary boundaries in order to transform community life."[44]

While Vaughan has correctly recognized certain affinities with the Porfirian education project, we would do well to also note the earlier attempts of Bourbon reformers to break the Catholic Church's hold via the schoolmaster or maestro.[45]

Uniquely, though, it was Cárdenas who combined this socialist education program with other interventionist policies seeking to radically transform rural community life, in particular Indian rural life. Himself of Tarascan Indian descent, Cárdenas hoped to break the "oppressive relations of power" within which the indigenous lived through the introduction of unionization and community reorganization. Furthermore, in an unprecedented move, Cárdenas also provided governmental protection to the first Protestant evangelical movement in Mexico, clearly supporting a competitor to the Catholicism to which the Indian majority was devoted. The deceptively named Summer Institute of Linguistics (SIL) targeted the most rural communities, including the indigenous communities of Chiapas. Although the government supposedly encouraged the SIL for their organizational abilities, their legacy of converts, like much that was first born of Cardenismo, has led to a peculiar political passivity within increasingly stratified indigenous collectivities.[46] It was thus Cárdenas who gave to indigenismo the very ethical and political ambiguity inherent in the postrevolutionary Mexican system.

In one of his final acts as president, Cárdenas hosted the first-ever Inter-American Indigenous Congress in Patzcauaro, Mexico, in 1940. With a message closer to Rivera than Gamio, Cárdenas in his address to the academic and indigenous delegates made his suspicion toward an overly culturalist stance explicit, while nevertheless reclaiming the Indian for his own project of revolutionary nationalism:

The formula of "incorporating the Indian into civilization," still has remains of the old systems that tried to hide the inequality of the situation, because this incorporation has generally been understood with regard to de-Indianizing and making less strange, that is to say, with putting an end to primitive culture: the uprooting of regional dialects, traditions, customs, and even the profound sentiments of the man rooted to his land. On the other hand, nobody is suggesting a resurrection of pre-Cortesian indigenous systems, or a stagnation incompatible with the currents of contemporary life. What we must support is the incorporation of the universal culture of the Indian, that is to say, the full development of all the potential and natural abilities of the race, the improvement of their living conditions, adding to their resources of subsistence and work all the implements of technology, of science, and of the universal arts, but always based upon a respect for the conscience and society of the racial personality."[47]

Revolutionary Experiences in Chiapas

Before the time of Cárdenas, though — a period that the Indians sometimes call *la revolución de los indios* (the revolution of the Indians) — the experience and legacy of the tragic decade in Chiapas was a very different and altogether less idealistic matter. It is even a common refrain that the revolution never arrived in Chiapas. It of course did, but it was not the social and populist revolution of later nationalist and party myth. Rather, the experience of Chiapas was similar to that of many regions outside of the northern and Zapatista zones: a partial, opportunistic, and parochial conflict between what were often long-established local rivals.

With the reforms of the Porfirian regime (1891–1911) that had resulted in an era of *caciquismo ilustrado*, Chiapas had experienced a period of uneven development with increased infrastructure and governmental investment concentrated in the commercial agricultural projects of the central lowlands and coastal zones. This governmental policy of *positivismo modernizador* (modernizing positivism) was initiated by the young Emilio Rabasa, who, with his transfer of the state capital from highland San Cristóbal to lowland Tuxtla, ensured that earlier divisions between the liberal/lowland and conservative/highland factions of the familia chiapaneca found themselves institutionally resolved in favor of the liberal lowland elite. Not surprisingly, therefore, the first "revolutionaries" in Chiapas turned out to be "essentially elitist, clerical and conservative in orientation."[48]

Called *el mano negro* (the black hand) or sometimes the iron circle, this group of highland lawyers and landowners expressed their opposition to the Díaz regime and the científicos as early as April 1911. Adopting the antireelectionist rhetoric of the Francisco Madero campaign, they raised an army of some eight hundred ladinos and, with both force and false promises, "recruited" several thousand mainly Chamulan Indians.[49] The rebellion was quickly quashed, and the highlanders, in fear of igniting another "caste war," accepted an unfavorable settlement. A more serious and prolonged rebellion began in 1914. After the victory of the revolutionary constitutionalist movement in central Mexico,

President Venustiano Carranza, in an effort to consolidate his government, dispatched a northern general and his troops to govern Chiapas. Although Chiapas had experienced an increase in violence and banditry since the turmoil in national rule began, it had not witnessed the massive destruction and upheaval experienced in other states. Conscious of this, the new military governor, General Castro, on his arrival in the state capital, addressed his somewhat startled Tuxtleco subjects in the following manner: "Chiapaneco cowards, while the north is struggling, you are enjoying peace but I will teach you to feel the effects of the Revolution."[50] Castro was true to his word, and over the next six years, both rural and urban Chiapas experienced the havoc, ambivalence, and often-arbitrary nature of revolutionary and counterrevolutionary violence.

Apart from Castro's renowned heavy hand — execution of opponents, burning of estates, theft of livestock, and looting of churches — the reforms that mobilized a counterrevolution known as *la revolución chiapaneca* were anticlerical, agrarian, and labor related. Castro's Ley de Obreros legally ended the practice of debt servitude that had shamed the state for so long. Imposing a minimum wage, he also cancelled workers' debts and, with the backing of his troops, liberated often-ambivalent servants and laborers. Suspicious of the northerners' claims and resistant to their saint-burning (*quemasantos*) practices, most Indians avoided joining the Carrancista revolution. In light of the clearly ethnic division within the state, the general himself seemed reluctant to arm a disparate Indian force. Emboldened by Carranaza's shaky hold on power after the occupation of Mexico City by Francisco Villa and Emiliano Zapata, an already incensed group of Chiapan *finqueros* (small estate owners) and *rancheros* (cattle farmers) formed their own revolutionary army, which they named Villista after the rebel general of the north. Through forging a variety of alliances, this group managed to hold the Carrancista forces to a fluctuating stalemate whereby the government could not control the countryside and the rebels could not hold the cities. Known as *los mapaches* (the raccoons) "because they moved at night and ate uncooked maize in the fields like their namesakes," the Villistas inspired no more confidence among the rural and Indian masses than their Carrancista opponents.[51] By 1920 the conflict was over, and due to the astute response of the Mapache leader, Fernández Ruiz, to maneuvers in the center of the country, notably the assassination of Carranza, the first postrevolutionary governorship of the state was his.

In the words of Thomas Benjamin, "Fernández Ruiz governed Chiapas as though the Mexican Revolution had never occurred."[52] He rescinded the Ley de Obreros, discouraged land reform, and rigged elections. For that reason, the "revolutionary victory" of 1920 was, for Chiapas at least, no revolution at all. Nevertheless, some of the more radical aspects of the revolution did survive. In 1919 the Partido Socialista Chiapaneca (Socialist Party of Chiapas) was formed, and, in combination with the remaining Carrancistas, it continued to champion many of the revolutionary social objectives surrounding land and labor reform, even if these goals were stymied by the local government of the official revolution. Although the government of Ruiz (himself a former student of the Porfirian governor Emilio Rabasa) did not endure past 1924, his Mapache collaborators continued to influence local rule, and in the moments when ex-Carrancistas found themselves in power, the limited concessions made by the local government to the rural masses rendered them seriously compromised by the stabilizing influences of the evolving party system. As Carlos Vidal, Ruiz's successor, commented, "the complete organisation of our [labour] Confederation, gives us absolute and firm control of local politics."[53] Although Vidal himself would meet a nasty end, he was not mistaken about the new system of governmental politics that had begun under Calles and that laid its most sturdy foundation with the creation of the Partido Nacional Revolucionario (PNR).

Community-Level Experience of "Revolution"

Depending on the village, Maya oral history tells a story about the upheavals of the Mexican Revolution quite different from those recorded by the ladino elite or the historians of the "official" revolution.[54] In Zinacantán, for instance, little reference is made to the first uprising of 1911, known locally as the Pajarito rebellion. *El Pajarito*, Jacinto Perez, was an Indian of the department of San Juan Chamula who became a general within the conservative "revolutionary" movement orchestrated by the ladino, and in particular clerical, elite of San Cristóbal—el mano negro, mentioned above. To understand why so many Chamulans would side with their traditional highland oppressors takes some explaining. Apart from the cynical promises of land redistribution made by the ladinos, historian Antonio García de León suggests that el Pajarito was an important individual in a new campaign of evangelization being undertaken among the Indians by the bishop of San Cristóbal, Francisco Orozco y Jiménez.[55] Having once served in the federal army, el Pajarito was fluent in both Spanish and Tzotzil and thus became a useful middleman between the church and the local native community. It seems Orozco y Jiménez was attempting once more to pull the Indians away from the more "idolatrous" aspects of their version of Catholicism and hoping, by doing so, to regain control of the highland indigenous populace.

Ever since the events of the so-called caste war of 1867, the Indians of the highlands had lived outside of the influence of a powerful clergy. This lack of church supervision, combined with the usurious labor-recruiting practices of the Díaz years, had affected the Indian communities in unexpected ways. In particular, the cycle of migrant labor that took Indians down to the coastal coffee fincas of Soconusco had led to the increased importance of Indian public rituals, such as the cofradía, as a means of asserting community identity and intercommunal prestige.[56] Though it may seem paradoxical, as the Indian villages had increasingly become mere reserves of labor for the lowland agriculturists, Indian life was given added structure and innovation by its attempts to incorporate both the new sources of income among some of the younger men and the fact that such men only had a limited physical presence within the community. Whatever the exact form of native government during this period, it is fair to say that highland Indians, when faced with the constant abuses of the *jefes políticos*, retreated into perhaps the only domain available to them: that of public ritual. In this way, the traditions of folk Catholicism or religious syncretism were once more opened to reinterpretation and renewal, and it was exactly these traditions that Orozco y Jiménez appears to have been keen to undermine.

Although he was by no means successful in all communities (Zinacantán was particularly resistant), over time the bishop was able to create a new faction among the Indians, with el Pajarito prominent among them, who pledged allegiance to the bishop rather than their traditional communities. When the conservative elite of San Cristóbal declared open rebellion against the Porfirian government of the lowlands, the bishop called upon this loyalty, but many Zinacantecos did not join the Pajarito band, and even in Chamula many refused him. More importantly, due to the rapid failure of the uprising itself, it appears that, if anything, the Indian communities of the highlands, including San Juan Chamula, became even more suspicious toward any future revolutionary claims. With the expulsion of the followers of the Pajarito band,

FIGURE 4.1 Tzotzil religious official, Chiapas, 1974. Photo by Gertrude Blom.

the traditional community set about reinforcing its binds of allegiance, increasingly restricting contact with ladinos to the minimum possible.[57] This experience perhaps also explains why Indian villagers often hid not only themselves but their saints when either Carrancistas or Mapachistas came to "liberate" their villages. Furthermore, after 1914, when Castro made his decrees for municipal freedom, it was the Chamulans who stipulated that the community's municipal president could not be bilingual but had to be a Tzotzil-speaking elder (*principal*) who had completed a career in the community's hierarchy of traditional civil and religious offices.[58]

The postrevolutionary period of the 1920s to the 1930s therefore appears to have been a period when not only was traditional culture undergoing a retrenchment but the guardians of this culture, the elders or *principales*, were increasingly being given a more formal and structured role within the organization of village government. This limited degree of autonomy in internal Indian affairs led to what Jan Rus has described as a "profound revitalization of traditional culture." As Rus explains,

> Fiestas that had not been celebrated since the late nineteenth century were revived and embellished; native curers were for the first time not only allowed but encouraged to conduct ceremonies in the community's church; even the dress of office-holders became more specialized.[59]

These acts of cultural renaissance must, however, be placed against the background of an all-but-nonexistent agrarian reform and the continued practices of *enganchadores*, who, although no longer receiving state support, continued to ensure that lowland *fincas* and jungle logging camps received a steady supply of native labor.[60] Thus, while relations within the Indian community had become subject to greater self-rule, relations outside of the community—that is, with non-Indian *ladinos*—remained highly exploitative and resistant to serious reform.

Several acts of resistance demonstrate the Indians' willingness to defend the new cultural freedom of their communities. First, it was claimed that in the early 1930s, Chamulans under the leadership of their *principales* (elders) murdered an *enganchador* and his two gun-toting companions as they sought to track down an Indian coffee laborer who owed them money. Then, a year later, one of the first postrevolutionary government schools was torched when it was built within a zone deemed to be residential by the community elders. Finally, when rumors of anticlerical *quemasantos* (saint-burners) reached Chamula, an armed guard was organized to protect the Indians' sacred religious artifacts.[61] This anticlerical aspect of the revolution was noted by Graham Greene when he traveled through Chiapas in 1938. Although churches were closed and the bishop of Chiapas was in exile, Greene came across many instances of native religiosity, in particular representations of saints that could supposedly talk.[62] It should be noted that in sharp contrast to the modernizing project of revolutionary nationalism that held a vision of a modern mestizo man at its center, Indian life nearly two decades after the revolution seemed to have carved an identity very much in opposition to ladino or mestizo national culture. Furthermore, as talk of party, progress, and class came to infuse the national discourse, Indian life continued to hold great respect for, and belief in, the transcendental, spiritual, or moral realm of daily and communal life.

While indigenistas had long been arguing for the specificity of such cultural adaptations, it was the indigenismo of Lázaro Cárdenas that sought to go beyond the level of community structure in a unique attempt to realize something of the indigenista agenda within the broader project of a national reconstruction of class relations. The arrival of Cardenismo in Chiapas, in part because of this unusual combination of culturalism with corporatism, was to lead to the deepest penetration, and finally corruption, of traditional Indian life of any Mexican governmentality.

Indigenismo in Chiapas

Well before Cárdenas made his address to the Inter-American Indigenous Congress in 1940, and even before he became president of the republic, the failure of revolutionary labor and land reform to reach the Indians of Chiapas was well known.[63] While the intellectual and academic debate surrounding the role of culture in the Indian's development was familiar to Cárdenas, his uniqueness lay in his adoption of indigenismo as another plank of his nationalist corporatist strategy to mobilize the rural masses within the structure of the revolutionary party. In Chiapas, therefore, although the Indians were clearly recognized as a special case, the fact that the Tzotzils and Tzeltals of the central highlands represented one-third of the population offered a significant political opportunity to direct the affairs of the state, via the combination of an Indian voting block with other loyal party sectors. However, since the state governor in 1934 was Victórico Grajales, a man strongly opposed to labor unions and land reform — to the extent that he even encouraged the formation of *guardias blancas*, ranchers' private guards — the arrival of Cardenismo was never going to be straightforward.[64]

Cárdenas's first move was to order a state labor commission that sought both to embarrass Grajales and to provide the excuse for federal intervention in state affairs. The report that the commission produced could not fail but record the obvious disparities between legislation and practice within the state, particularly with regard to treatment of the indigenous population. For instance, although nationally the minimum wage stood at 1.30 pesos per day, the report found that "Chamula workers labor for thirty centavos a day, and have to pay a twenty peso tax which state labor inspectors demand for authorizing the hiring, as well as various excises charged by municipalities for passage through the area."[65] Through the commission's report, the continued practice of enganche was exposed, and accusations of conditions of "virtual slavery" and the complicity of state officials led to the dismissal of several officials and eventually precipitated the downfall of Grajales in 1936. The new governor was a Cárdenas man, loyal to the party and free of compromising links to the local landed elite. One of his first acts was to name Erasto Urbina director of the freshly created state Departamento de Protección Indígena (Department of Indigenous Protection, DPI). Urbina had already distinguished himself through both his role within the earlier labor commission and his willingness and capacity to mobilize highland Indian communities in support of the party. Apart from his team of bilingual backwoods ladinos, who acted as bodyguards for his visits to rural highland communities, Urbina also had the unusual ability to speak both Tzotzil and Tzeltal fluently—"not like a ladino, but like us," according to Chamulans.[66]

In Chiapas, the creation of the DPI was closely followed by the founding of a Syndicate of Indian Laborers (STI). With these two institutions in place, it soon became possible for the government to play the role of intermediate between the coastal coffee plantations, the fincas, and their Indian labor supply—an involvement that, at least in the short term, was to improve conditions for the Indians. To achieve this end, however, it was also necessary to penetrate the traditional Indian political structure of the Tzotzil and Tzeltal Indian communities. Initially, this was realized through changing the ladino (non-Indian) secretaries who normally dealt with the Indian villages; later, however, it involved the more direct disruption of native political hierarchies. By demanding that a young bilingual Indian scribe be placed in the municipal presidency alongside the traditional Indian elder, who had reached his post only after completing years of ceremonial and community duties, the Cardenista reforms laid the seeds of a state-Indian complicity that, although briefly successful in altering the oppressive local non-Indian power structures of the period, would soon result in the creation of a new style of Indian oppression. It would be an oppression all the more potent because of its co-optation of the native traditional structure, whose legitimacy, due to its continued claim to uphold tradition, would remain unquestioned for some time.

The influence of the young bilingual Indian men whom Urbina had successfully negotiated into these communities — initially to perform the functions of translators and go-betweens in place of the ladino men who had previously fulfilled (and exploited) these roles — became more complicated by their additional positions within organizations beyond the confines of the community. The new scribe copresident of the Indian *municipio* (municipality) was also often the local labor union officer, the leader of the municipio's agrarian committee, the village representative to the regional committee of the Confederación Nacional Campesina (CNC), and perhaps most importantly, a leader of the local branch of the official party, the Partido Revolucionario Mexicano (PRM, previously the PNR, soon to become the PRI). Although there were two municipal presidents, the power that the younger man derived from his role as the principal link with the exterior political world was always subject to a degree of censorship from the traditional elder copresident. The traditional route to the presidency of the community had, after all, always required the completion of a certain number of obligations and responsibilities that were partially created to prove the commitment and ability of an individual to serve his community. So in 1942, when a young Chamulan scribe president, Salvador López Tuxum, volunteered to serve an important — and expensive — religious office, the grounds for the unification of traditional village power with external state and government power were prepared.

Previously, the serving of a civil-religious position within the community had been an expensive affair, often requiring the men to leave their *milpas* (corn fields), or absent themselves from migrant labor for a year, while they served the community. Rarely did men volunteer, and it was the community elders who chose candidates they felt were capable and appropriate. It was reasonable, therefore, to be suspicious of a young man's willingness to volunteer, and as Jan Rus has discovered, "during the same week that López Tuxum volunteered for religious office, . . . the DPI (Department of Indigenous Protection) quietly announced that it would permit liquor to be sold by current and *prospective* religious officials in Indian communities both out of respect for its ritual meaning, and to help defray the costs of the office."[67] This new opportunity for wealth creation that had not existed previously within the native civil-religious hierarchy led to a wave of new volunteers, and when Tuxum became sole municipal president the next year, the process of subversion of tradition was complete.[68]

While Cárdenas can therefore be seen as laying the institutional and social foundations of Mexico's indigenismo policy, the distinctive character of his reforms were nonetheless to be lost. "In other words," as Alan Knight writes of Cardenismo in general, "the jalopy was hijacked by new drivers; they retuned the engine, took on new passengers, and then drove it off in a quite different direction."[69] The new drivers were to be the conservative governments of the following years, and the new passengers, the "academic anthropological bureaucrats," who returned to a cultural understanding of the "Indian question" and its subsequent institutionalization.

The *"Comunidad Revolucionaria Institucional"*

With the change of governmental emphasis post-Cárdenas, the foundation of the Instituto Nacional Indigenista (INI) in 1948, and the opening of the first regional INI center in San Cristóbal de Las Casas in 1951, the Indians of the Chiapan highlands began to find that their newly constituted "traditional" hierarchies were also to become the official conduit for governmental development programs.

> Between the mid-1950s and the late 1960s, then, the state had not only recognized the scribe-principales as sole leaders of their communities, but by enriching them and supporting them politically, had given them power over those communities beyond any of their predecessors.[70]

In 1957, at the invitation of the INI, Evon Vogt, a professor of anthropology at Harvard University, established a fieldwork center in San Cristóbal de Las Casas. Over the next twenty years, more than 140 students would visit the Indian villages of the central highlands — Chamula and Zinacantán being the most consistently studied — with the express intention of "describing the inside of native structure."[71] There can be few ethnographic subjects that have received such intensive and consistent attention, and yet, in their exclusive adoption of the Boasian culturalist approach, the students of the Harvard project restricted themselves to representations that purposely ignored any external political dynamics.

This singularity of approach can in retrospect be seen as particularly unfortunate, for by the 1960s, long after the reforming zeal of Cardenismo had been swallowed up by the Mexican single-party system, the government had managed to co-opt not only the native leaders who were its direct collaborators, but ironically, the very community structures previously identified with resistance to outside intervention and exploitation: independent self-government, strict enforcement of community solidarity, and religious legitimation of political power. What anthropologists of the time were describing as "closed corporate communities" had in fact become "institutionalized revolutionary communities" harnessed to the state.[72]

It has been this situation, more than anything else, argues Rus — himself one of the last coordinators of the Harvard project — that "has led in recent years to the anomaly of the state enforcing 'native traditions' *against the natives themselves* to maintain order, and has forced many Maya peasants to search outside of their communities for alternative ways of organizing themselves."[73]

Such state influence, however, was not to go uncontested, and by the late 1960s, Indian communities all over the highlands were in conflict. At the center of this conflict lay the contradiction of a government policy that led to the education and training of a generation of younger men, equipped and keen, to realize their own business and personal plans without the requirement of traditional sanction. While the official party of the state, the PRI, has continued to support traditional Indian authority, the sociocultural and political landscape of Chiapas has become increasingly complex, with many Indians choosing the church (either Protestant or Catholic), opposition political parties, or independent unions as a means through which to explore what Jan Rus describes as "alternative ways of organizing communities that would be truer to their own sense of themselves."[74] In general terms, this has led to a large degree of migration away from the traditional centers of Indian life and a multiplication of often-competing nonstate sociopolitical structures through which Indian grievances have found expression, although not necessarily solution.

FIVE

Neoliberal Govern- mentality

Social Change, Contested Identities, and Rebellion

Ever since armed rebels attacked the military barracks of Ciudad Madera in Chihuahua, northern Mexico, on September 23, 1965, successive Mexican governments have been aware of the existence of *guerrilleros* willing to contest the country's status quo by military means.[1] One longtime student of Mexican guerrilla groups, Carlos Montemayor, identifies the Chihuahua attack as the beginning of a period of over three decades of nearly uninterrupted and "unofficial" warfare that continues to this day. Although figures never reached the horrific magnitude of the state-sanctioned campaigns in other Latin American nations such as Argentina and Chile, Mexico's own "dirty war" claimed the lives of thousands of suspected subversives[2] in operations that still remain virtually unknown outside of Mexico.[3] Whatever secrecy surrounded the government's stance toward dissident groups during this period was shattered, however, by an event that has become a landmark moment in the history of Mexican political activism and opposition. On October 2, 1968, just as Mexico sought to promote itself as a developed and sophisticated nation-state, as exemplified by its hosting of that year's Olympic Games, a peaceful demonstration by thousands of students in Mexico City's Tlatelolco Square was violently broken up with gunfire from military troops. Some 350 demonstrators were murdered in all, and although the government attempted to suppress media coverage of the massacre, a clear and unequivocal message was sent to all those citizens who wished to contest the rule of Mexico's Institutional Revolutionary

Party (PRI): whether clandestine or public, opposition would only be tolerated within dictated limits.[4]

From the 1920s until its defeat in 2000, the PRI was the only political party to rule Mexico. It has amazed political analysts not merely because of its perceived stability and evident durability but because of its continued international legitimacy, a status that has eluded other revolutionary regimes — most notably Cuba and the former Soviet Union. It was this ability to escape international criticism and sanction that led the Peruvian novelist Mario Vargas Llosa to dub Mexico "the perfect dictatorship." Since its creation in 1929, the PRI (then the PRM), as explained previously, has embodied a Comtean approach to society. Taking its inspiration from the positivism dominant at the end of the nineteenth century, the party has sought to realize the Comtean ideal of a "hierarchically organised non-competitive collectivism in which state and society were one."[5] By breaking society down into three main sectors — the labor sector, the agrarian sector, and the populist sector — and through creating the means for their political representation, the PRI's corporate approach to governance claimed a comprehensiveness that, theoretically at least, placed it above contestation.

In retrospect, some political analysts have sought to explain how it is that such a party has survived for so long. One suggestion has been the pendulum theory, which claims that it has been the PRI's political responsiveness that has ensured its longevity. By this analysis, the party itself has been astute enough to recognize shifts from left to right or vice versa among its electorate and has subsequently appointed presidents and governmental packages that have been able to swing as appropriate between the extremes of the traditional political spectrum. More convincing, and empirically better sustained, is the argument that it has been the PRI's institutionalized practices of clientism and corporatism that have ensured broad public support.[6] With methods ranging from the crude tactics of ballot-box stuffing, vote rigging, intimidation, and even murder to the more acceptable tactics of co-opting political troublemakers with the creation of new governmental posts or guaranteeing their political acquiescence via the enticement of conditional rewards, the PRI have long been considered experts in the simulation and manufacture of electoral support. Calls of protest against such clearly antidemocratic practices have, however, had little international resonance, for one oft-overlooked reason: Mexico's powerful northern neighbor.

Lying like a bridge between the economic and political Goliath of the United States of America and the once revolution-raked republics of Central America, throughout the 1960s and '70s, Mexico was considered a vital security concern by consecutive U.S. administrations. American involvement in counterrevolutionary activity in Central America (El Salvador, Nicaragua, Guatemala, Granada, and Panama) has already been well documented, but the full extent of U.S. operations in Mexico remains undisclosed.[7] Unlike its Central American neighbors, though, Mexico at no time faced a united countrywide revolutionary struggle. In fact, in a report he published in 1990, General Mario Acosta Chaparro of the Mexican military claimed that while there were at least some twenty-four subversive groups active in Mexico during the '60s and '70s, their various and competing leaders, in an ironic mirroring of PRI attitudes, often considered themselves "above the field of politics as the unique possessors of the true doctrine."[8] For the general, this, and not the counterrevolutionary tactics of the Mexican state, has been the principal reason behind the "consequent fragmentation and failure of the left to deeply root itself among the population."[9] Unusually, however, rather than reduce the existence of such subversive movements to the influence of ideology, even if the ideology was widely contested among the groups themselves, the general instead posits an alternative list of reasons for the continued existence of revolutionary movements: unemployment, lack of services and social policies, illiteracy, lack of democracy, injustice, low buying power, high foreign investment, agrarian problems, and corruption.[10] While the politically weighted use of labels such as "terrorists" or "subversives" serves to gloss over such primary causes, both the general and analysts such as Montemayor recognize that as long as such conditions exist, so too will the grounds upon which continued violent political opposition can take root.

It is perhaps unsurprising, therefore, that it was in the early years of the 1980s that six revolutionary socialists went to the state of Chiapas on Mexico's southeastern border with Guatemala to found the Zapatista Army of National Liberation (EZLN). Social, economic, and political conditions had reached a particularly low ebb in 1982 as Miguel de La Madrid began his six-year term as Mexico's latest PRI president. Faced with massive foreign debt, high inflation, and an unstable currency, De La Madrid's administration introduced the most radical changes in governmental style since the 1940s. Thus it was that at roughly the same time as the new Zapatista rebels were struggling to survive in the mountains of the southeast, the entire country once more experienced a transformation in governmentality that sought to reconfigure state-subject relations.

"Traditional" Communities in Crisis

By the mid-1970s there were an estimated 75,000 Chiapan Mayas working in migratory agricultural labor.[11] By the early 1990s, however, this figure had dropped as low as 40,000, while in the meantime the population of working-age men in the highland region had grown from 150,000 to 320,000.[12] In straightforward economic terms, during the 1980s, highland Chiapas began to suffer from a massive surplus of indigenous labor, which, like the pressures and forces brought to bear upon the communities and their leadership to supply labor in previous decades, can be traced to reforms within the centralized PRI federal government. For example, the adoption of neoliberal macroeconomic policies exposed the coffee producers to the ravages of the free market, and via the selective channeling of government funds and subsidies, increased support was given to lowland cattle farming, which was land intensive rather than labor intensive.[13] As a result of a short-lived oil boom, some Indians found temporary work as day laborers in Tabasco, others on the construction sites of hotel complexes in the latest Mexican tourist center, Cancun. Yet others attempted to eke out meager livings from subsistence farming on small plots in and around their traditional community centers, while a small but growing number made the grueling and dangerous journey north to work on the fruit plantations of southern California.[14] The majority of Indians in the late '80s and early '90s, though, began to fall into a vicious cycle of debt and poverty. The principal long-term effect of the radical economic restructuring, however, has been the creation of "social stratification and polarization within communities that formerly thought of themselves as egalitarian."[15]

Traditional self-understandings of the Tzotzil and Tzeltal Maya Indians who live in the highlands of Chiapas have long placed a social and cultural emphasis on agricultural labor. One example of this is the Maya belief that education is best understood as the slow acquisition of the soul. Such an education is not, however, to be found in the traditional locations of Western learning, the schoolroom or the university lecture hall; rather, the soul of a Maya Indian attains true maturity only through the careful tending of the corn field, more commonly referred to as the *milpa*. Although this conception has always remained something of an ideal rather than a reality, such a belief should neverthe-less serve as a warning to all those who would reduce the cultural and spiritual relationship of the Chiapan Indians with the land to one of mere functionalism. In Indian lore, the milpa can be seen to provide the tangible location for what is probably best comprehended as the nur-turing of a holistic understanding of what it might mean to be a Maya Indian, and furthermore what it might mean to be a Maya Indian who lives in harmony with the physical and spiritual world that surrounds him or her. For it is through working the milpa, through watching and responding to the slow passing of the seasons, through learning the right time to sow the seeds, how to nurture their growth, and how best to harvest their produce, that the Maya Indian also grows. In other words, it is through the natural process of agricultural care and atten-tion that the milpa teaches the Maya Indian the very human and social values of patience, gratitude, humility, and respect.[16]

For a long time, anthropologists have been understandably enchanted by the types of stories the Maya like to tell about themselves and the world they inhabit. In particular, they have been keen to see, and have sought to find, similarities between the beliefs and rituals of contem-porary Maya communities and the little that we know of their pre-Hispanic ancestors.[17] In this respect, the Indian communities of high-land Chiapas have been considered especially fitting. Municipalities such as San Juan Chamula and Zinacantán, with their strict observance of community obligations known as cargos, their complex and elabo-rate ritual calendar aligned with the annual agricultural cycle, and their belief in a world of supernatural spirits and animal co-essences, have exercised the intellects and imaginations of mainly American anthro-pologists for generations. In fact, as mentioned in the previous chapter, so worthy of study were the "closed communities" of highland Chiapas deemed that in the 1950s Harvard and the University of Chicago set up fieldwork centers in San Cristóbal de Las Casas so that students and professors might better conduct prolonged research studies.[18]

Through adopting a culturalist approach, such anthropological re-search has on the whole sought to show how isolated Indian communi-ties have maintained a simple culture of belief and ritual that makes little or no distinction between the spiritual and the temporal. Highland Maya communities have been understood as organizing themselves into civic-religious hierarchies that reflect their beliefs and that work toward the maintenance of community harmony and social equilib-rium.[19] One aspect in particular that has attracted considerable academic attention—and appears to confirm the structural functionalist approach to Maya community—has been the Indian belief in co-essences, animal spirits or souls. Occasionally manifesting themselves as either animals or winds, the spirits are more generally described as being "naturally incorporeal or invisible, of 'pure air' as the natives say."[20] Anthropologists have identified such spirits as manifestations of either a nagual or a *chanul*. As already explained in chapter 1, a nagual is generally understood as a spirit that, while not visible to the human eye, is capable of not only seeing but listening, protecting, or attacking. Its most feared power is its capacity to "eat" the souls of those who have seriously erred. The soul that a nagual attacks is quite often the chanul—the spirit companion, animal soul, or co-essence that each Maya Indian is said to possess. Such "Mesoamerican souls," writes Gary Gossen, "are fragile essences that link individuals to the forces of the Earth, society, the cosmos, and the divine."[21]

As anthropologists have been keen to map a "moral universe" or cosmology for the highland Maya that is separate and often opposed to the world of *kaxlanes* (non-Indians), the concatenation of the transcendental and the temporal that Indian soul beliefs entail has been central.[22] Talk of the "soul sickness" or "soul loss" of an individual has thus been thought to symbolize a disharmony within the local community that must be rectified. With the help of a *curandero* (an Indian curer and shaman), the victim of such a malady will reflect upon his past actions and dreams in an attempt to discover the act or omission that might have led to the sickness and to identify what course of action might best restore both his and his community's spiritual and temporal well-being.[23] By the early 1980s, however, even shamans had begun to divide into political factions. As greater pressure has been brought to bear upon indigenous communities, the shared cosmological framework of the Maya has begun to fragment.

Such classic anthropological research has proved particularly disenabling when it comes to explaining the conflicts that began to emerge in highland Chiapas during the 1970s and '80s. By concentrating exclusively on the ceremonies, rituals, and spiritual aspects of communities, many anthropologists only succeeded in perpetuating the myth that the Tzotzil and Tzeltal Maya existed in communities that had nothing or little to do with the non-Indian outside world, in particular the Mexican state. They failed to explore the communities' relations with government bodies and how such relations impinged upon what was viewed as traditional custom. As described in the previous chapter, during a period in the 1930s, with the increased interventionism of the government as part of its policy of indigenismo (itself based upon the same spurious American anthropological analysis of Indian community), the leadership of Chiapan Indian communities underwent a significant transformation. Through negotiating the appointment of young bilingual Indians to the positions of highest authority within the communities, the government successfully co-opted both native leaders and previously autonomous indigenous religious and community structures.[24]

Jan Rus believes that this situation, more than anything else, has led to a crisis in native community organization. As Indians witnessed outside authorities being employed to both legitimize and enforce "native rule," the priority of community loyalty that had been so vital in previous decades began to break down. As families and individuals began to look beyond their traditional communities, a sincere search for alternative ways to be "Indian" unfolded. In a very deep sense, this was a search for a new self-identity. It has been an experience all the more complicated not simply by the array of organizations that have come to involve themselves in Indian life in recent decades — opposition political parties, evangelical and Protestant groups, Catholic liberation theologists, unions, and new agrarian cooperatives — but by the fact that for so long the identification of what it was to be Indian for the highland Maya themselves has resided within the PRI-dominated "traditional" communities in which so many have since become marginalized.

Perhaps a short digression into the life of Miguel Kaxlan, a Chamula Tzotzil, might provide an insight into the complex reconfiguration of Indian life that has occurred over this period.[25] Miguel was one of the earliest converts to Protestantism in Chamula, a decision that would result in his expulsion from the community and finally in his assassination. His conversion and relocation to the non-Indian highland center of San Cristóbal de Las Casas represents the tortuous and dangerous path of re-identification that has troubled many a "traditional" Chiapan Indian soul. Having lost both his parents to influenza shortly after his birth, Miguel was taken in by his paternal uncle. Although poor, Miguel excelled at school, but with little opportunity locally, he had to leave the community to seek work. Laboring first on the coffee plantations of the lowlands and then on the construction of the Pan-American Highway, Miguel finally returned to the Chamula community center penniless. Disillusioned, he turned to drink and grudgingly reverted to the traditional Chamula lifestyle until one day he took a bath in the household *temescal* (sweat house) and had an unexpected revelation. In his vision, he was commanded to become a shaman, or curandero. For several years, Miguel lived off his income as a curer and interpreter of dreams. His life radically changed, however, when he was accused of stealing. His reputation ruined, he once again found himself broke and began to drink. It was then that Miguel encountered the North American Presbyterian missionaries Kenneth and Elaine Jacobs.[26]

Not only was Miguel converted, but he soon became an active and successful proselytizer himself. In a short time, the number of Protestants in Chamula numbered 120. While this is admittedly not a huge number, one of the converts' first actions was to refuse to pay the community tax mandatory to support the fiesta cycle. They also refused to participate in any way in the public religious life of the community, including the ritual consumption of alcohol. Although they were few in number, their stance sent shock waves throughout the traditional community. Their actions had, after all, set a worrying precedent for tax rebellion; but more seriously, they had openly challenged the moral authority of the community hierarchy and, in so doing, had also openly contested the cozy political arrangement with the PRI state and federal governments with which Chamula had first become entangled in the 1930s. The response was thus suitably severe. All the converts had their houses burnt to the ground; a few were killed, but most managed to flee to the safety of San Cristóbal de Las Casas. By the mid to late 1970s, Miguel Kaxlan was the outspoken leader of a group now numbering some two thousand Protestants expelled from San Juan Chamula. On behalf of this group, he pursued property claims through the courts for abuse of land rights while also becoming involved in wider state politics by allying himself with a national opposition party, the PAN (Partido de Acción Nacional). And then one day in 1982, some men from Chamula bundled him into a van; several days later, his dismembered corpse was recovered and buried. To this day, no charges have ever been brought for the murder of Miguel Kaxlan.

The life and death of Miguel Kaxlan, if nothing else, illustrate the serious and often violent influences of "tradition," community, state, party, globalization, economics, religious affiliation, and perhaps even the supernatural that play a part in what we might best call the new politics of indigenous identity that have engulfed Chiapas, if not all of Mexico, in the latter half of the twentieth century. While Miguel's choices and experiences were of course peculiar to him, he nonetheless gives some insight into the agonies of the Indian soul, once thought to need little more than the milpa to ensure a future of righteous living. In another important respect, his story also illustrates a fact fundamental for understanding at least one of the conditions that have made the Zapatista rebellion possible, that is, "the crisis in the basic unit of native social organisation — and thus of state control — in Chiapas, the traditional community."[27] As the PRI government continued its package of neoliberal reforms throughout the 1980s and '90s, the number of indigenous leaving their highland communities continued to grow. Many, with the help of religious organizations, joined what had become an exodus to the Selva Lacandona (the Lacandon jungle), where new experiments in the organization of indigenous community were already taking place. One experiment, however, would prove to be more radical than any other.

The International Revival of (Neo)Liberalism

It is generally agreed that it was in 1982, during the presidency of Miguel de La Madrid, that Mexico first entered the neoliberal stage of governmental rule. Although the necessity for structural adjustment was initially imposed by the soaring debt crisis and the consequent conditionality of IMF and World Bank loans, the breadth and scope of the reforms introduced have shown that Mexico's metamorphosis cannot be reduced simply to the imposition of an external economic vision; rather, it represents the conjuncture of a new breed of national rulers with a dominant international conception of how a modern nation-state should be run. A vital component, then, in the Mexican neoliberal transformation, has been the role of its political elite. Unlike in previous national governments, since the early 1980s the constitution of the political elite has increasingly been drawn from those equipped with postgraduate educations in disciplines such as economics and administration.[28]

The majority of these individuals who have made it to the cabinet level during the 1980s and '90s received their doctorates from universities in the United States — Harvard, MIT, Stanford, Yale, and Chicago featuring prominently among them. All three presidents from that period — de La Madrid, Salinas, and Zedillo — had studied economics or administration, and not coincidentally, all had served in the budgeting and finance departments of the administration previous to theirs.[29] It is also revealing to note that all became president without ever having held any previous elective office. As expertise becomes the route to government, it also fulfills another important task in the exercise of power. "The elite's faith in the rationality of economics not only helped determine the kinds of policies adopted by it but also served to exclude rival claims to knowledge," writes Miguel Ángel Centeno. What's more, he continues, "these educational qualifications further increase the social exclusivity and homogeneity of the ruling elite by requiring financial and professional commitments to education that only a select few can make."[30] Dubbed the *técnicos* by the press and public — and not at all unlike their *científico* predecessors — this new generation of rulers set about dismantling the Mexican state.

Since Mexico quite clearly had been run according to a certain system ever since Lázaro Cárdenas put in place its central components, legitimating changes to such a durable governing structure was a difficult task. The strategies of corporatism, clientism, and patronage that have kept the same party in rule for seventy years did not conform at all well to the new ideal of a streamlined minimal state, at least not in their pre-neoliberal guise. Removing subsidies, reducing union power, firing hundreds of thousands of civil administration workers, and exposing manufacturing goods and producers to an aggressive international market were all neoliberal initiatives that disturbed, if not destroyed, the very ties that had linked the PRI to its traditional sectorial power bases in the past. Just how disruptive such policies have been for the ruling party was made startlingly apparent in the 1988 presidential election, when Carlos Salinas, even with the assistance of a manufactured computer crash, only just scraped a victory with less than 50 percent of the vote — a result unprecedented in PRI history.[31] What, then, we must ask, made this new elite so determined to institute such radical change in a system of governance that had for so long been their sole guarantor of unquestioned national power?

The answer to this question, as has often been the case with Mexico's major moments of governmental transformation, lies outside of the nation-state's borders, and in this instance it can perhaps be traced to the conscious plotting of a group of European intellectuals at the Swiss hotel Mont Pèlerin in 1947.[32] At the center of this group stood the individual most often cited as responsible for the new liberal revival — or new neoliberal order, as it is more commonly known — that has come to dominate the international economic and political landscape from the late 1970s on. His name was Friedrich von Hayek. In the 1950s, at a time when the relevancy of liberalism seemed to be in decline and the insights of Keynesian macroeconomic planning had achieved the status of orthodoxy, Hayek's attempts to create a liberal international order were considered out of step. Nevertheless, in light of the totalitarian regimes that had brought Europe to war and the increasingly collectivist nature of state planning, it was Hayek's fervent belief that the seeds for new totalitarian orders were unconsciously being put in place. To counter this slide, Hayek sought through the establishment of numerous think tanks such as the Mont Pèlerin Society (and later the famous British Institute of Economic Affairs) to rearticulate the principles of classical liberalism and, in so doing, to influence the content of public policy.[33]

Key to Hayek's project, and to those of his similarly influential collaborators, Milton Friedman and Ludwig von Mises, was a far greater and more passionate belief in the freedom of the individual than their liberal predecessors had possessed.[34] In an important respect, however, this freedom was constructed in opposition to the continued challenge of socialist and communist thought, for what Keynes and Marx had in common, according to Hayek, was an overbearing and liberty-depriving conception of the role of the state.[35] True freedom, Hayek claimed, lay in the liberty to act and make choices without the intervention of state structures. It cannot be considered wholly coincidental, then, that it was only in the wake of the increasingly bipolar social, military, and economic relationship that developed during the Cold War between the European and North Atlantic states and the Soviet Union that Hayek's liberals first began to find receptive audiences and increased influence.[36]

Beginning with the retreat from the welfare-state model of government that became widespread among the Western states in the 1970s, neoliberal theory began to make the transition into a neoliberal formula of rule. Most clearly apparent in domestic terms, during the administrations of Ronald Reagan and Margret Thatcher, the removal of state structures became synonymous with the policies of privatization, deregulation, and "rationalization," and the political rhetoric of neoliberal freedom began to take on an increasingly international and evangelical hue.[37] In one recorded instance at a British Conservative Party policy meeting in the 1970s, a member had prepared a paper arguing for a "middle way." Before the individual had finished his presentation, however, the new party leader, Margret Thatcher, reached into her briefcase and took out a book. As one man who was present recalls, "it was Friedrich von Hayek's *The Constitution of Liberty.*" Interrupting the presenter, she then held the book up for all to see. "'This,' she said sternly, 'is what we believe,' and banged Hayek down on the table."[38] Perhaps this glimpse into the notoriously autocratic nature of Thatcherite rule also suggests the manner in which such neoliberal theory embodied a central contradiction.[39]

Despite the ubiquity of the term "free" in the neoliberal political discourse—free market, free trade, and free choice—the very meaning of freedom has always been something of a philosophical chimera. To believe that a time has existed or will ever exist when there are no claims upon our conduct, no restrictions upon our desires, and no limits upon our options is to believe in such an empty and abstract conception of freedom as to rob the notion of any of the political and ethical content by which we might render the term meaningful. Conversely, a situated freedom—that is to say, the concept of freedom placed in a historical and political context—leads us to question the very concrete limits upon a person's conduct and to ask in what ways our conduct is or has been governed.[40] Historically, as chapter 2 also demonstrated, it has been this apparently unencumbered and consequently empty vocabulary of freedom that has been both central to liberalism's appeal and key to understanding the contradiction that the governmentalization of such a political vocabulary entails.

"The freedom upon which such modes of government depend," writes Nikolas Rose, "and which they instrumentalise in so many diverse ways, is no 'natural' property of political subjects, awaiting only the removal of constraints for it to flower forth in forms that will ensure the maximisation of economic and social well-being."[41] Quite the contrary, for the withdrawal of the state as owner, director, and financier of the public sector in areas such as industry, health, and administration has not so much released the individual from an overbearing centralizing influence as it has inaugurated the increased intervention of newly "liberalized techniques of government"—for example, medical advisers, psychologists, marital guidance counselors, business, marketing, management consultants, and so forth. All such newly privatized mechanisms for self-government have had the further consequence of reducing the level of accountability that can be leveled at a government. Also, perhaps tragically in some cases, they have led to a reconceptualization of notions of need, sickness, normalcy, and success, creating what some analysts have identified as an increasing internalization of notions of the "good" and heralding a consequent decline in communitarian understandings of society.[42]

That this neoliberal style of governmental rule should become internationally dominant can only be explained in reference to three interrelated factors. First, powerful states such as Britain and the United States adopted such neoliberal rhetoric and policies in the highly charged international environment of the Cold War, adding an increased geopolitical aspect to what is already a highly international approach to domestic policy. Second, international liberal institutions such as the World Bank, the International Monetary Fund (IMF), and the GATT, all of which had been in existence since the end of the Second World War, began in the late 1970s and early '80s to take an increasingly instrumental role and interventionist approach to the realization of neo-liberalism among debtor nations.[43] Finally, the institutionalization and implementation of this neoliberal governmental style could only have been possible with the "understanding" and belief of a new breed of national leaders, the creation of which can be traced to the foundation of think tanks and international scholarships between the universities and research institutes of the North Atlantic states and those of the Southern Hemisphere.

Neoliberal Governmentality in Mexico

After López Portillo's dramatic decision to nationalize the banks in 1982, and his personal influence in the choice of his successor, international financial institutions such as the World Bank and their donor nations were clearly nervous about Mexico's political and economic future. However, from the very start, new president Miguel de La Madrid expressed himself in the vocabulary of the neoliberal right, reassuring those with an interest in the nation's direction. "To rationalize" he declared, "is not to state-ize (*estatizar*)." Then, so as to leave nobody in doubt, he underlined the approach of his new administration: "we shall not state-ize society."[44] Furthermore, in his inaugural speech, he made uncharitable reference to his predecessor's "financial populism" and attacked the creation of a "fictional economy," giving a warning and an insight into the "new realism" of neoliberalism when he admitted that, "the first months of the government will be arduous and difficult." He explained the necessity for cuts with the curt justification "the situation requires it. The austerity is obligatory."[45]

As the eighties wore on, de La Madrid set about reversing many of Portillo's policies; in particular, he opened the national banking system to partial ownership by the private sector. In his addresses to the nation, he went out of his way to compliment the activities of a growing enterprise culture and to emphasize the importance of an efficient governmental system. With drastic cuts to public expenditure, except in military funding, and the closing of many of the parastatals founded under Echeverría, de La Madrid marked a watershed in Mexican governmental style, leaving large social sectors traditionally managed by the PRI, such as labor and agriculture, increasingly exposed. As one Mexican technocrat of the time explained, "the decision-making process relies more on the indirect scientific-economic rationale for the social construction of reality than on the direct political/ideological commitment to a given class."[46] However, examples of such self-reflection on the constitutive nature of neoliberal economic discourse were rare, and as de La Madrid's term came to a close, and the process of selecting his successor began, there was a heightened sense of consensus among the technocratic elite. In a clear abjuration of moral responsibility, the elite claimed that they (and their educations) were not responsible for the inevitability of socioeconomic policy but rather that "the *reality* of the global economic system forced Mexico to abandon its protectionist isolation and accept the limits of its role as a supplier of cheap labor and as a mendicant in the world financial market."[47]

This "reality" nearly resulted in a historic defeat for the PRI when in 1988 Cuauhtémoc Cárdenas, son of the famous former PRI president Lázaro Cárdenas, defected from the party and led a leftist coalition against the official PRI candidate, Carlos Salinas de Gortari. Thanks to a (now debunked) supposed computer crash, Salinas was voted in by the narrowest of electoral margins, clearly illustrating that theories viewing electoral liberalization as a natural effect of market liberalization, at least in Mexico, did not concur with experience.[48] Perhaps because of this electoral shock, Salinas, although certainly the most neoliberal of presidents, was also the first to incorporate a social aspect into Mexican neoliberalism.[49] Although previous PRI administrations had also introduced large-scale development programs, one of the features that was new about Carlos Salinas's National Solidarity Program (PRONASOL) — and in an important sense integral to realizing something of the rhetoric of social liberalism that accompanied it — was that its programs and available credit were directed either at freshly created Solidarity committees or at individuals.[50] In fact, the concentration on the role of *autogestión* — that is, self-help — and the civic construction of autonomous groups fit extremely neatly into more general ideas about the aims of neoliberal government.

While analysts such as Denise Dresser are correct to point out that the program created another means by which popular groups can be incorporated into a newly structured party machine — and to conclude therefore that the program is political in a traditional Mexican clientist sense — there is still a more subtle sense in which Salinas is partially right about creating "a new relationship between the people and the State."[51] This relationship, irrespective of how convincing or unconvincing it appears, can be seen in the attempt to present PRONASOL as an "apolitical political project." For example, the roles of business advisers who attempt to counsel agricultural producers on the best ways to commercialize their product, or of technical advisers who recommend more scientific farming practice, are presented as instances of independent expertise, and as such they attempt to transform the relations of authority and subjectivity as they have previously been understood to have been linked to government in the past.[52]

To a certain extent, this is the primary aim of neoliberalism: that expertise both among the political elite and among the "independent" advisers who help institute its programs should come to be the central means through which citizens relate to the state, to their society, and to themselves. This goal is desirable because, as Rose explains it, such expertise both "depoliticises and technicises a whole swathe of questions by promising that this machinery (that of the knowledge of the expert) will operate according to a logic in which technical calculations — as to the best way to economic growth, industrial organization, social harmony and individual well-being — will overrule a logic of contestation between opposing interests."[53] Not wishing to leave such faith in the technologies and mechanisms of neoliberal governmental expertise to chance, the Salinas programs also involved the requirement for newly created social and popular movements to sign *convenios de concertación,* "agreements of concert." This strategy appears to have first been created after the Mexican earthquake in 1985, but it was widely deployed by Salinas, as one former government minister explains, to achieve very traditional ends:

> In signing the agreement, groups agreed, in effect, to work with and not against the state. The accord therefore cleverly brought groups "into line," and put an end to "popular protests." In this way, the convenio is consistent with long-standing inclusionary corporatist state-society relations in Mexico.[54]

However, in light of the combined emphasis on personal responsibility and identification with the state, Princeton sociologist Miguel Ángel Centeno makes the more radical claim that

> PRONASOL could even be seen as moving the regime away from its traditional authoritarian willingness to accept passive acquiescence, by now requiring a more active mobilization and voicing of support more akin to totalitarian systems.[55]

Certainly in Mexico the legitimization of the neoliberal program has been dressed in nationalistic terms, and as a consequence, criticisms of the PRI have been treated as "offences against the integrity of the

nation," as one observer has written.⁵⁶ This contempt with which dis-
senting opinion has been greeted reveals not only the presumption of
the transcendental nature of neoliberal politics—a politics that is conducted above and beyond the squabbling of national party politics—
but also that such an apolitical politics can only be understood as democratic under the most narrow of definitions.

Recalling the Bourbon reforms of the late eighteenth century, and
the positivists' authoritarianism of the late nineteenth century, Mexico
seems in the late twentieth century to have returned to a style of governmental rule that is so convinced of its correctness that little attempt
is made to accommodate the popular, representative, and responsive
aspect supposedly characteristic of democratic politics. Where once the
PRI party sought to unite and control the nation through a sectorial
system of corporate representation, the neoliberal style of rule seems to
suggest that sectorial understandings must be broken and replaced with
stronger, individualistic political and social understandings through
which new techniques of governance—principally scientific and economic expertise—will provide the social binding that labor, agricultural, and union officials used to provide. At their cost, early liberals
in nineteenth-century Mexico assumed that *Homo economicus* existed;
later "scientific" liberals, in contrast, recognized the need to create such
subjects; and late-twentieth-century neoliberals seem struck once again
with the need to create subjects that will control themselves and thus
leave the government of politics to culturally recognized experts.

By the early 1990s, in a publication not noted for its promotion of
conspiracy theories, the extent of the adoption of the new neoliberal
elitist governmental style was acknowledged:

> A continental network of Harvard, Chicago, and Stanford grads are
> back [in Latin America] atop businesses and ministries spreading the
> new market mind-set. They're using old school ties to reach across
> Latin America's borders, signing joint ventures and free trade agree-
> ments with fellow alumni.⁵⁷

While neoliberalism had become the dominant governmentality
in Latin America, few other nations matched the dramatic nature of
Mexico's transformation or its ambition. Having already signed up to
the GATT in 1986, in the late 1990s Mexico sought to secure its international status through negotiating an entry into the North American
Free Trade Agreement (NAFTA).⁵⁸ This process was conducted at an

elite level, and debate as to the implications or benefits of entry into either agreement was never seriously entertained. The country as a whole was never consulted.[59] By late 1993, the government's policies of privatization and deregulation had created a new generation of billionaires, twenty-four of whom now featured in the *Forbes* World's 100 rich list. On the eve of 1994, as Mexico sought to promote itself as an international model of development, the highly partial, coercive, and elite nature of Mexico's neoliberal revolution was about to be laid bare.

The "New" Communities of the Lacandon Jungle

With few contacts and no experience of living in jungle conditions, the six rebels who went to Chiapas's Selva Lacandona to foment revolution in November 1983 very soon learned a lesson that would become central to their transformation from a vanguardist revolutionary movement to an indigenous revolutionary movement.[60] Humbled by the harshness of life in the mountains, lacking both food and supplies, and occupied principally with fighting disease and illness rather than state oppressors, the original Zapatistas came to respect, value, and rely on the advice and generosity of the indigenous communities for their continued existence as a clandestine organization. However, although the Indians did not betray the rebels, neither did they immediately embrace the idea of an armed struggle, especially one that was to be led by outsiders who knew little or nothing of life within the communities. After all, the Indians, although long since marginalized from the political process, had recently been the subject of significant cultural, demographic, and community transformations — changes that were, in effect, nothing less than the reorganization of Chiapas's native society.

The fact that this reorganization did not follow traditional lines can in large part be explained by the growing rejection of the corrupted civil-religious hierarchies of the highland communities; but what also made the selva "a unique space of social construction" were the diversity of ethnic groups that migrated there and the number of religious organizations with which such groups had become involved.[61] Thus, apart from the Tzeltal and Tzotzil speakers from the highlands, there were speakers of Chol, Tojolabal, Mame, Kanjobal, Chuj, Jacalteco, Mocho, and Cakchiquel, alongside small groups of Spanish-speaking mestizos and other Guatemalan Maya refugees, who began to arrive in the early 1980s. Furthermore, within this ethnic mosaic we find not only Catholics (followers of liberation theology as well as traditionalists)

FIGURE 5.1 Zapatista soldier, 1998. Photo by Pedro Valtierra.

but also Adventists living alongside Presbyterians, Pentecostals, Baptists, Jehovah's Witnesses, Nazarenes, members of the New Rising of Christ, of the Column of the Living God, of the Light of the Good Shepherd, of the Light of the World, of the Church of God the Prophesier, and various other minor Pentecostal sects.[62] The combined effect of this intermixing of ethnicities and religions has been the creation of hybrid cultures that resist easy classification.

While traditional Catholic missionaries were the first to visit the new communities of the Lacandon, it was the Protestant missionaries who initially began to attract converts and transform the organization of native community.[63] In theory at least, the Protestant emphasis on the individual and the personal above the collectivity, alongside the belief in a salvation through God that ignores the flagrant inequities of the temporal status quo and prepares instead for a life to come, would seem to suggest a deeply conservative influence on Indian life.[64] However, in just one of many contradictions, Protestant missionaries also promoted the right to cultural difference, and true to this belief, they initiated programs of Bible translation into the indigenous languages. Having been taught to read and write and encouraged into the habits of Christian reflection, many Indians soon put their new organizational skills to more political effect, aligning themselves with oppositional agricultural unions and federal political parties.[65]

Nevertheless, the most potent instrument of change in Chiapas has undoubtedly been the more overtly political activism of the "new" Catholic Church that became influential throughout the region in the early 1970s. For this reason, some historians consider the pivotal date in Chiapan history to be 1974, the year when the Catholic diocese of San Cristóbal de Las Casas held its first Indian Congress, ostensibly to commemorate the quincentennial of the death of Fray Bartolomé de Las Casas, but more importantly to facilitate the realization of a pastoral approach known as "the preferential option for the poor."[66] Based in the theology of liberation that surfaced throughout Latin America in the 1970s and propelled by the very personal conversion of the bishop of San Cristóbal de Las Casas, Samuel Ruiz, the change in diocesan policy was explained to me by one local priest as the transformation from "a church of the cult to a church of service."[67] Just what this service was to include could be seen reflected in the topics discussed by community-level groups at the congress, themes such as land tenure, marketing, education, housing, and health. The church also invited students and lecturers of Mexican history, economics, and agrarian law to address local Indians, and arguably it was at this conference that the indigenous themselves became cognizant of their shared plight, a plight that went beyond their local municipalities and involved wider state and federal governmental structures.

A key element in the transformation of the church is the commitment to apply the Christian liturgy to Indian culture, an undertaking that, while similar to that of their Protestant brothers, is further advanced by the attempt to create an indigenous church that is aware of the socio-economic situation of its members. Through a network of Indian catechists, and later deacons, the Catholic Church was able not only to instruct a significant portion of the 150,000 Indians who inhabit the Lacandon but also to assist in the creation of production and transport cooperatives and cooperative shops, the education of women, and the training and implementation of community health projects. However, perhaps one of the most lasting and influential initiatives undertaken by the Catholic Church was to invite members of the Maoist movement Línea Proletaria and their leader, Adolfo Orive, to Chiapas.[68] Although it was a relationship that did not last, Línea Proletaria, in keeping with their Maoist constructivist line, set about assisting the indigenous communities of the selva to form organized unions that could better present their demands to the state government.[69] Their creation of the union Quiptic ta Lecubtesel laid the foundations for the uniting of numerous smaller organizations into the first nongovernmental Chiapan supraregional organization, the Asociación Rural de Interés Colectivo (ARIC), commonly known as the "Union of Unions."[70]

By the late 1980s, life in the Indian communities of the Lacandon had changed radically. Unlike in the highlands, the number of positions of responsibility (*cargos*) within the community had multiplied. In keeping with the Catholic Church's belief in the sanctity of community and its commitment to serve that community, public servants were made directly responsible to the members of the Indian collectivity. It is an ethos best reflected in the phrase *mandar obedeciendo* (command obeying), a principle of local organization since elevated to the level of national debate by the Zapatista rebels.[71] The aim of the catechists and *tu'uneles* (deacons) has been to break down the hierarchies and vertical networks of power as practiced in the corrupted traditional communities. Being Indian themselves, and educated to act as a de facto indigenous priest class, the catechists have sought to encourage community dialogue, involving all sectors and age groups of the community in decisions and appointments. Their position, after all, is only tenable with the support of the collectivity. In this way, catechists often find themselves assigned to other posts as well, and with the involvement of children and elders in the process, the community works by consensus, the method considered by the missionaries to be the best preparation for the practice of democracy.[72]

The realm of the Indian supernatural is still present in the communities, and the Maya of the selva can still be heard to talk of the nahual, but the role of the curandero no longer carries a monopoly within the collectivity, and religion, be it Protestant or Catholic, has encouraged greater critical reflection on the part of the indigenous toward their own rituals and customs. As the Indian communities have established themselves and their new forms of organization throughout the selva, it has become clear that while being "Indian" can evidently take multiple forms at an individual level, the social cohesion and political unity that have come to characterize the Lacandon communities are based on a belief in, and mobilization of, a reinvented understanding of ethnic identity. "These processes of re-invention," writes Rosalva Aida Hernández Castillo, "have not been voluntary strategies to create 'fictitious identities,' but historical processes of social construction through which the indigenous peoples of the frontier have re-defined their sense of belonging to a collectivity in a dialectic of resistance and adaptation to external ideologies."[73]

Religious conversion should therefore not be seen as a straightforward process of acculturation, for to interpret it this way would be to fail to see the indigenous as complex social subjects in their own right, subjects with the capacity to contest and restructure their new religious beliefs, and subjects possessing the agency to opt for change should they so choose. To fail to recognize this capacity within the indigenous would be to run the risk of objectifying and reifying a particular notion of Indigenous culture, tradition, and identity and thus to deny the indigenous the very real and hazardous possibility of being the subjects of their own history.[74] While most Indians initially restricted their choices to the churches, the unions, and the village councils, soon the option of armed insurrection that had long existed clandestinely began to attract greater support.

Political Violence

To understand the radicalization of the indigenous communities of Chiapas, it is thus important to recognize that the reassertion of indigenous identity it represents is an identity that to a very large extent has been carved in opposition. While opposition was initially directed toward the repressive tendencies of corrupted local Indian hierarchies (caciques), with the exodus to the selva came greater wrangles with government-run bodies over land rights. Prior to the Zapatistas, the most famous dispute in Chiapas had surrounded an attempt by the government to partition the Lacandon into clearly defined sectors irrespective of the number of newly founded colonies that might be located within a particular zone.[75] Known as the battle for *"la brecha,"* it was a conflict that at times involved the creation of human barriers to stop eviction and bulldozing of communities. The issue involved the demands of logging concerns, oil drilling, the legal rights of the Indian ejidos (cooperative parcels of land sanctioned by the Mexican constitution), and the socio-economic plans of the PRI administration. It was through fighting the proposals of "la brecha" that many of the diverse ethnic communities recognized the need to present a unified front.[76]

Prospects for cross-community, interreligious, and most significantly, pluriethnic unity were, however, severely challenged by the appointment of General Absalón Castellanos Domínguez to the governorship of Chiapas in 1982. In light of the revolutions that affected the Central American states to the south of the Chiapan frontier, the choice of a military man for the post should not be considered coincidental. Already an established cattle rancher and large landowner in the Lacandon, the general set about ensuring the "integrity of national security" in a manner that brought an unprecedented level of repression to bear on the state's new independent peasant organizations. One of his first acts was to reform the state's penal code, increasing both his own powers and the nature of liability for "crimes against internal security." It was also during this time that Chiapas began to receive greater numbers of Guatemalan Maya refugees fleeing the civil war. Camps had been created close to the border to house the refugees, but as a result of bombing raids and a helicopter attack by the Guatemalan military in 1984, it was decided to transfer the refugees to "less sensitive areas."

In an interview with Ronald Wright, Ricardo, a Mexican worker in the refugee camps at the time, confirms this necessity but also adds another interpretation for the relocation of the increasing Maya populace. In reference to the Tzotzil and Tzeltal Indians, who are also Maya and who had begun to settle the Lacandon zone some years earlier, Ricardo explains how the different groups of Indians began to help each other:

RICARDO: It was a sort of Maya reunion, something very beautiful to see. They began sharing their languages, their textiles — it was a Maya cultural interaction. In one little camp where we worked there were people from six language groups, and the children were learning to speak all six, as well as Spanish. The powers-that-be didn't like this solidarity between indios of Mexico and Guatemala. Not long afterward I was at the United Nations. I happened to see a recommendation from the United States government to our government demanding that even local Mexican Indians be cleared from the border area to create a 'clean zone,' a kind of — what did they call it in Vietnam?

WRIGHT: DMZ?

RICARDO: Yes a DMZ! The U.S. wanted a line of defense against 'communist subversion.'[77]

It is perhaps not surprising, then, that as conservative elements within the Mexican government began to worry about "guerrilla infiltrations on the southern border," the growing militancy of the new social movements of the Lacandon jungle was met with an increasingly violent response.[78] Indian protagonists in land invasions, public demonstrations, and even official negotiations often found themselves attacked, imprisoned, or killed. Such was the scale of the repression that by 1987 a report by the Mexican Academy of Human Rights claimed that since the appointment of General Castellanos Domínguez in 1982, Chiapas had witnessed an average of two politically motivated killings per month.[79]

This, combined with the policies of President de La Madrid and the beginning of the neoliberal period of rule, also meant that the communities of the Lacandon began to witness the withdrawal of the little state support their agricultural lifestyle had previously received. Initially, the PRI government attempted to manipulate the communities and their land use by removing subsidies and credit for "traditional crops" such as coffee and corn and increasing support instead for cash crops and cattle ranching. However, by the late 1980s, as Carlos Salinas de Gortari began his term as Mexican president, government cuts and reform became increasingly drastic.

By the end of 1989 it was clear that the future of the agricultural sector would be subordinated to the economic goals of the Salinas administration: the reduction of inflation via wage and price controls, privatisation of state enterprises and trade liberalisation.[80]

As the Indians of Chiapas saw the prices of their crops plummet, they knew that the opening of the market to competition from cheaper U.S. grains had direct links to the decisions of international financial institutions such as the IMF and the World Bank. After all, writes Neil Harvey,

> the Bank conditioned the disbursement of new structural adjustment loans to a radical overhaul of the agricultural sector, recommending the privatisation of state-owned enterprises and the gradual elimination of price supports and other input subsidies.[81]

Increasingly sucked into a cycle of debt and poverty, with all the incumbent illness and death that that implies in rural Mexico, thousands of growers had to abandon crop production. Not surprisingly, the number of protests and demonstrations by Indian communities and peasant unions grew. The reaction of local government bodies was fierce. Indian leaders were arrested or "disappeared," the government invested in the construction of new jails, and the use of violent armed teams (*guardias blancas*) by local land owners to evict families from land wanted for cattle ranching was given implicit state sanction.[82] As human rights abuses such as arbitrary arrest and even torture became increasingly commonplace, a new governor instituted a further reform in Chiapas's penal code that effectively outlawed protest and dissent, allowing for the detention of all those seen to be disturbing public order.[83] The reform was attacked throughout the country as a violation of civil and human rights, "eventually forcing its repeal in law, if not in practice."[84] It has now been documented that "between 1988 and 1993, Chiapas's Indians suffered 8,109 reported human rights violations, out of a national total 11,608 violations against the country's native population."[85] Such repressive tactics on the part of the government effectively forced opposition underground, and it was at this time that the Zapatistas' long-standing offer to act as the indigenous communities' army began to receive increasing numbers of recruits.

Nevertheless, far removed from the local reality of the Chiapan Indians, decisions concerning Mexico's ongoing transition to a free market economy continued apace. In a seemingly logical extension of the neoliberal rationale, the Salinas administration sought to realize Mexico's potential as an emerging market by entering into the North American Free Trade Agreement with the United States and Canada. For the

FIGURE 5.2 Women in Xoyep, 1998. Photo by Pedro Valtierra.

realm of agriculture, the lifeblood of the majority of Mexico's ten million indigenous inhabitants, ratification of NAFTA held serious implications. The first step was the reform of article 27, a political decision that effectively ended any hopes the new communities had of legalizing the ejidos (agricultural cooperatives) in which they had worked and lived for decades. As Neil Harvey explains,

> the rationale for NAFTA is that each country and region should produce goods and services in which they have comparative advantages. This argument implied that over two million small producers in Mexico could not continue to survive as maize (corn) producers.[86]

Irrespective of the disparities in technology, infrastructure, climate, and subsidies that clearly placed Mexico at a considerable disadvantage, it was agreed that NAFTA would come into being on January 1, 1994. New Year's Day 1994, however, witnessed the dramatic manifestation of the rebel army that had for so long existed in secret. Those Indians made invisible by the modernist image and practice of a neoliberal Mexico made themselves visible for the first time under the banner of the Zapatista Army of National Liberation.

From the balcony of the municipal presidency of San Cristóbal de Las Casas, a masked Commander Marcos, speaking on behalf of the rebel army, declared,

> Today the North American Free Trade Agreement begins, which is nothing more than a death sentence for the indigenous ethnicities of Mexico, who are perfectly dispensable in the modernization program of Salinas de Gortari. Thus the compañeros decided to rise up on this same day to respond to the decree of death that the Free Trade Agreement gives them, with the decree of life that is given by rising up in arms to demand liberty and democracy, which will provide them with the solution to their problems. This is the reason we have risen up today.[87]

Before leaving the balcony and in front of a still-stunned Chiapaneco populace, Marcos issued a historic reminder: "Don't forget this: This is an ethnic movement!"[88]

SIX

Visible Indians

Subcomandante Marcos and the "Indianization" of the Zapatista Army of National Liberation

The Zapatista Uprising

And so, on the morning of January 1, 1994, Mexico was once more dramatically and violently awakened to the all-but-obscured social reality of an incensed indigenous populace that had reached the limits of human endurance. With the armed occupation of seven of the main towns in the southeastern state of Chiapas, the soldiers of the Zapatista Army of National Liberation (EZLN) provided the world and Mexico with a palpable reminder — lest they had been completely convinced by the Mexican government's insistent claims to first-world status — that here in Mexico, despite all assertions to the contrary, there still existed levels of malnutrition, discrimination, and exploitation that betrayed any claim to the feverously coveted title of "developed nation."

The fighting did not last long, principally because of the indignation provoked by the media coverage of captured Zapatistas with their hands tied behind their backs and bullet holes through their heads. A cease-fire was called, the Catholic Church and Msgr. Samuel Ruiz offered to act as mediators, and the government offered the rebels — or "professionals in violence," as they were then called — an official pardon. This was the Zapatista response:

> What do we have to ask forgiveness for?
> What are they going to "pardon" us for?
> For not dying of hunger?
> For not accepting our misery in silence?

For not humbly accepting the huge historic burden of disdain and
abandonment?

For having risen up in arms when we found all other paths closed?

For not heeding Chiapas's penal code, the most absurd and repressive
in history?

For having shown the country and the whole world that human dignity
still exists and is in the hearts of the most impoverished inhabitants?

For having made careful preparations before beginning our fight?

For having brought guns to battle instead of bows and arrows?

For having learned to fight before having done it?

For being Mexicans, every one of us?

For being mostly indigenous?

For calling the Mexican people to fight, through whatever means, for
what rightfully belongs to them?

For fighting for freedom, democracy, and justice?

For not following the leaders of previous wars?

For refusing to surrender?

For refusing to sell ourselves?

For not betraying one another?

Who should ask for forgiveness and who can grant it?

Those who, for years and years, sat before a full table and satiated
themselves while we sat with death, as such a daily factor in our
lives that we stopped even fearing it? Those that filled our pockets
and souls with declarations and promises?

The dead, our dead, who mortally died "natural" deaths, that is, of
measles, whooping cough, dengue, cholera, typhoid, mononucleosis,
tetanus, bronchitis, malaria, and other gastrointestinal and
pulmonary diseases?

Our dead, who die so undemocratically of grief because nobody did
anything to help them, because all the dead, our dead, would simply
disappear without anyone paying the bill, without anyone finally
saying, "ENOUGH!"

Those who give feeling back to these dead, our dead, who refuse to ask
them to die over again, but now instead ask them to live?

Those that denied us the right to govern ourselves?

Those who treat us as foreigners in our own land and ask us for papers
and to obey a law whose existence we ignore?

Those that torture, seize, and assassinate us for the great crime of
wanting a piece of land,

not a big piece,
not a small one,
just one on which we could grow something with which to fill our
    stomachs?

Who should ask forgiveness and who can grant it?

The president of the republic?
The secretaries of state? The senators? The deputies? The governors?
The municipal presidents? The police? The federal army?
Powerful businessmen, bankers, industrialists, and landowners?
Political parties? Intellectuals? Galio and Nexos?
The media? Students? Teachers? Our neighbors?
Workers? Campesinos? Indigenous people?
Those who died useless deaths?

Who should ask forgiveness and who can grant it? [1]

With the cease-fire the Zapatistas repeated their demands, and slowly a process of negotiation began. Their central demands were threefold: freedom, democracy, and justice. When the time arrived for face-to-face talks with the government, these demands were elaborated into thirty-four concrete proposals, among which featured calls for agrarian reform, improvements in education and health, indigenous autonomy, and the recognition of the Zapatistas as a belligerent force,[2] a recognition that was never to be granted.[3] Although certain accords on indigenous rights and culture were signed, the talks broke down in August 1996 when it became clear that the government lacked both the political will and the intention to fulfill its word. Since 1996, therefore, Chiapas has been embroiled in what has been termed "low-intensity warfare." In concrete terms, this means pro-Zapatista communities have had to confront the terror of paramilitaries, the classic governmental tactics of using aid to divide and conquer, and the more constant intimidation that has come with the continued military encroachment on their villages. Monologue has replaced dialogue, and the government strategy for "peace" has become unilateral.[4]

During this time, the masked figure of Subcomandante Marcos has emerged as the chief spokesperson and interlocutor for the rebel movement. Through publication of his press releases and letters to the nation, we have come to learn more about how the Zapatista Army of National

Liberation came into being, and in the process we also learn what it is that is so distinctive about the nature of Zapatista politics.

Subcomandante Insurgente Marcos

Marcos, or *el Sup,* as he is better known, was born on January 1, 1994, or so the legend goes. There are, of course, those who deny this, not least among them the Mexican government and its national intelligence service (CISEN). They would instead have us believe that the masked figure who is both military commander and spokesperson for the rebel EZLN is none other than one Rafael Guillen, a Jesuit-educated former university lecturer born in 1957 in Tampico, in northern Mexico.[5] The story they wish to tell is of a man corrupted by the texts of Marx and Mao, a man so frustrated with the apathy of metropolitan campus life that he allowed himself to become embroiled in the more radical politics of violent subversion.[6] To some extent, they may in fact be right — but only, as academics might say, within the terms of their own discourse.[7] And it is with this discourse — the discourse of Mexican officialdom, the discourse of "government knows best," of "government has the legitimacy to represent," of fact over fiction — that Marcos and the Zapatista rebels with whom his life is now so inextricably linked take issue.

It is not so much that Marcos never came from the city to the countryside to preach the revolutionary doctrines of Marxism-Leninism, for this he freely admits, while still refusing to confirm his alleged identity. His own story, however, places greater emphasis on his encounter with Indian culture, an encounter that he claims changed him and the very principles upon which the thousands of Zapatista soldiers thought it necessary to fight. The nature of this change, and consequently the nature of the revolutionary movement to which Zapatismo gives its name, has become the principal focus of the speeches and texts to which he has dedicated himself ever since. That Marcos should often choose the narrative form of the short story (usually employing the literary creation of a pipe-smoking beetle, Don Durito, as his alter ego), or the wise parables of the Indian elder *el Viejo Antonio,* or sometimes simply the direct inquiries of Mayan children, as his preferred means to illustrate the motives behind the 1994 New Year's Day uprising should not be mistaken as the signs of a purely literary indulgence, a vice to which he is by no means immune.[8] Equally, his less prolific but similarly telling choice of poetry as a favored form of expression should not be acknowledged simply on the grounds of literary merit,

FIGURE 6.1 Subcomandante Insurgente Marcos in Chiapas, 1994. Photo by Pedro Valtierra.

but instead, it should be recognized as a conscious and political statement concerned with just how, and by whom, the realm of experience can best be communicated.[9]

His now-famous communiqués to the national and international press are thus in and of themselves an attempt to disrupt and disturb the government's monopoly on truth and fact.[10] His texts seek to reveal everything that has been excluded from the realm of official discourse in a way every bit as vital to the Zapatista revolution as the unexpected physical apparition of thousands of armed Indians that first exposed the thin veneer of an inclusionary and developmentalist rhetoric upon which governmental claims to legitimacy had been based. What follows is essentially Marcos's version of the "slow accumulation of forces" that resulted in the January 1994 uprising and the continued Zapatista rebellion of today.

La palabra dura — *The Hard Word*

Even now, few people live in the deepest, densest parts of the Lacandon jungle — not even the Indians.[11] So on November 17, 1983, when six individuals arrived in Chiapas to found the Zapatista Army of National

Liberation, they knew that in the terms of the clandestine, few places could compete with the seclusion of the Chiapan jungle.[12] Buoyed up on the intellectual opiates of Marxist-Leninist theory, the group was poorly armed, badly equipped, deficient in the practice of political conversion, and lacking in all but the most skeletal of local indigenous contacts upon which to base a guerrilla movement. Faced with the sheer severity of the jungle environment, they fought their first battles with the mountains, with hunger, with sickness, and with the cold. In view of this, they named their first camp *la pesadilla,* "the nightmare," and ironically the area in which it was located, in contrast to the intense volume of its vegetation, had long been known as *el desierto,* "the desert."[13] By all accounts, it was not an auspicious beginning.

In 1984, Marcos himself arrived. At this time, the group consisted of only three Indians and three mestizos. The Indians already had a long experience of political movements; they also had seen the inside of prison, had suffered torture, and were only too familiar with the internal squabbles of the Mexican left. As a teacher, Marcos was set the task of instructing them to read and write and schooling them in what they most demanded: *la palabra política,* "the political word." The word in this instance was history—history in general, and in particular the history of Mexico and its struggles. Still, for all the bookish knowledge Marcos may have had of the triumphs and failures of Mexican history, it soon became evident that his role as teacher would be limited to the informal classroom of the camp. Outside, it was the Indians who taught him how to negotiate the jungle, how to walk so as not to exhaust himself, how to hunt, and how to prepare and cook what he caught—how to make himself, as they put it, "part of the mountain." Even for the Indians, though, it was not an easy time. It was unusual for them to spend such a long period away from their communities, and while the jungle was completely alien to the urban-dwelling mestizos, for the indigenous, the fact that they were living in an uninhabited sector of the mountains had an added cultural significance.

Slowly Marcos realized that this desert of solitude was, for the Indians, a place far more culturally potent than he had ever imagined. It was, in his words,

the home of the dead, a place of spirits, and of all the histories that they populate, and that still populate the night in the Lacandon jungle, and for which the Indians of the region have much respect. Much respect and much fear.[14]

For Marcos, it was his first experience of an indigenous world of phantasms, of gods reborn, and of spirits that took the form of animals or objects. As he began to listen to the myths and stories of his Indian companions, it was, he would later reflect, the slow beginning of a process that he now calls the "Indianization" of the Zapatista Army of National Liberation.[15] First, however, there were harsher lessons to learn.

Both the importance and the amorphous nature of Indian culture were to make themselves painfully felt when the group made its first attempts to proselytize among the communities that lived closest to the jungle interior. In retrospect, Marcos talks of entering these communities and trying to teach

the absurdities that we had been taught; of imperialism, social crisis, the correlation of forces and their coming together, things that nobody understands, and of course neither did they.[16]

When he asked if they understood, their response was honest:

They would tell you that they had understood nothing, that your words were not understandable, that you had to look for other words; (they would say,) "tu palabra es muy dura, no la entendemos" [your word is very tough, we don't understand it].[17]

It became clear that the rhetoric of Marxism-Leninism did not ring true to the Indians of the selva, and so the search for "the words with which to say it" began in earnest.

It was around this time that Marcos wrote one of his first few published poems. It is a piece that perhaps reflects the frustration he felt in trying to communicate his sincere belief in the necessity for revolution, and the fact that he chose the poetic form should by no means be considered accidental. We might also approach his constant search for examples as further evidence of a teacher still unsure of whom he is addressing. Appropriately enough, it is entitled "Problems."

PROBLEMS:

This thing that is one's country is somewhat difficult to explain
But more difficult still is to understand what it is to love one's country.
For example
they taught us that to love one's country is, for example,
to salute the flag

to rise upon hearing the National Anthem
To get as drunk as we please when the national soccer team loses
To get as drunk as we please when the national soccer team wins
and a few et ceteras that don't change much from one presidency to
   the next . . .

And, for example,
they didn't teach us that to love one's country can be
for example,
to whistle like one who's becoming ever more distant, but
behind that mountain there is also a part of our country where nobody
   sees us
and where we open our hearts
(because one always opens one's heart when no one sees them)
And we tell this country,
for example,
everything we hate about it
and everything we love about it
and how it is always better to say it,
for example,
with gunshots and smiling.

And, for example,
they taught us that to love one's country is,
for example,
to wear a big sombrero,
to know the names of the Boy Heroes of Chapultepec,
to shout "Viva-arriba Mexico!,"
even though Mexico is down and dead.
and other et ceteras that change little from one Presidency to the
   next . . .

And, for example,
they did not teach us that
to love one's country
could be,
for example,
to be as quiet as one who dies,
but no,
for beneath this earth there is also a country

where no one hears us
and where we open our hearts
(because one always opens one's heart when no one is listening)
and we tell our country,
the short and hard history
of those who went on dying to love her,
and who are no longer here to give us their reasons why,
but who give them all the same without being here,
those who taught us
that one can love one's country,
for example,
with gunshots and smiling.[18]

Lunas escondidas — Hidden Moons

Any difficulties the Zapatistas may have had in explaining their notion of revolution to the Indians were, of course, only compounded by the seemingly simple barrier of language. Since the newcomers spoke only Spanish, it was unavoidable that the original Indian Zapatistas would have to act as translators on behalf of their urban, educated, non-Indian companions. Since the Zapatistas were keen to spread *la palabra política* (the political word), the grounds of an engagement nearly always centered on the question of history. However, as these initial conversations became increasingly marked by misunderstanding and incomprehension, it became clear that the indigenous held a different — and to the non-Indian, a curious — conception of time. As Marcos recalls,

> You weren't always sure about which era they were speaking; when they spoke, they could be talking about a story that happened that very week, or that happened five hundred years earlier or even when the world began.[19]

Initially, the mestizo Zapatistas paid scant attention to the importance of such cultural differences; their outlook was fixed. From their perspective, that of educated urban guerrillas, they were the vanguard, and the Indians were simply "the exploited people — those who had to be organized and shown the path."[20] The universalism of their Marxist analysis and reading of history precluded any meaningful differentiation between sectors in society, and the notion of culture held little purchase outside of the realm of the disdained elite bourgeoisie. To their mind, "it was the same to talk to a member of the proletariat, a peasant, an employee, or a student. All would understand the word of the revolution."[21] So when the Indians told them they didn't, it was a profound blow.

Marcos explains:

> It's very difficult when you have a theoretical scheme that explains the whole of a society and then you arrive in that society and you realize that your scheme explains nothing. It's difficult to accept, to recognize that you have dedicated all of your life to a project, and that this project is fundamentally warped. It can't even explain the reality into which you are trying to integrate yourself. It was something truly serious.[22]

It was at this point, then, that the mestizo Zapatistas realized that their problems were not simply issues of translation. They became aware that the Indian language had its own referents, its own cultural markers, which were different from theirs, and that if they hoped to have any further or successful contact with the indigenous communities, these were differences that had to be understood.

These initial difficult conversations thus started what Marcos calls "a process of cultural contamination, in the sense of seeing the world, one that obliged us to reconsider our politics and the way in which we viewed our own historical process and the historical process of the nation."[23] It was during this period, as Marcos would later admit, that the non-Indian Zapatistas learned to listen. What previously had been purely an object of passing curiosity now became an issue of central importance. As they sat around the fire at night, the Indians' stories of Sombreron, of Votan, of Ik'al, of the Black Lord, the stories of the talking boxes and of Ix'paquinte, became not simply a form of entertainment but also the primary means through which the mestizos became aware of the cultural richness and otherness of the Indians of southeastern Mexico.[24] When the mestizos inquired further, and asked where the Indians had learned these stories, they were told that they in turn had heard them from *los viejos*, the community elders.

The mestizos learned that the viejos were a central source of legitimacy within the communities and that, in fact, the Indians who were at that time their companions in the jungle camp were only there by approval of the elders. Still unsettled by the seeming confusion of temporalities that littered the indigenous histories, the mestizos found it difficult to understand the legitimacy and respect accorded to such stories and the elders who told them. Slowly, however, they came to recognize that outside of the schoolroom and the university, this was how history worked: because of the high level of illiteracy within the community, it had become necessary to choose someone whose task it would be to memorize the history of that community, someone who could act, as it were, like a "walking book."[25]

It was this experience of history, and the constant invocation of inherited oral history, that provided the basis upon which the language of Zapatismo was constructed. By listening to the Indians' own experience and history of exploitation, of humiliation, and of racism, the Zapatistas found the keystones upon which to build a new politics. The local history revealed just how partial non-Indian claims to a national history were, and to a large extent, the Zapatistas learned firsthand what it meant to be erased from the history books. In this context, we would do well to ponder the political consequences of an academic knowledge that claims a comprehensiveness and transparency that do not exist. Scholars of international relations, in particular, could do worse than accept a poem by Marcos appropriately entitled "a gift and a lesson in politics."

A GIFT AND A LESSON IN POLITICS:

A little piece of the moon . . .
though really it's not one at all,
but two:
A piece from the dark side,
and one from the bright.
And what must be understood
is that the little piece of the moon
that shines
shines because there is a dark side too.
The dark side of the moon
makes possible the bright.

Us too.
When we are the dark side,
(and we must take turns)
it doesn't mean we are less,
only that it's time
to be the dark side,

so that everyone can see the moon
(to tell the truth,
when it comes down to it, the dark side
is more important,
because it shines in other skies,
and because to see it
you have to learn to fly
very high).

And so it is,
only a few
are willing to suffer so
others won't,
and die
so others live.
And this is so,
given that boots and moon and et cetera
are there.[26]

El Viejo Antonio — Old Man Antonio

As these founding Zapatistas experienced a transformation of their role
from that of teachers to that of pupils, one Indian village elder in particular took on the mantle of cultural compass for Marcos especially.
His name was el Viejo Antonio, and it was he who in large part gave
legitimacy to the Zapatistas' tentative early presence in the Indian communities. He was, in the words of Marcos, the one "who explained us,
who we were and who we should be."[27] As Marcos would later admit,
it was the time spent with el Viejo Antonio, "Old Man Antonio," that
had the most profound influence on the unconscious transformation of
the quasi-Marxist guerrilla army into an Indian rebel army. He was,
for the Zapatistas, a vital bridge, and for Marcos in particular, a mirror in which to reconsider and recreate the nature of the revolutionary
struggle to which he had chosen to dedicate his life.

Typically, el Viejo Antonio would appear in a quiet moment when
Marcos or his companions had cause to visit his community. Without greeting, he would sit beside Marcos and begin to roll one of his
homemade tobacco cigars while Marcos would take the opportunity
to repack and relight his own pipe. After these moments of individual
preparation, and after both had savored their first draws of smoke, it

FIGURE 6.2 Zapatista soldier, 1994. Photo by Pedro Valtierra.

was nearly always incumbent upon Marcos to break the now-heavy silence that hung amid them and their respective fumes. Most often, Marcos would begin with a question, and after a dignified pause, el Viejo Antonio would characteristically and enigmatically respond with a story.

They were stories of gods who sacrificed themselves to make the sun and the moon, of why carbon is black and yet nonetheless produces light, of lions and mirrors, of night and stars, of colors, of clouds and rain, of questions, of trees, stones, ants and water, and of rainbows.[28] Each story was in its own right a parable, and although Marcos probably never did receive a straight answer to his questions, he came to consider el Viejo Antonio his teacher, perhaps even his mentor. And the most important lesson he learned was patience.

With only a short-wave radio as their principal means of receiving news from the outside world, the guerrillas often felt isolated and out of step with the wider changes that were taking place in the international arena. As Radio Havana, Voice of America, and Radio France Internationale informed them, the Soviet Union was collapsing, peace deals and elections were taking place in Central America, and Reaganism was becoming the ideology of preference among the developed and lesser-developed nation-states. In fact, the rebels' decision to come to the mountains of southeastern Mexico to foment revolution at times looked increasingly anachronistic. It was during these moments of tempered despair and doubt, however, that el Viejo Antonio's parables directed Marcos' attention back to the environment around him. Rather than looking outward for signs of confirmation, el Viejo Antonio taught him to look within.

As Marcos has said,

You come from the city accustomed to managing time with relative autonomy. You can extend the day with a light well into the night, to read, to study, to do many activities after dark. But not in the mountain. The mountain says to you, "from here on in, it's the turn of another world," and we enter effectively another world, other animals, other sounds, another time, other air, and another form of being with people, that includes the indigenous who were with us. In the night you are made truly more timid, more introspective, more close, as if looking for a handle on something that has always been prohibited: a night in the mountain.[29]

For Marcos, it was during this period that a lasting transformation took place among the Zapatistas:

> The idea of a more just world, everything that was socialism in broad brushstrokes, but redirected, enriched with humanitarian elements, ethics, morals, more than simply indigenous. Suddenly the revolution transformed itself into something essentially moral. Ethical. More than the redistribution of the wealth or the expropriation of the means of production, the revolution began to be the possibility for a human being to have a space for dignity. Dignity started to be a word with much strength. It wasn't our contribution, it didn't come from the urban element; this was the contribution of the [Indian] communities. In such a way that the revolution would be the guarantee for dignity, so that it might be respected.[30]

In more intimate terms, he has written:

> There is in the world a mirror.
> It allows us to know who we are,
> who we were and who we can be.
>
> The first image is not always so agreeable,
> the second explains why,
> and with the third we show our promise.
>
> The problem is in knowing how to find the mirror.
> It's not so easy.
> But the really dangerous part
> is to dare oneself to look inside.
> A little distance from oneself,
> assisted by a smile, will help things.[31]

El lento despertar — *The Slow Awakening*

While Chiapas itself has been home to Mayan Indian groups for over a thousand years, the indigenous with whom Marcos and the Zapatistas made their initial contact were, as explained in the previous chapter, relative newcomers to the Lacandon jungle zone. Beginning in the 1940s, small numbers of Indians mainly from the highland areas of

Chiapas were encouraged by the federal government to colonize the uncultivated land in the southern parts of the state, close to the border with Guatemala. Although the number of communities originally established was small, their creation laid the foundations for a later period of substantially greater migration that some, in conscious invocation of the biblical connotations, have described as an exodus.[32] By 1980, the migrant population had risen to around 100,000 from an estimated 10,000 in 1960, and the current figure of 150,000 is expected to reach 200,000 by the year 2000.[33]

Apart from the sheer numbers that such an upheaval and resettlement involved, the factor that gave the Lacandon jungle its distinctive cultural identity was that within this body of migrants existed differences in language, ethnicity, religion, and political affiliation that, when combined, resulted in what has already been described as a "unique space of social construction."[34] In light of the already well-established influences — such as the church, both Protestant evangelical and Catholic liberation theologist, as well as the long-active Maoist-inspired political unions — the indigenous culture that the Zapatistas encountered was one both resistant to easy definition and recalcitrant to external political control.[35] It is perhaps not surprising, then, that when the indigenous eventually came to embrace the Zapatista politics of clandestine subversion, they did so under conditions of severe economic hardship, and only after the exhaustion of various legal attempts at political expression.[36]

The true extent of the "Indianization" of the Zapatista Army of National Liberation was, however, only finally formalized after the communities themselves had decided to go to war. With the creation of the Clandestine Revolutionary Indigenous Committee (CCRI) in 1993, the Zapatista general command became completely Indian, and the organizational structure at last reflected the earlier ideological change that had taken place among the movement's non-Indian members.[37] Consisting of representatives of the four main ethnic groups (Tzeltal, Chol, Tzotzil, and Tojolabal) from the three central regions of Zapatista influence in the state (the north, the highlands, and the jungle), the CCRI became the central means of coordination and information dissemination necessary in the preparation for the planned rebel offensive.[38] It was around this time, also, that Marcos was appointed chief military commander for the rebel forces.

Nobody was really sure how the 1994 New Year's Day rebellion would go. It had the potential to be a disaster, a horrific bloodbath. As it turned out, the rebel force of some six thousand successfully occupied seven of Chiapas's main towns with little bloodshed. In the days that followed, however, once the Mexican military had recovered from the surprise, many hundreds of lives — Zapatista, military, and civilian — would be lost. The government was not slow to employ Swiss- and U.S.–manufactured planes and helicopters to bomb the rebel positions, although their superior firepower was to be quickly tempered not so much by the guerrilla tactics of the Zapatistas themselves as by the national and international media attention they had unleashed with their dramatic declaration of war in San Cristóbal some days earlier. By January 12, the government had declared a cease-fire, and most analysts were hopeful that a peaceful resolution to the conflict might be possible.

La lucha sigue — *The Fight Continues*

It has been over nine years since those first days of violent insurrection in Chiapas, and still to this day blood is shed in the defense of Zapatismo. The Mexican federal government has been accused of attempting to "administer" the war rather than sincerely seeking its resolution.[39] The government's strategy, both domestic and international, has combined the showmanship of rhetorical and gestural politics, common to much of late-twentieth-century statecraft, with the more classical tactics of countersubversion already tried and tested in the mountain villages of Mexico's Central American neighbors. It is a battle fought on two fronts. Locally in Chiapas, the Indian communities have found themselves surrounded by a military force estimated to be some eighty thousand strong.[40] While their constant patrolling and increasingly regular incursions leave the communities intimidated and tense, it has been the training and arming of unofficial paramilitary groups throughout the region that has given rise to a refugee population of some sixteen thousand and, most horrifically, resulted in the December 1997 massacre of forty-six Tzotzil Indians, mainly women and children, in the community of Acteal.[41]

In contrast to this painful realism of low-intensity warfare under which large parts of Chiapas continue to suffer today, the other aspect of the governmental response has been directed toward the more nebulous frontier of public and international opinion. It is in this connected realm, where the politics of representation and discourse have been most fiercely contested, that we must locate and understand the initial governmental obsession with the unmasking of Marcos. For since the first declaration of the Lacandon jungle on New Year's Day 1994, it has fallen upon Marcos as both product and expression of the Zapatista struggle to communicate why the indigenous chose to fight and why they continue to fight to this day.

After so many secretive years of survival in the mountains, the sudden arrival of journalists, photographers, and camera crews in the Lacandon communities has, instead of making the struggle seem more real, often made the world of national and international politics appear increasingly *sur*-real. At times, Marcos has drawn an analogy between his and the Zapatistas' apparition in this new world and that of Lewis Carroll's Alice when she stepped through a looking glass.[42] At other times, he has compared his actions and those of his companions to those heroic moments of madness immortalized in Cervantes's tale of the exploits of Don Quixote de la Mancha and his loyal footman, Sancho Panza. For Marcos, the saddest part of Don Quixote was always the moment when he was returned to a life of normality, the moment when he said of himself, "I was mad, and now I am sane." It has been Marcos's belief that the Zapatistas have to continue battling in the madness until the very last.[43] To this end, Marcos has created his own Sancho Panza in the literary character of a tough little beetle known as Don Durito.[44]

All this might appear too much, too playful, too lightweight in contrast to the daily plight of Indian life in Chiapas, were it not for the fact that such stories, such literary allusions and poems, have at their core one key message. For the Mexican governmental administration so determined to follow the schematic rules of neoliberal reform, a government whose only recourse is to call on the cold and sometimes savage rationalism of economic analysis in sterile defense of its contested legitimacy, the Zapatista message is difficult to counter. Not directed at the head—because the Zapatistas believe they have little to add to existing analyses of Mexico's continued economic crisis—their message aims for "the heart, the part most often forgotten."[45] This does not mean that they simply hope to elicit sympathy. As Marcos puts it,

> We are not saying that we want to create a sentimental discourse, one that's apolitical, or atheoretical, or antitheoretical; but what we want is to bring theory down to the level of the human being, to what is lived, to share with the people the experiences that make it possible to continue living.[46]

It is precisely this appeal to the human — a humanness not articulated in any theory, ideology, or doctrine but reflected within the literature and speeches of Zapatismo and made intimate through the jungle encounters that have attracted thousands to Chiapas since the conflict first began — that makes the Zapatistas unique.[47] It has led some to term the struggle the "first post-modern revolution of the twenty-first century,"[48] and while remaining sensitive to the hyperbolic appropriation such a claim entails, we must also admit that there might also be some truth here. Mexican history, after all, seems to show us that the Indians of Chiapas have fallen under one modernist vision after another, leaving an Indian invisible in Mexican and world politics, a situation that the Zapatista rebels seem to uniquely contest. As we enter the twenty-first century, however, the result of such contestation must remain open-ended.

Conclusion

Modernist Visions and the Invisible Indian

It would be easy and understandable to characterize the Zapatista movement as romantic. To a certain extent it is. But what the seemingly romantic elements of the rebellion invite is not criticism for their perceived lack of realism but self-reflection upon our own received expectations of real politics. We must ask ourselves how it is that we have come to presume that the true nature of politics involves top-down instrumental and structural proposals. As we are forced to look away from the official and traditionally recognized centers of power, so too should we be forced to question how we understand the nature of such power as it is lived and not merely prescribed. In academic fields such as international relations, this failure to decouple politics from its institutional and theoretical locale has centered mainly on an overevaluation of the role and function of the modern sovereign state.

Outside of what are often considered to be the traditional boundaries of the discipline, scholars like Quentin Skinner have looked to the history of political thought as it was understood prior to our distinctly modern understanding of the state "as the sole source of law and legitimate force within its own territory, and as the sole appropriate object of its citizens' allegiances."[1] Within the transformations and dynamics of Renaissance political thought and their later influence upon the Reformation and Counter-Reformation, Skinner has sought to explain how a "decisive shift was made from the idea of the ruler 'maintaining his state'—where this simply meant upholding his own position—to the idea that there is a separate legal and constitutional order, that of the state, which the ruler has a duty to maintain."[2] The curious legacy of modern international theorizing has been its studied indifference to the implications of such historical research for contemporary political analyses of the state. It is as though, once the existence of the state had been identified, little more thought needed be given to how the body politic itself continued to exist. Its actions, its relations, and its very agency have as a consequence been attributed a coherence, a logic, and a reified position that provide the primary foundation for the theorizing that has followed.

One thinker who could be read as picking up where Skinner left off is Michel Foucault. Only too well aware of the shackles such state-centric thinking can impose, in a passage not directly aimed at the discipline of international relations but nonetheless expressive of a similar problematic, Foucault makes a critique and a suggestion:

The excessive value attributed to the problem of the state is expressed, basically, in two ways: the one form, immediate, effective and tragic, is the lyricism of the monstre froid we see confronting us; but there is a second way of overvaluing the problem of the state, one which is para-doxical because apparently reductionist: it is the form of analysis that consists in reducing the state to a certain number of functions, such as the development of productive forces and the reproduction of relations of production, and yet this reductionist vision of the relative impor-tance of the state's role nevertheless invariably renders it absolutely essential as a target needing to be attacked and a privileged position needing to be occupied. But the state, no more probably today than at any other time in its history, does not have this unity, this individual-ity, this rigorous functionality, nor, to speak frankly, this importance; maybe after all, the state is no more than a composite reality and a mythicized abstraction, whose importance is a lot more limited than many of us think. Maybe what is really important for our modernity — that is, for our present — is not so much the étatisation of society, as the "governmentalisation" of the state.[3]

In the chapters that have preceded this conclusion, I have taken inspiration from such a suggestion. I have thus attempted to provide not so much a history of the Mexican state per se as a history of the "gov-ernmentalization" of the Mexican state. While Foucault began writing about the history of thought and practice involved in the creation of the modern Western European state, I have been surprised to discover how Western and European the models of Mexican governance have been in their basis. However, although there has been a notable overlap of political thought and governmental rationale within this history, my account has also sought to chart a distinctively Mexican dynamic that the genesis of the Western state did not involve. This additional dynamic, of course, has been the existence of a native culture and society prior to the arrival of the Spanish colonists that, since that time, has been known as "Indian." With this history of Mexican governmental thought, therefore, there has also been intertwined a parallel narrative of Indian subjugation, what might best be described as a necessarily partial and subjugated history of Indian resistance.

Because the event that first triggered this study was the Zapatista uprising of 1994, this attempt to tell a story concerning the relations between governmental thought and Indian subjectivity should by no means be considered accidental. In fact, it has been my intention to approach the Zapatista rebellion as a window of opportunity through which we would be led back through Mexican history to consider the different manners in which the Indian has been thought of and treated. In doing so, we have been able to consider the effects of the adoption of diverse mentalities of rule, effects that have led to the Indian's being made both invisible and visible in very particular ways. As the traditional approach in international relations has been to treat the state as a monolithic actor in its own right, my approach hopefully acts as a necessary corrective to the erasure of the all-too-human and contested subjectivities that constitute the living modern polis. In this way, I have sought to work from a deep-seated ontological viewpoint—that is to say, the entry point chosen for the study of international relations is not the modern state and its institutions but the human and social subject upon which such political rationales have come to be inscribed.[4]

Concentrating on the Maya Indians of Chiapas in particular, I have attempted to fuse the two histories to provide a context and a perspective from which to better understand the current condition of Mexican governmental politics and Zapatista Indian rebellion at the beginning of the twenty-first century. As the preceding chapters have indicated, history is both complex and multilayered, and much else that might have been of significance and interest remains outside this particular narrative. This study, like every narrative of historical life, remains hostage to the limits of representation. Nevertheless, while I have thus far tried to be sensitive to the routes not traveled, I shall now turn my attention

FIGURE 7.1 Peace demonstrations in Mexico City, not long after the Acteal massacre, demanding the withdrawal of the Mexican military, the disarming of paramilitary groups in Chiapas, and the fulfillment of the San Andrés peace accords, 1998. Photo by author.

to a necessarily more schematic and perhaps more useful summary of the political and social history recounted so far.

A History of Mexican Governmental Thought

The first chapter concerned itself with the impact, both European and native, of the discovery and described the system of government imposed by the colonists. It argued that while Europe may well be understood to have begun a period of modernity at this time, for the American natives and the government of the colony, the periodization "medieval" is more appropriate. This is to argue that (a) modernity has distinct trajectories depending on concrete historical conditions; and (b) Mexico (then New Spain) experienced little of the Reformation/Counter-Reformation dynamic that would prove so divisive in Europe and, as a consequence, maintained a system of order that, owing to its religious and feudal forms, is best described as medieval.

It was not until the end of the Hapsburg dynasty and the establishment of the Bourbon line that the transformations in the European "art of government" began to make themselves felt in the Americas. Chapter 2 set out what I argue is the first moment of modernity in Mexican history, the period of "enlightened despotism," which began in the late eighteenth century and ended with the wars of independence, creating the governmental entity that we now know as Mexico. Ethnohistorians, like Serge Gruzinski, describe this period as a "second acculturation" for the Indians of New Spain. While the first period of acculturation came with the discovery and colonization of the Americas, this second encounter with European culture involved an attempt to remove the natives from the influence of both the church and the local *encomenderos* (plantation owners). It was, in fact, the first attempt to bring the Indian under the administrative and bureaucratic control of what was now becoming recognizable as the techniques of governance of the modern European nation-state. It is perhaps not surprising that the external imposition of such a novel system of government should conflict with the prior Hapsburg modus operandi that had been functioning for hundreds of years. However, the role of the indigenous population in the ensuing wars needs explaining.

Although I disagree with the assertion of historians Jacques Lafaye and David Brading that the Indian rebellion supporting Hidalgo and the battle to defend the dark-skinned Virgin of Guadalupe presents the founding moment of a "Mexican national consciousness," I nevertheless suggest that the religious form the rebellion adopted should alert us to the continued significance of a native religiosity that was at odds with the modernism of the governmental elite. Independence, when it eventually came, has been widely acknowledged to have embodied a compromise among diverse creole (non-Indian native-born American) elites. The choice of a loosely defined liberal constitutionalism as the preferred basis of government was clearly not made by the Indian masses, and when the constitution effectively rendered the Indian juridically invisible, the few remaining rights that being subject to a foreign monarchy had afforded disappeared. Postindependence Mexico was a country that neither functioned well as a state nor constituted a nation. It would not be until the late nineteenth century that Mexico could fairly be judged to have adopted a coherent and effective governmental rationale.

In the third chapter, I discussed the establishment of the Mexican governmental state and the importance of science in the creation of a governmental politics. In particular, I highlighted the work of Auguste Comte and Saint-Simon for the influence it had on a group of government officials known as the *científicos*. Analogies cannot fail to be

Table 1. Historical problematiques of the Mexican state

Problem	System	Expertise	Techniques
Order/legitimacy	Colonial	Theologians	Encomienda
		Courtiers	Repartimiento
			Reducción
			Religion
Efficiency/ productivity	Bourbon	Physiocrats	Statistics
			Tax/administration
			Hispanicization
			Church censorship
Order/strength/ productivity	Liberal Authoritarian	Positivists	Police
			Foreign investment
			Infrastructure
			Sectorial understanding
Order/unity	Corporatist	Positivists	Sectorial representation
			Education
			Church censorship
			Unions
Efficiency/ productivity	Neoliberal	Economists	Privatization
			Finance
			Foreign investment
			Specialization
			PRONASOL
			Concertación

drawn between the científicos' increasingly instrumental and interventionist style of politics and the earlier period of enlightened despotism. The thirty-year period presided over by the dictator Porfirio Díaz was Mexico's self-consciously "modern" moment. That it was also one of the darkest periods for the country's native population should not be considered an innocent coincidence. The chapter considered how the prominence of a liberal economic logic led to an understanding of the indigenous as a resource rather than a distinct people or culture and thus legitimized some of the worst treatment and conditions that Mexican history has bestowed upon its Indian inhabitants.

The social revolution of 1910–1920 put an end to some of the more flagrant excesses of the Mexican governmental state, but in significant respects, the postrevolutionary establishment of a single party (initially the PNR, then PRI) that claimed to represent all sectors of society perpetuated an instrumental and sectorial understanding of the indigenous that, while for the first time offering some form of representation, did so under the monolithic category of "worker." Chapter 4 demonstrated how this new form of corporatism came to impinge upon the life of the indigenous. In particular, employing the work of anthropologist Jan Rus, I described how the national project of indigenismo eventually led to the subversion of tradition within the highland Indian communities of Chiapas, resulting in a situation whereby "culture," as understood by the government, became an object of political control.

Chapter 5 brings us to the present high modern period of Mexican governmental rule. Here I discussed the roles of international financial structures (World Bank, IMF) and Mexican elite education (U.S. and European) in the introduction of the neoliberal method of governmental rule. I paid specific attention to the effects of this latest Mexican governmentality on the indigenous of Chiapas. I also described the arrival of other social actors, including protestant evangelicals, liberation theologists, and mestizo (non-Indian) revolutionaries, in the state. The chapter concluded with an analysis of the nation as it was on the eve of 1994.

In light of this analysis, although the history of Mexico's modernity cannot be considered purely analogous to that of the European state, it is possible to claim that the forms of government that Mexican political elites have chosen are all of European inspiration. Appreciating that every society is burdened with the task, under its concrete condition, of creating a sociopolitical order, we can now ask, what has been distinctive about the Mexican "governmentality"? The argument propounded here claims that Mexico has experienced three distinct moments of governmentality: the early modern period of the late eighteenth and early nineteenth centuries, the modern period of the late nineteenth and early twentieth centuries, and the high modern period of the late twentieth century. By this analysis, globalization, or the late-twentieth-century project of neoliberalism, becomes merely the latest, even if by far the most pervasive, in a series of governmentalities that the Mexican Indian has experienced. This brings us back to the second dynamic of the book.

A History of Subjugated Indian Identity and Resistance

As we have already seen, governmental power and practice do not necessarily produce the desired results. Colonial Indians took on much of Hispanic Christian practice without becoming Spanish. They neither subsumed the religious beliefs of Catholicism within their own culture nor synchronized the two; rather, they lived and experienced something new. In chapter 1 we witnessed in dramatic fashion how an indigenous religiosity was capable of reappropriating the symbols of conquest in a short-lived reversal of supernatural and temporal power known as the Cancuc rebellion of 1712. The Hapsburg colonial system, for all its barbarity and abuse, seems by its very promotion of a duality between the Christian transcendental and the monarchical to have avoided the psychological and symbolic rupture that would have left no space for a preexisting Indian imaginary.

In chapter 2, the permanently suspect question of conversion was made increasingly apparent. As enlightened Bourbon rule sought to reform the role of the Catholic Church within the Spanish Empire, public displays of native religiosity faced censure. As priests were encouraged to perform increasingly bureaucratic and regulatory tasks, Indian culture, which had always been more than its public expression, appears to have grudgingly reverted to the clandestine. The disruption caused by this new governmentality, with its imposition of peninsular Spaniards in place of the colonial-born locals, created the unrest that led to the Hidalgo revolt of 1810. The Indian role in the subsequent battles, as already mentioned, remains questionable, but the work of Eric Van Young on the Bajío Indians suggests that any claims to a Mexican nationalism were partial and limited to the creole elite at most. Millenarian beliefs and the desire to rout the *gachupines* (peninsular Spanish) while claiming the brown Virgin of Guadalupe for themselves again point to the persistence among the indigenous of mythical, transcendental, and spiritual elements that do not sit at all comfortably with notions of a modern nation-state.

While attempts had been made by both European and Mexican intellectuals to appropriate the civilization of the ancient Mexica — or Aztec, as they have since come to be known — as a means to legitimize independence and create a national identity, any suggestions that the existing Indian populace might have a more legitimate claim to such a cultural heritage were dismissed. Postindependence legislation in fact sought to juridically eradicate the living Indian as a subject with an identity separate from the abstract liberal citizen who now theoretically populated the former colony of New Spain. Such an act clearly reveals the inability of the liberal governmentality to accept the pluriethnic constitution of the Mexican territory. Chapter 3 demonstrated how this liberal myopia permitted rival mestizo groups to carve up the countryside of Chiapas, forcing the Indians into debt while excluding them from every aspect of public life.

What has since come to be misnamed the "caste war" of 1867 effectively illustrated how the persistent and understandable native devotion to autonomous acts of spiritual and supernatural worship could be presented as a threat to the new order. Empty constitutional formalism, combined with the continued sanction of Indian exploitation, led indigenous communities to once again animate the only refuge over which they had some control: the divine. The "talking stones" of Tzajahemel and the autonomous culture that briefly flourished around them provide powerful testimony to the vital and energizing presence of nonmaterial, transcendental, and spiritual realms within native culture. The vicious manner in which the public display of such beliefs was met should remind us once again of both the incapacity of Mexican liberalism to allow such nonnational allegiances to exist and its failure to replace Indian religiosity and ethics with its own means of cultural governance. This lack at the heart of Mexican rule was, of course, recognized by the científicos of the Díaz era.

Informed by a conscious developmentalism, the científicos made little attempt to uphold the constitutional liberties so keenly defended only decades earlier. Internal security instead took on an increasingly repressive role as individual rights were openly subsumed under more general nationalist economic priorities. The Indians as a group were no longer governmentally overlooked, but neither was their condition eased. In fact, their economic potential became subject to more systematic and regularized forms of exploitation, such as the *enganche* and seasonal plantation labor. Once more, Indian identity seems to have found expression in public village ritual. With the relaxing of church censorship and the new economic opportunity offered via the sale of aguardiente, the cofradía regained a central role in community life. The national revolution that Díaz's authoritarianism eventually triggered saw only limited participation by the Maya of Chiapas. One exception was the Pajarito rebellion, recounted in chapter 4. Nevertheless, this short-lived foray into (counter-) revolutionary activity only served to confirm the more dominant Indian stance of noninvolvement.

The immediate postrevolutionary years appear to have involved something of a renaissance in Indian cultural life, allowing for the elaboration of village rituals and cofradía celebrations. Nationalist revolutionary victory was thus locally supported on the basis of this unusual period of noninterference. Sadly, as chapter 4 demonstrated, when the revolution eventually adopted its lasting institutional form, the corporate inclusion of Indian hierarchies into a party alliance led to a

Table 2. Modern Mexican governmentalities

State-Building History or History of Governmentality	System	Subjugated Indian History
Colonial	Medieval/Christian	Cancuc rebellion, 1712
Bourbon	Enlightenment	Hidalgo Indian uprising, 1810
Liberal	Constitutionalist	"Caste war," 1867
Liberal-authoritarian	Científico	Pajarito rebellion/ postrevolutionary renaissance
Postrevolutionary	Corporatist	Corruption of Indian communities
Neoliberal	Free market/ self-enterprise	Zapatista Rebellion, 1994

corruption of the very Indian cultural structures of self-defense that had nourished the populace for so long. The eventual weariness, frustration, and fragmentation that such elite co-optation created led in large part to the acceptance and adoption of diverse creeds, mobilizations, and community experiments that finally resulted in the Zapatista rebellion of 1994.

Modernist Visions . . .

Viewed from this historical perspective, the Maya Indians' experience of modernity has been one characterized by struggle and repression. However, the notion that the modern Mexican state has become, in Weberian terms, "the sole source of law and legitimate force within its own territory, and the sole appropriate object of its citizens' allegiances" does not appear to hold.[5] If anything, the Maya of Chiapas have fought continually to maintain an ongoing allegiance to a culture of their own making, a historical trend only understandable with reference to the scant opportunity they had to participate in and benefit from the legitimized practices of the modern state. These practices, and the political rationales within which they are mobilized, are what give modernity its distinctive character.

It is quite clear that while the early colonial period of Hapsburg rule permitted numerous abuses to occur, the dual nature of Spanish imperial rule also involved a Christian pastoral aspect. This religious element provided a system of self-government that not only granted legitimacy through association with the divine but permitted each and every royal subject an equal opportunity to create a relationship with a higher power through the practices and rituals that individuals and communities could conduct. In retrospect, the modern moment could be said to occur precisely when religious practice is redeployed within the realm of government. Certainly in Europe this was no overnight process, and the transformation of the theocratic state into the modern state relied heavily on the reorientation of such Christian pastoral practices within newly understood governmental practices. The creation of a new governmentality, however, involved not only the ability of rulers to see their subjects differently, but the capacity for such subjects themselves to become active participants in this vision.[6]

It is also relatively obvious in our historical narrative of governmental thought that it is with the new practices of the Physiocrats and the beginnings of tabulation of population and its particular specificities that we witness the first modernist vision settle on Mexican soil and subjectivity. When the Bourbon empire collapsed, this vision remained limited to the *hombres de bien* (educated elite) of the newly independent Mexican state. These often Jesuit-educated Enlightenment men formed a governmental elite that confronted a rebellious nation with a predatory U.S. neighbor and sought legitimacy through an abstract constitutionalism that they lacked the institutional means to enforce. The second modernist vision that might best be understood in the more holistic terms of a governmentality thus appears with the ascension of the *científicos* to power. Their employment of a rural police force and their support for the dictatorial authoritarianism of Porfirio Díaz should be seen as evidence of their recognition of the unnatural character of the modern state and consequently the necessity of adopting violent internal security measures to create the cohesion that the nation so obviously lacked. Again, assisted by the evolutionist and linear concepts of Comtean progress, these experts were able to see Mexico as an object in need of strong guardianship.

This paternalism, at first sight, seems paradoxical given the modern state's reliance on institutional government and expertise. In fact, as the Mexican Revolution dramatically underscored, the lack of legitimacy and the weariness of top-down governance eventually generated significant resistance. That many of the positivists' ideas, and even the personnel themselves, were able to survive the revolution and return to positions of power should only confirm the transformation not of the institution of government but of the people in the practice of govern-

FIGURE 7.2 Peace demonstrations in Mexico City in the wake of the Acteal massacre, 1998. Photo by author.

ment that the heavy hand of Díaz did indeed produce. The corporate system chosen after the revolution as a means to bind the citizen to the state was seen as an effective way of overcoming the elite/masses division that had been so prominent in Mexican rule previously. The educational projects, the experimental introduction of Protestantism, and the nationalist character of the cultural projects of this period all reflect a massive effort to unite the territory and the people behind the modern state endeavor and, to a large extent, the myth of the revolution. That this system lasted seventy-one years should be seen as sufficient proof of the effectiveness of its (often coercive) practices of loyalty enforcement.

Although in 1988 Cuauhtémoc Cárdenas of the left-wing Partido Revolucionario Democrático (PRD) was denied victory by a manufactured computer crash, with the July 2000 elections, Mexico has for the first time voted in a presidential candidate from an opposition party. The success of Vicente Fox Quesada of the right-wing Partido Acción Nacional (PAN) should be recognized as the latest development in the neoliberal governmental rationale that has dominated Mexico since the early 1980s. This final and current modernist vision, although introduced by the long-dominant Institutional Revolutionary Party (PRI), necessitated the breakdown of the traditional corporate power structure of the one-party state. Attempts to replace the old system of clientism and bossism with new networks of power led to a period of unprecedented corruption, enrichment, and human rights abuse. Again, the alienation characteristic of failed or radical governmentalities could only be mediated through the highly coercive use of internal security measures.[7] The paradoxical element of neoliberalism, however, was its consciously international nature. With the attempts to reorganize national practices in line with international financial prerogatives came increased attention from international media and nongovernmental organizations. Also, the eruption of the Zapatista rebellion in 1994 and the scrutiny it commanded should be seen as contributive to the cleaning up of the electoral process.

The success of the PAN, however, should also alert us to the establishment of a new sector of the Mexican populace that the Zapatistas do not represent. The small-business owners and entrepreneurs that neoliberalism has created are seen to be the major supporters of the PAN. That they are predominantly from the north of Mexico, and have experienced greater industrialization and urbanization than the rural citizens of the south, is also vital for understanding their allegiance to an economic governmentality, and not to a traditional party that tried to encompass all sectors. Many international commentators would like to believe that Mexico's "democratic transition" will be the means to contain and give expression to the diversity of allegiances that exist within the contemporary modern Mexican state. To adopt such an optimistic conclusion, however, would be to overlook the central contention of this book and to perhaps miss the historic opportunity that the Zapatista rebellion has presented.[8]

. . . and the Invisible Indian

As globalization—understood as an international process of harmonization in terms economic, cultural, and political—raises the perhaps worrying specter of a modernity untamed, events such as the ongoing Zapatista rebellion act as "untimely" reminders of what is at stake in such processes. Through seeking to uncover a genealogy of Maya Indian subjectivity, I hope in this book to have contributed to an understanding of governmentality as a historical process that endeavors to create both internal changes in an individual's self-understanding and large-scale, external change in institutional and political structures. While in the West such changes are understood to have been less dramatic, owing to a shared history of political subjectivity, in the case of southern countries such as Mexico, the strength and unpredictability of a prior cultural and spiritual self-understanding leads to a very particular disruption of the totalizing and individualizing aspects at work within the modern governmentalized state project.

Recently international relations has become more attuned to the implicit normative aspects present in world politics. Much of what has been termed normative international relations, however, has been concerned with the purely abstract and philosophical construction of what might be best understood as the moral basis for engagement. This book, in contrast, seeks to contribute to another (related) strand of scholarship that finds itself more loosely preoccupied with both the ethical and the political.[9] In other words, this history belongs to a body of work that labors to a large extent to create a novel insight into, and awareness of, political change through an attentive analysis of its costs and consequences as experienced at the margins of traditional political or moral preoccupation.[10] Clearly, Michel Foucault has been one major influence in this type of scholarship. While much of his later work sought to uncover the increasingly internalized nature of governmentality in the modern Western political subject, this history hopes to illustrate the contrasting dynamic of indigenous subjectivity that seeks justification for its resistance not in large metatheoretical or institutional terms but in the personal, individual, and human terms that modern Mexican governmental politics appears so ill equipped to provide.

The deep-seated conflict in Mexico is therefore between different historical and cultural self-understandings and the power embodied within each. With the outbreak of the Zapatista uprising, Mexico for the first time faced an opportunity to reorient and reconsider its national and cultural constitution. The originality of the Zapatistas, therefore, has been their attempt to make nationally and internationally visible what had been made invisible: an Indian populace that had both political opinions and sociocultural visions. The story of Zapatista politics appears to be one of a movement that not only sought to put difference at the heart of Mexican citizenship but perhaps also suggested a politics constructed on the basis of diverse cultural ontologies. This is to suggest that the Zapatistas' lack of a clearly discernible large-scale governmental strategy or policy was not a failure of political vision on their part but rather the result of an alternative historical and political perspective that clashes with the modernist governmentalities of the orthodox political elite.

If we allow ourselves, therefore, to consider the Zapatista uprising as a post- or perhaps countermodern rupture in an otherwise modernist history, where, then, might we consider Mexican modern governmental rule to lie? I believe we can now attempt a generalization of sorts — for all the Mexican modernist visions that have come to make themselves methods of rule have had one thing in common, and that thing could be called a gaze. This gaze has come to view either all humans as the same or all humans as sharing the same evolution, even if differing in their relative position and role within such a hierarchy. Either way, the gaze is totalizing, allowing for little contestation of context or of individual particularity. It should come as little surprise that, as this gaze has made itself governmentally felt through various practices, human conduct has not necessarily fulfilled its ascribed role. It has long been known that power also breeds resistance. However, what is novel about Mexico is that the subjective experience of power should breed such an inclusive vision of government. In this regard, rather than reduce the Zapatista movement to an instance of realization of a contemporary sociopolitical theory such as postmodernism, I believe it is more convincing to view the sociocultural practices and experiences of Chiapan Indians themselves as producing another modernist vision, one that we might productively call a cultural humanism.

After the experience of the exclusionary practices of traditional political bosses, and with the multiple ethnicities that could often be counted in just one village, the Indians of the selva could be said to have naturally come to adopt democratic methods of community rule. That some are Catholic, some Protestant, some union members, some not, some women, some Chol, some Tojolobal, and some Tzeltal, and yet nearly all indigenous, has also led to a more flexible construction of what it is that can be called Indian culture. Thus, rather than the static, ahistorical conception of anthropological culture that has proved so damaging to Mexican Indians in the past, culture in this context should be understood as a constantly moving, changing, and evolving psycho-symbolic realm. While it is not the only motivating factor in an individual's or a community's life, culture nevertheless has an important ethical and political influence on relations toward the self and others. Neither can humanism be considered in essentialist terms. Rather, by

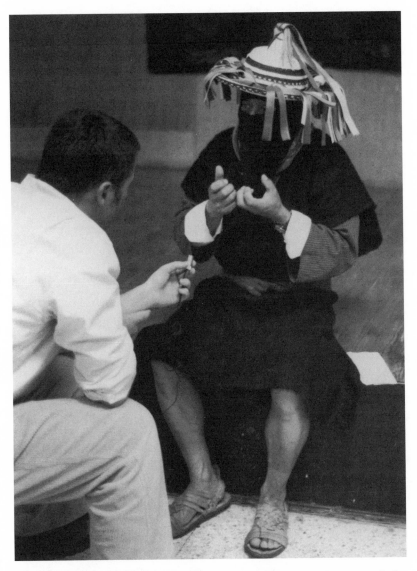

FIGURE 7.3 Comandante David, representative of the General Command of the Revolutionary Indigenous Clandestine Committee (CG-CCRI), being interviewed by the author on the occasion of the Zapatista march to Mexico City, March 2001. Photo by Yen Nomikos.

encouraging an awareness of its historicity and the importance such history plays in the life of any one human being, such humanism holds a self-ironic perspective that remains open ended in its conception of what it means to be human.

As the Zapatistas themselves have written,

Behind our black mask,
behind our armed voice,
behind our unnamable name,
behind what you see of us,
behind this we are you.
Behind this, we are the same simple and ordinary men and women
 who are repeated in all races, painted in all colors, speak in all
 languages and live in all places.

Behind this, we are the same forgotten men and women,
the same excluded, the same untolerated,
the same persecuted, the same as you.

Behind this, we are you.[11]

Perhaps not surprisingly in light of this vision, as Zapatista cultural humanism confronts the question of government, its response is necessarily democratic.[12] However, in recognition of the diversity of the Mexican populace, and of the multiplicity of sociopolitical identities that exist within it, the Zapatistas do not look for a complete political consensus. Rather, their conception of democracy is probably closest to what Judith Shklar calls "agonistic democracy."[13] It is for this reason as well that the question of indigenous autonomy has been raised, for the Zapatistas do not want to rule the country; they do not want to impose their "ideology." Rather, they hope for a more plural, active, and understanding political culture that need not reduce all its diverse political constituents to the same faceless, voiceless category. This amplification of the political space and vision has looked to those strata of the national populace, most often referred to as civil society, that are not linked to any political party and that might provide the best environment for nurturing the democratic impulse. And just as the strategy of rule with which it conflicts has an international character, so too does the Zapatista vision encompass that transnational community of individuals, human rights groups, and solidarity groups that is also often called international civil society.[14]

In local terms, rural Chiapas and the Indians and non-Indians who live there have seen their lives dramatically transformed since the Zapatista uprising. There have also been significant national cultural changes, but what perhaps remains beyond the purview of political analysis, although not outside of the ambition of modernist governmentalities, is that most intangible element of indigenous life, the Indian soul. As Indians in Chiapas continue to talk of the powerful *ch'ulel* of Marcos,[15] as the local retelling of history resituates the events of 1994 in less academically defined narratives of myth and countermyth,[16] as new reports of miraculous apparitions emanate from Chiapas[17]—there must remain factors that defy not only the neat conclusions of academic theses but also the desired transparency of governmental decree. Cultural humanism, at least as an ethos, should remain sensitive to this invisible aspect of Indian and human life and thus leave open the future of Mexico's Indian/government dynamic while all the time pointing to the elements within our latest modernist visions that seek to deny this presence that is also an absence.[18]

It was the 1992 Maya Indian Nobel Peace Prize laureate who wrote in her now-famous (if recently contested) autobiography, *I, Rigoberta Menchú*, "we Indians have always hidden our identity and kept our secrets to ourselves. This is why we are discriminated against. We often find it hard to talk about ourselves because we know we must hide so much in order to preserve our Indian culture and prevent it from being taken away from us. So I can tell you only very general things about the *nahual*. I can't tell you what my *nahual* is because that is one of our secrets."[19] In her more recent book, Menchú also writes that identity "is what cannot be seen or touched but is lived and experienced." It is that, she claims, which "is invisible to the human eye."[20] While anthropologists like Gary Gossen would seek to take such testimony further and argue on behalf of something as structural as a Maya cosmology,[21] I would instead like to argue that the indigenous of Chiapas have shown, both in their pluralistic manner of living in local communities and in their willingness to defend such collectivities, that indigenous "culture" has no essential quality.

In light of this, I believe the indigenous who have become Zapatista rebels can perhaps teach us an important lesson: that people, whether Indian or not, as the central subject of politics both local and global, are

more than what can be described through economic or social reduction-
ism, and that sometimes the expression of that analytically invisible self
can be worth dying for. International relations, as a discipline so long
defined by both war and peace, can hopefully learn from such all-too-
human rebel lives and deaths; and hopefully, too, this history in its very
telling has contributed to a deeper understanding of both political subjectivity and the critique of its essentially contested habitus: the modern
governmental state.

Notes

Introduction

1. The research described here has since been published as Nicholas P. Higgins, "The Politics of Humanitarian Intervention: The Ethiopian-Eritrean Experience," in *New Thinking in Politics and International Relations*, ed. Hazel Smith (Kent Papers in Politics and International Relations, series 5, no. S2, University of Kent at Canterbury, 1996).

2. "Testimonies from the First Day," *La Jornada,* January 19, 1994, reprinted and translated in *Zapatistas! Documents of the New Mexican Revolution* (New York: Autonomedia, 1994), 62.

3. Christine Sylvester, *Feminist Theory and International Relations in a Postmodern Era* (Cambridge: Cambridge University Press, 1994).

4. Edward H. Carr, *The Twenty Years' Crisis, 1919–1939* (1940; repr., New York: Harper & Row, 1968), 8 (my emphasis).

5. Edward H. Carr, *What Is History?* (1961; 2nd ed., with an introduction by R. W. Davies, London: Macmillan, 1986).

6. Carr, *Twenty Years' Crisis,* 70.

7. Quoted in Torbjørn L. Knutsen, *A History of International Relations Theory,* 2nd ed. (Manchester: Manchester University Press, 1997), 236.

8. Hans J. Morgenthau, *Politics among Nations* (New York: Knopf, 1978); Martin Wight, *Systems of States* (Leicester: Leicester University Press, 1977); and Kenneth N. Waltz, *Theory of International Politics* (Reading, MA: Addison-Wesley, 1979).

9. See Barry Buzan, "The Timeless Wisdom of Realism?" in *International Theory: Positivism and Beyond,* ed. Steve Smith, Ken Booth, and Marysia Zalewski, 47–65 (Cambridge: Cambridge University Press, 1996).

10. Michael Banks, "The Inter-Paradigm Debate," in *International Relations: A Handbook of Current Theory,* ed. Margot Light and A. J. R. Groom (London: Pinter, 1985), 7. See also his earlier essay, "The Evolution of International Relations Theory," in *Conflict in World Society: A New Perspective on International Relations,* ed. Michael Banks, 3–21 (Brighton: Wheatsheaf Books, 1984).

11. Michael Nicholson, "Imaginary Paradigms: A Sceptical View of the Inter-Paradigm Debate in International Relations" (Kent Papers in Politics and International Relations, series 1, no. 7, University of Kent at Canterbury, 1992), 17; and more recently, Michael Nicholson, "What's the Use of International Relations?" *Review of International Relations* 26, no. 2 (April 2000): 183–198.

12. Steve Smith, "The Forty Years' Detour: The Resurgence of Normative Theory in International Relations," *Millennium* 21, no. 3 (1992): 493–494.

13. Ibid., 495.

14. Chris Brown, "Turtles All the Way Down: Anti-foundationalism, Critical Theory and International Relations," *Millennium* 23, no. 2 (Summer 1994): 214.

15. This division was first suggested to the discipline as a result of a debate between Mark Hoffman and Nick Rennger; it has since been recognized by Smith to be "the most important one for the future of international theory." See Steve Smith, "The Self-Images of a Discipline: A Genealogy of International Relations Theory," in *International Relations Theory*, ed. Ken Booth and Steve Smith (Cambridge, UK: Polity Press, 1995), 30.

16. Post-positivists can be split into two camps, as evinced by the work of Der Derian, Connolly, George, Klein, Ashley, Shapiro, Campbell, Sylvester, and Bleiker, in the first instance; and Hoffman, Linklater, Brown, Cochrane, Frost, Neufeld, and Rennger, in the second. See my "A Question of Style: The Politics and Ethics of Cultural Conversation in Rorty and Connolly," *Global Society* 10, no. 1 (1996): 25–42.

17. This is the central thesis of Richard Rorty, *Philosophy and the Mirror of Nature* (Oxford: Blackwell, 1980).

18. For a general introduction to this theory, see D. J. O'Connor, *The Correspondence Theory of Truth* (London: Hutchinson, 1975).

19. Thomas Nagel, *The View from Nowhere* (Oxford: Oxford University Press, 1986).

20. Thomas Kuhn, *The Structure of Scientific Revolutions* (Chicago: University of Chicago Press, 1962). See also Kuhn's *The Essential Tension* (Chicago: University of Chicago Press, 1977) and Ian Hacking's edited volume, *Scientific Revolutions* (Oxford: Oxford University Press, 1981).

21. Donald Davidson, "A Coherence Theory of Truth and Knowledge," in *Truth and Interpretation: Perspectives on the Philosophy of Donald Davidson*, ed. E. Lepore (Oxford: Blackwell, 1986). Also see Davidson's *Inquiries into Truth and Interpretation* (Oxford: Oxford University Press, 1984). Alternatively, for a general introduction to philosophical work on this topic, see Ralph Walker, *The Coherence Theory of Truth* (London: Routledge, 1989).

22. See Davidson's essay "Mental Events" in his *Essays on Actions and Events* (Oxford: Oxford University Press, 1985), and also his contribution to *Causation and Conditionals*, ed. E. Sosa (Oxford: Oxford Readings, 1975). Or, in closer relation to Descartes and Nagel, his "Myth of the Subjective," in *Relativism: Interpretation and Confrontation*, ed. Michael Krausz (Notre Dame: University of Notre Dame Press, 1989).

23. The philosophical story I have told so far owes its principal debt to Richard Rorty, *Philosophy and the Mirror of Nature*. His political stance and his interpretation of the implications of such an antifoundationalist pragmatist conclusion are to be found in the writings that followed that book; see *Consequences of Pragmatism*

(Minneapolis: University of Minnesota Press, 1982); *Contingency, Irony, and Solidarity* (Cambridge: Cambridge University Press, 1989); *Philosophical Papers*, vol. 1, *Objectivity, Relativism, and Truth* (Cambridge: Cambridge University Press, 1991); *Philosophical Papers*, vol. 2, *Essays on Heidegger and Others* (Cambridge: Cambridge University Press, 1991); and most recently, *Philosophical Papers*, vol. 3, *Truth and Progress* (Cambridge: Cambridge University Press, 1998).

24. Rorty, *Philosophical Papers*, vol. 1, *Objectivity, Relativism, and Truth*, 2.

25. This is the kind of charge raised by Nancy Fraser in "From Irony to Prophecy to Politics: A Response to Richard Rorty" in *Pragmatism: A Contemporary Reader*, ed. Russell B. Goodman (London: Routledge, 1995); and in her "Michel Foucault: A 'Young Conservative'?" *Ethics* 96 (1985). See also Honi Haber, "Richard Rorty's Failed Politics," *Social Epistemology* 7, no. 1 (1993); and Christopher Norris, *What's Wrong with Postmodernism: Critical Theory and the Ends of Philosophy* (New York: Harvester Wheatsheaf, 1990). A similar debate has also occurred in the pages of international relations journals. See, for example, Sankaran Krishna, "The Importance of Being Ironic: A Postcolonial View on Critical International Relations Theory," *Alternatives* 18, no. 3 (Summer 1993); and James Der Derian's response in "The Pen, The Sword, and the Smart Bomb: Criticism in the Age of Video," *Alternatives* 19 (1994). Also see William Wallace, "Truth and Power, Monks and Technocrats: Theory and Practice in International Relations," *Review of International Studies* 22, no. 3 (1996); Ken Booth, "Discussion: A Reply to Wallace," *Review of International Studies* 23, no. 3 (1997): 371–377; and Steve Smith, "Power and Truth: A Reply to William Wallace," *Review of International Studies* 23, no. 4 (1997): 507–516. And more recently, Colin Wight, "MetaCampbell: The Epistemological Problematics of Perspectivism," *Review of International Studies* 25, no. 2 (1999); and David Campbell's response, "Contra Wight: The Errors of Premature Writing," *Review of International Studies* 25, no. 2 (1999): 317–321.

26. This lecture has been reprinted as "Feminism and Pragmatism" in Goodman, *Pragmatism: A Contemporary Reader* (see note 25). What follows in the next two sections is based upon my "'Supposing Truth to Be a Woman?' Pragmatism and the Feminist Problematique," in *Women, Culture, and International Relations*, ed. Vivienne Jabri and Eleanor O'Gorman, 137–163 (London: Lynne Rienner, 1999).

27. Feminism thus came to be placed alongside such esteemed company as "for example, Plato's Academy, the early Christians meeting in the catacombs, the invisible Copernican colleges of the Seventeenth century, groups of working men gathering to discuss Thomas Paine's pamphlets" (Rorty, "Feminism and Pragmatism," 138).

28. Ibid., 140.

29. As an example of his even-handed antifoundationalist approach, consider Rorty's "Human Rights, Rationality and Sentimentality," in *On Human Rights: The 1993 Oxford Amnesty Lectures* (New York: Basic Books, 1993); also see the essays "Priority of Democracy to Philosophy" and "Postmodern Bourgeois Liberalism" in Rorty, *Philosophical Papers*, vol. 1, *Objectivity, Relativism, and Truth*.

30. See Rorty, "Priority of Democracy," for a full account of the ongoing "experiment" that liberal democracy comes to represent once foundationalist philosophical liberalism has been abandoned. In particular, see pp. 192–193 for the resigned admission that such a stance might entail an unavoidable condition of paradox and self-referentiality.

31. See Rorty, "Method, Social Science, Social Hope," in *Consequences of Pragmatism*, 203–208, especially note 16, for an explicit account of his endorsement of the liberalism of Mill and Dewey. See also Rorty, "Moral Identity and Private Autonomy: The Case of Foucault," in *Philosophical Papers*, vol. 2, *Essays on Heidegger and Others*, for a further elaboration of the procedural role of the public/private distinction. In this instance there might also be good reason to assume that Rorty's conception of freedom remains particularly enamored of Mill's project of self-realization as expressed in *On Liberty*. In this respect, see John N. Morris, *Versions of the Self: Studies in English Autobiography from John Bunyan to Stuart Mill* (New York: Basic Books, 1966). Clearly, Mill's early feminist thoughts are also of relevance here; see J. S. Mill, *The Subjection of Women* (1869).

32. See Rorty, "Private Irony and Liberal Hope," in *Contingency, Irony, and Solidarity*, 73–95.

33. Rorty, "Feminism and Pragmatism," 146, quoting Chris Weedon, *Feminist Practice and Poststructuralist Theory* (Oxford: Basil Blackwell, 1987), 31.

34. Ibid., 139.

35. Ibid.

36. Ibid., 128. This should also be recognized as the key difference between Rorty and a thinker like Habermas, an antifoundationalist/foundationalist divide.

37. Ibid.

38. See Nancy Fraser, *Unruly Practices: Power, Discourse, and Gender in Contemporary Social Theory* (Cambridge, UK: Polity Press, 1989).

39. Rorty, "Feminism and Pragmatism," 128.

40. Wilfred Sellars, *Science, Perception, and Reality* (London: Routledge & Kegan Paul, 1963), 170.

41. Ian Hacking, "Five Parables," in *Philosophy in History: Essays on the Historiography of Philosophy*, ed. Richard Rorty, Quentin Skinner, and J. B. Schneewind (Cambridge: Cambridge University Press, 1984), 109. I would like to thank Quentin Skinner for directing me to this particular article. For a similar use of Hacking's insights for the discipline of anthropology, see Paul Rabinow, "Representations Are Social Facts: Modernity and Post-Modernity in Anthropology," in *Writing Culture: The Poetics and Politics of Ethnography*, ed. James Clifford and George E. Marcus, 234–261 (Berkeley and Los Angeles: University of California Press, 1986).

42. Hacking, "Five Parables," 119. Hacking also recognizes his position's extremely close affinity to Gaston Bachelard's "applied rationalism and technical materialism."

43. See also Ian Hacking, "Making People Up," in *Reconstructing Individualism: Autonomy, Individuality, and the Self in Western Thought*, ed. Thomas Heller, Morton Sosna, and David Wellbery (Stanford: Stanford University Press, 1986).

44. For a more comprehensive account of Rorty's political project, see Rorty, *Contingency, Irony, and Solidarity*.

45. For an excellent introduction to the political role of histories of the present, upon which my own perspective is based, see Graham Burchell, Colin Gordon, and Peter Miller, eds., *The Foucault Effect: Studies in Governmentality* (Chicago: University of Chicago Press, 1991); and Andrew Barry, Thomas Osborne, and Nikolas Rose, eds., *Foucault and Political Reason: Liberalism, Neo-Liberalism and Rationalities of Government* (London: UCL Press, 1996).

46. See Ian Hacking, *The Emergence of Probability* (Cambridge: Cambridge University Press, 1975) and *The Taming of Chance* (Cambridge: Cambridge University Press, 1990).

47. Ian Hacking, "How Should We Do the History of Statistics?" in Burchell, Gordon, and Miller, *Foucault Effect*, 194.

48. Hacking, "Five Parables," 122.

49. Fraser, *Unruly Practices*.

50. See Rorty, "Feminism and Pragmatism," 144 n. 22, and Rorty, "The Contingency of Selfhood," in *Contingency, Irony, and Solidarity*, as examples of this tension.

51. Marie Cardinal, *The Words to Say It* (London: The Women's Press, 1993).

52. Marie Cardinal, *In Other Words*, trans. Amy Cooper (London: The Women's Press, 1996), 41.

53. See Nikolas Rose, *The Psychological Complex: Psychology, Politics and Society in England, 1869–1939* (London: Routledge, 1985); *Governing the Soul: The Shaping of the Private Self* (London: Routledge, 1990); and *Inventing Ourselves: Psychology, Power and Personhood* (New York: Cambridge University Press, 1996). For a clear example of Hacking's similar methodological approach, as well as a revealing overlap in their research interests, see Ian Hacking, *Rewriting the Soul: Multiple Personality and the Sciences of Memory* (Princeton: Princeton University Press, 1995).

54. In this regard, Cardinal represents the positivity within the freedom of psy, and we would do well to remember the negativity that such sciences also create. See Kate Millet's moving account of her experience of psychiatric treatment—treatment that is still very much an unpleasant reality within British medical institutions, perhaps unlike those of America or France—in *The Loony Bin Trip* (London: Virago Press, 1991). The fact that Millet was a high-profile feminist before she was put into psychiatric care [see Millet's best-seller, *Sexual Politics* (London: Virago Press, 1970)], and that Cardinal only became one after her literary treatment of psychoanalysis, may also remind readers that feminists are very much situated within the relations of power that our contemporary practices of freedom entail—thus the need to try to conceptualize such freedom in a more politically sophisticated manner.

55. Nikolas Rose, "Assembling the Modern Self," in *Rewriting the Self: Histories from the Renaissance to the Present*, ed. Roy Porter (London: Routledge, 1997), 241–242.

56. Nikolas Rose, "Towards a Critical Sociology of Freedom" (inaugural lecture, Goldsmiths College, London, May 5, 1992; Folio paper, Goldsmiths College, University of London, 1993), 3.

57. Friedrich Nietzsche, "On the Uses and Disadvantages of History for Life," chap. 2 in *Untimely Meditations*, trans. R. J. Hollingdale (Cambridge: Cambridge University Press, 1983).

58. See, for example, Michel Foucault, *Madness and Civilization: A History of Insanity in the Age of Reason*, trans. Richard Howard (New York: Random House, 1973); *Birth of the Clinic*, trans. Alan Sheridan (London: Tavistock, 1976); and *Discipline and Punish: Birth of the Prison*, trans. Alan Sheridan (New York: Vintage Books, 1979).

59. Foucault, "Afterword: The Subject and Power," in *Michel Foucault: Beyond Structuralism and Hermeneutics*, by Hubert L. Dreyfus and Paul Rabinow (Hemel Hempstead: Harvester Wheatsheaf, 1982), 208.

60. For attempts to apply the genealogical method in IR, consider James Der Derian, *On Diplomacy: A Genealogy of Western Estrangement* (Oxford: Basil Blackwell,

1987); and Jens Bartelson, *A Genealogy of Sovereignty* (Cambridge: Cambridge University Press, 1995).

61. Foucault, *Power/Knowledge: Selected Interviews and Other Writings, 1972–1977,* ed. Colin Gordon (Hemel Hempstead: Harvester Wheatsheaf, 1980), 117.

62. Ian Hacking, "The Archaeology of Foucault," in *Foucault: A Critical Reader,* ed. David Couzens Hoy (Oxford: Basil Blackwell, 1986), 36.

63. Ibid., 37.

64. James Tully, "The Pen Is a Mighty Sword: Quentin Skinner's Analysis of Politics," *British Journal of Political Science* 13 (1983): 505. This reading owes as much to Quentin Skinner as Ian Hacking. For Skinner's admission of the influence of a Foucauldian archaeological method on his own research, see Quentin Skinner, *Liberty before Liberalism* (Cambridge: Cambridge University Press, 1998), 112.

65. Hacking, "The Archaeology of Foucault," 39.

66. Foucault, "Afterword: The Subject and Power," 212.

67. Many of these lectures remain unpublished; however, various fragments from this period have been made public. It has also been claimed that Foucault was engaged in plans for further collective work on governmental rationalities shortly before his death. Primary sources include Foucault, "On Governmentality," *Ideology and Consciousness,* no. 6 (1979): 5–21; *"Omnes et Singulatim:* Towards a Criticism of 'Political Reason,'" in *The Tanner Lectures on Human Values,* vol. 2, ed. Sterling McMurrin (Cambridge: Cambridge University Press, 1981); and various course résumés: "Foucault at the Collège de France I: A Course Summary," *Philosophy and Social Criticism* 8, no. 2 (Summer 1981), "Is It Useless to Revolt?" *Philosophy and Social Criticism* 8, no. 1, (Spring 1981), "Foucault at the Collège de France II: A Course Summary," *Philosophy and Social Criticism* 8, no. 3 (Fall 1981), all three translated and introduced by James Bernauer. The secondary literature on governmentality and related themes is more extensive; see in particular the contributions to Burchell, Gordon, and Miller, *Foucault Effect;* Barry, Osborne, and Rose, *Foucault and Political Reason;* and Mike Gane and Terry Johnson, *Foucault's New Domains* (London: Routledge, 1993); as well as Nikolas Rose, *Powers of Freedom: Reframing Political Thought* (Cambridge: Cambridge University Press, 1999).

68. Colin Gordon, "The Soul of the Citizen: Max Weber and Michel Foucault on Rationality and Government," in *Michel Foucault: Critical Assessments,* ed. Barry Smart (London: Routledge, 1995), 4:431.

69. Foucault, *"Omnes et Singulatim,"* 242.

70. Ibid., 245–6.

71. See Michel Foucault, *The History of Sexuality,* vol. 1, *An Introduction,* trans. Robert Hurley (London: Allen Lane, 1979).

72. Gordon, "The Soul of the Citizen," 432.

73. Foucault, *"Omnes et Singulatim,"* 252.

74. Ibid., 254.

75. See Foucault, *The History of Sexuality,* vol. 2, *The Use of Pleasure,* translated by Robert Hurley (New York: Vintage, 1986) and vol. 3, *The Care of the Self,* trans. Robert Hurley (London: Allen Lane, 1986); and also "On the Genealogy of Ethics: An Overview of Work in Progress," in *The Foucault Reader,* ed. Paul Rabinow, 3rd ed. (London: Penguin Books, 1991), especially 342, 345.

76. Foucault, "On the Genealogy of Ethics," 369–370.

77. Foucault, *"Omnes et Singulatim,"* 253.

78. Foucault, "Afterword: The Subject and Power," 211.

79. Foucault, "Polemics, Politics, and Problematizations," in Rabinow, *Foucault Reader,* 385.

Chapter One

1. Quoted in Michel de Montaigne, *Des cannibales* [On the Cannibals] (1588).

2. Translated into English for the first time by Margarita Zamora; see Zamora, "Christopher Columbus's 'Letter to the Sovereigns': Announcing the Discovery," in *New World Encounters,* ed. Stephen Greenblatt (Berkeley and Los Angeles: University of California Press, 1993). The passage quoted appears on p. 7.

3. See Anthony Grafton, *New Worlds, Ancient Texts: The Power of Tradition and the Shock of Discovery* (Cambridge, MA: Harvard University Press, Belknap Press, 1992), 48–82.

4. See S. Y. Edgerton Jr., "From Mental Matrix to *Mappamundi* to Christian Empire: The Heritage of Christian Cartography in the Renaissance," in *Art and Cartography,* ed. D. Woodward, 10–50 (Chicago: University of Chicago Press, 1987).

5. See Edmundo O'Gorman, *La invención de América* (Mexico City: Fondo de Cultura Económica, 1984).

6. See Grafton, *New Worlds, Ancient Texts,* 35–48.

7. See Hartman Schedel, *Liber chronicarum* [the Latin version of the *Nuremberg Chronicle*] (Nuremberg, 1493) for illustrations of these fantastical "ethnographic" oddities. They can also be found reprinted in Luisa Martin Meras, *Cartografía marítima hispana: La imagen de América* (Madrid: Lunwerg Editores, 1993).

8. Zamora, "Letter to the Sovereigns," 4, 8.

9. Quoted in Tzvetan Todorov, *The Conquest of America: The Question of the Other* (New York: Harper & Row, 1984), 15.

10. Quoted in Grafton, *New Worlds, Ancient Texts,* 82.

11. For an alternative interpretation that is in itself revealing for its Eurocentric and unreflective stance, see Leonardo Olschki, "What Columbus Saw on Landing in the West Indies," *Proceedings of the American Philosophical Society* no. 84 (1941): 633–659.

12. John Leddy Phelan, *The Millennial Kingdom of the Franciscans in the New World* (Berkley and Los Angeles: University of California Press, 1956), 22.

13. Ibid.

14. Zamora, "Letter to the Sovereigns," 6.

15. Todorov, *Conquest of America,* 28.

16. Ibid., 48.

17. Aldo Scaglione, "A Note on Montaigne's *Des Cannibales* and the Humanist Tradition," in *First Images of America: The Impact of the New World on the Old,* ed. Fredi Chiappelli (Berkeley and Los Angeles: University of California Press, 1976), 1:63.

18. Ibid., 65.

19. Stephen Toulmin, *Cosmopolis: The Hidden Agenda of Modernity* (Chicago: University of Chicago Press, 1990).

20. Ibid., 21–44.

21. Myron P. Gilmore, *The World of Humanism, 1453–1517* (New York: Harper & Row, 1962), 205.

22. Ibid.

23. On Dante, see Wilson Coates, Hayden White, and J. Salwyn Schapiro, *The Emergence of Liberal Humanism* (New York: McGraw-Hill, 1966), 8–9. On Augustine, see William E. Connolly, *The Augustinian Imperative* (New York: Sage, 1995).

24. See Quentin Skinner, *The Foundations of Modern Political Thought* (Cambridge: Cambridge University Press, 1978), 2:349.

25. Toulmin, *Cosmopolis*, 26–27.

26. Most notable among which are the writings of Cervantes, Rabelais, Montaigne, Erasmus, and Shakespeare. More excessive — and universal rather than merely European — claims concerning Shakespeare and the new understanding of the human can be found in Harold Bloom, *Shakespeare: The Invention of the Human* (New York: Riverhead Books, 1998).

27. Coates, White, and Schapiro, *Emergence of Liberal Humanism*, 5.

28. Toulmin, *Cosmopolis*, 25.

29. Charles G. Nauert Jr., *Humanism and the Culture of Renaissance Europe* (Cambridge: Cambridge University Press, 1995), 151.

30. Ibid., 155.

31. I have referred to the Penguin edition, Michel de Montaigne, *The Complete Essays*, trans. M. A. Screech (London: Penguin Books, 1991).

32. See Clifford Geertz, *The Interpretation of Cultures: Selected Essays* (New York: Basic Books, 1973).

33. Montaigne, *On the Cannibals* (1588), in *Complete Essays*, 239.

34. Ibid., 231.

35. The true colonial ethnographer was, of course, Las Casas. See Anthony Pagden, "*Ius et Factum:* Text and Experience in the Writings of Bartolomé de Las Casas," in Greenblatt, *New World Encounters*, 85–100.

36. On the move from Renaissance humanism to seventeenth-century exact science, see Stephen Toulmin, "The Recovery of Practical Philosophy," *The American Scholar* 57, no. 3 (Summer 1988): 337–352, and also his co-authored work with Albert R. Jonsen, *The Abuse of Casuistry* (Berkeley and Los Angeles: University of California Press, 1988).

37. Toulmin's book should be seen as an attempt to answer questions that more "philosophical" accounts of modernity have ruled out — in particular, the accounts proposed by John Dewey and Richard Rorty, two American philosophical pragmatists who identify Descartes as the reason that "modern" philosophy has reached an intellectual cul-de-sac. For Toulmin, the fact that these accounts make no attempt to understand why Descartes should have been so appealing to the European culture of the seventeenth century means that they fail to recognize the importance of historical situation and context. This is no minor point, for by providing purely philosophical accounts, such philosophers perpetuate the split between rhetoric and logic that in itself led to the Cartesian dead end. See Toulmin, *Cosmopolis*, 35–37.

38. This is to claim, alongside Toulmin, that while we can trace the continuance and even development of a certain humanistic modernist mentality within the realms of literature, poetry, and drama (Shakespeare being the most obvious example), in the realms of science, philosophy, and politics, definitions of the "human"

became narrow, overdetermined, and relative to scientific and institutional definition. This is clearly an argument that finds certain affinities with the work of Michel Foucault and his claim that man as a subject of science was invented around the end of the eighteenth century. See Foucault, *The Order of Things: An Archaeology of the Human Sciences* (London: Tavistock, 1970).

39. Todorov, *The Conquest of America*, 5. There is now, however, some reason to believe that Todorov does share in the identification of the modern with the advent of humanist thought. See his latest publication, *Le jardin imparfait: La pensée humaniste en France* (Paris: Bernard Grasset, 1998), in which he tells the story of a development from Montaigne to Constant to Rousseau. For another brief but suggestive account of this historical moment, see J. H. Elliot, "A World United," in *Circa 1492: Art in the Age of Exploration*, ed. Jay A. Levenson, 647–652 (New Haven: Yale University Press, 1991).

40. In keeping with the general interpretative thrust of this chapter, this is not to argue that the American Indian always played a positive role in the formation of a European modernist mentality. Later uses of the "noble savage theme" could well be considered regressive, but such transformations in perception only serve to highlight the antagonisms within modernity's genealogy, rather than suggest any fixed notion of the nature of Indian humanity as such. See Hayden White, "The Noble Savage: Theme as Fetish," in Chiappelli, *First Images of America*, 1:121–135.

41. See Phelan's *Millennial Kingdom* for a fascinating account of the influence and perseverance of medieval thought in the Americas. Also see Grafton's *New Worlds, Ancient Texts* for the central importance of medieval texts in the orientation of the Spaniards as they confronted the New World. It is also worth considering anthropologist Olivia Harris's "The Coming of the White People: Reflections on the Mythologisation of History in Latin America," *The Bulletin of Latin American Research* 14, no. 1 (1995): 9–24, for an argument that claims that Columbus's arrival as a historical date does not hold the same kind of significance for contemporary indigenous peoples as it claims within European historical narratives both in Europe and as adopted and adapted by Latin American nationalist historians. In Mexico, good examples of just this dynamic can be found in Miguel León-Portilla, "El Nuevo Mundo, 1492–1992: Una disputa interminable?" in *Raíces indígenas: Presencia hispánica*, ed. Miguel León-Portilla (Mexico City: Colegio Nacional, 1993), and in Edmundo O'Gorman, *La invención de América* (see note 5).

42. See J. H. Elliot, *Imperial Spain* (London: Pelican, 1970), 62.

43. See Luis de Valdellano, "Historia de las instituciones españoles de los orígenes al final de la Edad Media," *Revista de Occidente* (1968): 522.

44. Leslie Byrd Simpson, *The Encomienda in New Spain: The Beginning of Spanish Mexico* (Berkeley and Los Angeles: University of California Press, 1950), ix. I shall return to a definition and analysis of these practices in a following section.

45. Ibid., xi. On Cortés, see the excellent revisionary essay by Inga Clendinnen, "'Fierce and Unnatural Cruelty': Cortes and the Conquest of Mexico," in Greenblatt, *New World Encounters*, 12–47.

46. Montesino's sermon was related in Bartolomé de Las Casas, *Historia de las Indies*, ed. Augustín Milares Carlo, with a preliminary study by Lewis Hanke (Mexico City: Fondo de Cultura Económica, 1965), 1:263. The historical relevance of this incident is argued both in Lewis Hanke, "The Dawn of Conscience in America:

Spanish Experiments and Experiences with Indians in the New World," *Proceedings of the American Philosophical Society* 107, no. 2 (1963): 89; and in Anthony Pagden, *Spanish Imperialism and the Political Imagination: Studies in European and Spanish-American Social and Political Theory, 1513–1830* (New Haven: Yale University Press, 1990), 14–15. Unless otherwise noted, all translations from Spanish-language sources are my own.

47. For more detailed accounts of the spiritual world of the Middle Ages, see Dom Jean Leclerq, et al., eds., *A History of Christian Spirituality*, vol. 2, *The Spirituality of the Middle Ages* (New York: Seabury Press, 1982); Ludger Holscher, *The Reality of the Mind: Augustine's Philosophical Arguments for the Human Soul as a Spiritual Substance* (London: Routledge & Kegan Paul, 1986); and Dyan Elliott, *Fallen Bodies: Pollution, Sexuality, and Demonology in the Middle Ages* (Philadelphia: University of Pennsylvania Press, 1998).

48. Lewis Hanke, *Aristotle and the American Indians: A Study in Race Prejudice in the Modern World* (London: Hollis and Carter, 1959).

49. Aristotle, *Politics*, trans. Stephen Everson (Cambridge: Cambridge University Press, 1996), 11.

50. Las Casas's and Vitoria's Thomist championing can be seen to have inspired and shaped the content of Spain's New Laws for the Indies, and Vitoria himself has also been hailed as the founding father of international law. See James Brown Scott, *The Spanish Origin of International Law: Francisco de Vitoria and His Law of Nations*, vol. 1 (Oxford: Oxford University Press, 1934); and Etienne Grisel, "The Beginnings of International Law and General Public Law Doctrine: Francisco de Vitoria's *De Indiis prior*," in Chiappelli, *First Images of America*, 1:305–326.

51. Hanke, *Aristotle and the American Indians*.

52. Grafton, *New Worlds, Ancient Texts*, 137–138.

53. J. A. Fernández-Santamaría, *The State, War and Peace: Spanish Political Thought in the Renaissance, 1516–1559* (Cambridge: Cambridge University Press, 1977), 5.

54. Ibid., 6.

55. Ibid., 17–23.

56. Ibid., 271.

57. See Edward M. Peters, *Inquisition* (London: Free Press, 1988); and Bernard Hamilton, *Medieval Inquisition: Foundations of Medieval History* (London: Holmes & Meier, 1981).

58. As a means of locating this debate within the wider European dynamic, see Robert Bireley, *The Counter-Reformation Prince: Anti-Machiavellianism or Catholic Statecraft in Early Modern Europe* (Chapel Hill: University of North Carolina Press, 1990); and Skinner, *Foundations of Modern Political Thought*, vol. 2, *The Age of Reformation*, in particular chap. 5, "The Revival of Thomism."

59. See the interesting work of Anthony Pagden in *Spanish Imperialism and the Political Imagination*.

60. See Simpson, *Encomienda in New Spain*, 15.

61. There is reason to believe that this was not necessarily the case throughout New Spain nor the Kingdom of Guatemala, under whose direction Chiapas remained until 1823. See Robert Wasserstrom, *Class and Society in Central Chiapas* (Berkeley and Los Angeles: University of California Press, 1983), 12.

62. Robert G. Keith, "Encomienda, Hacienda and Corregimiento in Span-

ish America: A Structural Analysis," *Hispanic American Historical Review* 51, no. 3 (August 1971): 439. The official name for the reducción was the *corregimiento*. The system was backed by a peninsula-inspired legislative order.

63. Antonio García de León, *Resistencia y utopia: Memorial de agravios y crónica de revueltas y profecías acaecidas en la provincia de Chiapas durante los últimos quinientos años de su historia*, 2nd ed. (Mexico City: Ediciones Era, 1998), 44. See also Jan de Vos, *Vivir en frontera: La experiencia de los indios de Chiapas* (Mexico City: CIESAS and Instituto Nacional Indigenista, 1994), 96–98, where de Vos claims this account is a version passed on via oral tradition that is borne out by his detailed study of the incident in *La batalla del Sumidero: Historia de la rebelión de los chiapanecas, 1532–1534, a través de testimonios españoles e indígenas* (Mexico City: Editorial Katun, 1985).

64. Nelida Bonaccorsi, *El trabajo obligatorio indígena en Chiapas, siglo XVI* (Mexico City: Universidad Nacional Autónoma de México, 1990), 49–59.

65. Some of the best work on the Spanish project of acculturation has been done by Serge Gruzinski. See his *The Conquest of Mexico: The Incorporation of Indian Societies into the Western World, 16th–18th Centuries* (Cambridge, UK: Polity Press, 1993).

66. Sidney David Markman, *Architecture and Urbanization in Colonial Chiapas, Mexico* (Philadelphia: American Philosophical Society, 1984); in particular see chap. 6, "The Religious and Cultural Conversion of the Indians as a Determinant of Town Planning and Architecture of Pueblos de Indios," 28–37.

67. Gerónimo de Mendieta, *Historia eclesiástica indiana* (Mexico City: Editorial Salvador Chavez Hayhoe, 1945), 3:106, quoted in Elsa Celia Frost, "Indians and Theologians: Sixteenth-Century Spanish Theologians and Their Concept of the Indigenous Soul," in *South and Meso-American Spirituality*, ed. Gary H. Gossen (New York: Crossroad Publishing, 1993), 137.

68. Silvio Zavala, *Sir Thomas More in New Spain: A Utopian Adventure of the Renaissance* (Cambridge, UK: W. Heffer & Sons, 1955), 17.

69. Mendieta, *Historia eclesiástica*, 106, quoted in Frost, "Indians and Theologians," 137; also see Phelan, *Millennial Kingdom*.

70. Torbio de Benavente Motolinia, *Memoriales o libro de las cosas de la Nueva España y de los naturales de ella*, ed. Edmundo O'Gorman (Mexico City: Universidad Nacional Autónoma de México, 1971), 158, quoted in Frost, "Indians and Theologians," 133.

71. Andrés Aubry, ed., "Extractos de una carta pastoral IX, San Cristóbal 1698, por Fr. Francisco Obispo de Chiapa," *Boletín del Archivo Histórico Diocesano* (San Cristóbal de Las Casas, Chiapas), June 1983, 8.

72. Ibid.

73. Alfonso Villa Rojas, "El nagualismo como recurso de control social entre los grupos Mayanses de Chiapas, Mexico," in *Estudios Etnológicos: Los Mayas* (Mexico City: Universidad Nacional Autónoma de México, 1985), 536.

74. Ibid. (my emphasis).

75. Ibid., 537.

76. Ibid.

77. Ibid.

78. There is good reason to think that such ideas can trace their genealogy even further back, possibly even to the Olmecs of 1200 BC. See Gary H. Gossen, "From

Olmecs to Zapatistas: A Once and Future History of Souls," *American Anthropologist* 96, no. 3 (1994): 553–570.

79. Dennis Tedlock, trans., *Popol Vuh: The Mayan Book of the Dawn of Life* (New York: Touchstone, 1996), 15.

80. Ibid., 21.

81. Ralph L. Roys, trans., *The Book of Chilam Balam of Chumayel* (Washington, DC: Carnegie Institution of Washington, 1933), 4.

82. Pedro Sánchez de Aguilar, *Informe contra idolorum cultores del Obispado de Yucatán* (Madrid, 1639), 95, quoted in Roys, *Chilam Balam*, 5.

83. J. Eric S. Thompson, *The Rise and Fall of Maya Civilization* (Norman: University of Oklahoma Press, 1954), 162.

84. Miguel León-Portilla, *Time and Reality in the Thought of the Maya*, 2nd ed. (Norman: University of Oklahoma Press, 1988), 112.

85. See Roys, *Chilam Balam*, 3.

86. Ibid., 10.

87. Serge Gruzinski, "Individualization and Acculturation: Confession among Nahuas of Mexico from the Sixteenth to the Eighteenth Century," in *Sexuality and Marriage in Colonial Latin America*, ed. Asunción Lavría (Lincoln: University of Nebraska Press, 1989), 96.

88. Ibid., 97.

89. Ibid., 98. Also see Juan Pedro Viqueira, "Matrimonio y sexualidad en los confesionarios en lenguas indígenas," *Cuicuilco: Revista de la ENAH* (Mexico), no. 12 (January 1984), for an account that considers the colonial attempt to reconstruct the practices of sex and marriage mainly among the Indians of the north of Mexico. Also consider Louise M. Burkhart, *The Slippery Earth: Nahua-Christian Moral Dialogue in Sixteenth-Century Mexico* (Tucson: University of Arizona Press, 1989); and María Cristina Sacristán, *Locura e inquisición en Nueva España, 1571–1760* (Mexico City: Fondo de Cultura y Económica, 1992).

90. Alonso de Molina, *Confesionario mayor en lengua mexicana y castellana* (Mexico City: Antonio de Espinosa, 1569), 5–6, quoted in Gruzinski, "Individualization and Acculturation," 98.

91. Gruzinski, "Individualization and Acculturation," 99.

92. Pablo Escalante, "Sentarse, guardar la compostura y llorar: Entre los antiguos Nahuas, el cuerpo y el proceso de civilización," in *Familia y vida privada en la historia de IberoAmérica*, ed. Pilar Gonzalbo Aizpuru and Cecilia Rebell Romero (Mexico City: Colegio de Mexico and Universidad Nacional Autónoma de México, 1996).

93. Gruzinski, "Individualization and Acculturation," 99. Gruzinski's work in this area is, of course, a self-acknowledged extension of the research of Michel Foucault in *History of Sexuality*, vol. 1, *An Introduction*. It was Foucault's contention in that book that the practice of confession became more important during the Counter-Reformation in Europe; see pp. 52–56.

94. Juan de La Anunciación, *Doctrina cristiana muy cumplida donde se contiene la exposición de todo lo necesario para doctrinar los indios* (Mexico City: Pedro Balli, 1575), 141, quoted in Gruzinski, "Individualization and Acculturation," 98.

95. This is in fact the approach of Murdo J. MacLeod; see his "Papel social y económica de las cofradías indígenas de la colonia en Chiapas," *Mesoamerica* 5 (1983).

96. Ibid., 69–70.

97. For an elaboration on this insight, see Robert Wasserstrom, "Spaniards and Indians in Colonial Chiapas, 1528–1790," in *Spaniards and Indians in Southeastern Mesoamerica: Essays on the History of Ethnic Relations*, ed. Murdo J. MacLeod and Robert Wasserstrom (Lincoln: University of Nebraska Press, 1983), 106.

98. MacLeod, "Papel social," 71. See also Wasserstrom, "Spaniards and Indians."

99. On the role of the Virgin in Mexico, see Jacques Lafaye, *Quetzalcoatl and Guadalupe: The Formation of Mexican National Consciousness, 1531–1851* (Chicago: University of Chicago Press, 1976). Also see Michael P. Carroll, *The Cult of Virgin Mary: Psychological Origins* (Princeton: Princeton University Press, 1992); Marina Warner, *Alone of All Her Sex: The Myth and the Cult of the Virgin Mary* (London: Picador, 1985); and Eamon Duffy, *Madonnas that Maim? Christianity and the Cult of the Virgin* (Glasgow: Blackfriars, 1999).

100. There is now an impressive literature available on the Tzeltal rebellion of 1712. See Juan Pedro Viqueira, *María de la Candelaria, india natural de Cancuc* (Mexico City: Fondo de Cultura Económica, 1993); Kevin Gosner, *Soldiers of the Virgin: The Moral Economy of a Colonial Maya Rebellion* (Tucson: University of Arizona Press, 1992); and Victoria Bricker, *The Indian Christ, the Indian King: The Historical Substrate of Maya Myth and Ritual* (Austin: University of Texas Press, 1981). For an account of how these events are still recalled in contemporary Mayan Indian oral history, see Domingo Gómez Gutiérrez, *Letras mayas contemporáneos* (Mexico City: Instituto Nacional Indigenista, 1992). The 1712 revolt was the largest organized Indian resistance of the colonial period. In contemporary Mexican history, the current and ongoing Zapatista rebellion emanating from Chiapas represents incontrovertible proof that Indian-government relations still fall tragically short of the modern democratic ideal of mutual respect. The historical link between the two movements was first raised by the publication of a short article by the highly respected Mexican historian Enrique Florescano in the Mexico City daily *La Jornada* during the first weeks of the Zapatista uprising in January 1994. For details, see Kevin Gosner, "Historical Perspectives on Maya Resistance: The Tzeltal Revolt of 1712," in *Indigenous Revolts in Chiapas and the Andean Highlands*, ed. Kevin Gosner and Arij Ouweneel (Amsterdam: Centre for Latin American Research and Documentation, 1996), 28. In addition, for an interesting and suggestive linkage of contemporary oral history to the current Zapatista conflict, see Carlos Montemayor, *Chiapas: La rebelión indígena de México* (Mexico City: Editorial Joaquin Mortiz, 1997), chap. 6.

101. "Declaración de Juan Perez, indio de Cancuc de 18 años. Cancuc, 28 de noviembre 1712," quoted in Juan Pedro Viqueira, *Indios rebeldes e idólatras: Dos ensayos históricos sobre la rebelión india de Cancuc, Chiapas, acaecida en el año de 1712* (Mexico City: CIESAS, 1997), 96.

102. Bricker, *Indian Christ*, 60.

103. Ibid.

104. Ibid.

105. See Gosner, "Historical Perspectives," 37–38, on the nature of Indian coercion.

106. See Viqueira, "Indios rebeldes," 97; and Bricker, *Indian Christ*, 61.

107. Gosner, "Historical Perspectives," 38.

108. Quoted in Bricker, *Indian Christ*, 63.

109. Wasserstrom, "Spaniards and Indians," 112.

110. Ibid., 114.

111. Perhaps the form of contestation is not so unusual. In this regard, we might do well to consider the work of anthropologist Michael Taussig in *Mimesis and Alterity* (Chicago: University of Chicago Press, 1992) and *Shamanism, Colonialism, and the Wild Man* (Chicago: University of Chicago Press, 1987).

112. This understanding of subjectivity and the "human" is clearly derived from Michel Foucault and his inheritors. See Foucault, "The Ethics of Concern for the Self as a Practice of Freedom," in *Ethics: Subjectivity and Truth*, ed. Paul Rabinow, trans. R. Hurley (New York: Free Press, 1997); and Nikolas Rose, "Towards a Critical Sociology of Freedom" (see introduction, note 56), and "Authority and the Genealogy of Subjectivity," in *De-traditionalization: Authority and Self in an Age of Cultural Change*, ed. P. Healas, P. Morris, and S. Lash (Oxford: Blackwell, 1996).

113. The classic article is William Masden, "Religious Syncretism," in *Handbook of Middle American Indians*, vol. 6, *Social Anthropology*, ed. Manning Nash (Austin: University of Texas Press, 1967), 369–391.

114. The available literature is considerable; however, a representative cross-section might include David G. Scotchmer, "Convergence of the Gods: Comparing Traditional Maya and Christian Maya Cosmologies," in *Symbol and Meaning beyond the Closed Community: Essays in MesoAmerican Ideas*, ed. Gary H. Gossen, 197–226 (Albany: University at Albany, Institute for MesoAmerican Studies, 1986); Munro S. Edmonson, "The Maya Faith," in Gossen, *South and Meso-American Native Spirituality*, 65–85; Eugenio Maurer Avalos, "The Tzeltal Maya-Christian Synthesis," in Gossen, *South and Meso-American Native Spirituality*, 228–250; and John M. Watanabe, "In the World of the Sun: A Cognitive Model of Mayan Cosmology," *Man* 18 (1983): 710–728. A useful overview can be found in appendix B of Miguel León-Portillo's *Time and Reality*. Also, to gain some idea of the sheer volume of work constantly being produced on the Maya, consider the research essays in *Latin American Research Review*, especially Barbara Tedlock, "Mayans and Mayan Studies from 2000 B.C. to A.D. 1992," *LARR* 28/3 (1993): 153–173.

115. There are, of course, exceptions to these criticisms, authors to whose pioneering work I am greatly indebted, and not surprisingly, they are generally scholars who have adopted a historical approach to the study of Indian life. See Murdo MacLeod, Jan de Vos, Jan Rus, Juan Pedro Viqueira, and Robert Wasserstrom. An excellent collection of just such work can be found in Juan Pedro Viqueira and Mario Humberto Ruz, eds., *Chiapas: Los rumbos de otra historia* (Mexico City: Universidad Nacional Autónoma de México, 1998).

116. For a broad geographic, demographic, and anthropological overview, see Alain Breton and Jacques Arnauld, coords., *Los mayas: La pasión por los antepasados, el deseo de perdurar* (Mexico City: Editorial Grijalbo, 1994).

117. I will return to this theme in more detail in chap. 4.

118. See Viqueira, *Indios rebeldes*, 137–140.

Chapter Two

1. For a useful analysis of Humboldt's contribution to modern scientific thought, see Margaret Bowen, *Empiricism and Geographical Thought: From Francis Bacon to Alexander von Humboldt* (Cambridge: Cambridge University Press, 1981).

2. Incredibly detailed diagrams and cross-sections of volcanoes and land formations can be found in Alexander von Humboldt, *Examen critique de l'histoire de la géographie du nouveau continent* (1813). For the delicate life studies of plants, flowers, and animals, see the illustrative folios of his multivolume collection *Atlas géographique et physique des régions équinoxiales du nouveau continent* (Paris: Libraire de Gide, 1814–1834).

3. Anthony Pagden, *European Encounters with the New World: From Renaissance to Romanticism* (New Haven: Yale University Press, 1993), 108.

4. Mary Maples Dunn, introduction to *Political Essay on the Kingdom of New Spain*, by Alexander von Humboldt (New York: Alfred A. Knopf, 1972), 6.

5. Quoted in Pagden, *European Encounters*, 106.

6. For a detailed account of Humboldt's life, see Hanno Beck, *Alexander von Humboldt*, 2 vols. (Wiesbaden, Germany: F. Steiner, 1959–1961).

7. A rare, and incomplete, original edition of Humboldt's *Atlas géographique* can be seen in the Glasgow University special collections unit, Glasgow, Scotland. On this topic, see also White, "The Noble Savage."

8. This approach is best exemplified in Humboldt, *Vues des cordillères et monuments des peuples indigènes de l'Amérique* (Paris, 1810).

9. Georges Lefebvre, "Enlightened Despotism," in *The Development of the Modern State*, ed. Heinz Lubasz (London: Macmillan, 1964), 52

10. John G. Gagliardo, *Enlightened Despotism* (London: Routledge & Kegan Paul, 1968), 87.

11. Bruce D. Porter, *War and the Rise of the State: The Military Foundations of Modern Politics* (New York: Free Press, 1994), 20.

12. On the Physiocrats, see Elizabeth Fox-Genovese, *The Origins of Physiocracy: Economic Revolution and Social Order in Eighteenth-Century France* (Ithaca: Cornell University Press, 1976); on their influence on the thinking of Adam Smith, see Andrew S. Skinner, "Adam Smith: The French Connection" (University of Glasgow Discussion Papers in Economics, no. 9703, 1997); and on their pivotal role in the creation of modern economics, see Charles Gide and Charles Rist, eds., *A History of Economic Doctrines: From the Time of the Physiocrats to the Present Day*, trans. R. Richards (London: George G. Harap, 1915; 7th ed., 1950), 21–68.

13. Michel Foucault, "Governmentality," trans. R. Braidotti, in Burchell, Gordon, and Miller, *Foucault Effect*, 92.

14. See John Lynch, *Bourbon Spain, 1700–1808* (Oxford: Basil Blackwell, 1989); and Richard Herr, *The Eighteenth-Century Revolution in Spain* (Princeton: Princeton University Press, 1958).

15. John Leddy Phelan, "Authority and Flexibility in the Spanish Imperial Bureaucracy," *Administrative Science Quarterly* 5 (June 1960): 47–66; and Brian R. Hamnett, "The Mexican Bureaucracy before the Bourbon Reforms, 1700–1770: A Study in the Limitations of Absolutism" (Institute of Latin American Studies Occasional Papers 26, Glasgow University, Glasgow, 1979).

16. For a detailed account of Gálvez's visitation, see H. I. Priestley, *José de Gálvez, Visitador-General of New Spain, 1765–1771* (Philadelphia: Porcupine Press, 1916; 2nd ed., 1980).

17. Ibid., 123–134.

18. Similar reforms were also taking place in the Kingdom of Guatemala, the province under which the colonists and Indians of Chiapas remained until 1824

(after which it became part of Mexico); see Miles L. Wortman, *Government and Society in Central America, 1680–1840* (New York: Columbia University Press, 1982), esp. pp. 172–183 on how the reforms affected the Indians.

19. Priestley, *José de Gálvez*, 322–329.

20. For more detail on the extent of Bourbon reform, see David A. Brading, *Miners and Merchants in Bourbon Mexico, 1763–1810* (Cambridge: Cambridge University Press, 1971), 33–92.

21. On the expulsion of the Jesuits, see Jacques Lafaye, *Quetzalcoatl and Guadalupe*, 99–112.

22. Priestley, *José de Gálvez*, 228.

23. Serge Gruzinski, "La 'segunda aculturación': El estado ilustrado y la religiosidad indígena en Nueva España (1775–1800)" Estudios de Historia NovHispania 8 (Mexico City: Universidad Nacional Autónoma de México, 1985).

24. On the Bourbon methods of control of the clergy, see Nancy M. Farris, *Crown and Clergy in Colonial Mexico, 1759–1821: The Crisis of Ecclesiastical Privilege* (London: Athlone Press, 1968); David A. Brading, *Church and State in Bourbon Mexico: The Diocese of Michoacán, 1749–1810* (Cambridge: Cambridge University Press, 1994); and Brading, "Tridentine Catholicism and Enlightened Despotism in Bourbon Mexico," *Journal of Latin American Studies* 15, no. 1 (1983): 1–22.

25. Gruzinski, "La 'segunda aculturación,'" 190.

26. Bourbon success in this endeavour is evinced by the increase in the number of parishes that included "Castilian schools" from 84 in 1754 to 237 in 1755. See Silvio Zavala, *El castellano, lengua obligatoria?* (Mexico City: Centros de Estudios de Historia de México, Condumex, 1977).

27. See Georges Duby, ed., *A History of Private Life*, 5 vols. (Cambridge, MA: Harvard University Press, Belknap Press, 1987).

28. See Brading, *Church and State*, 131–170.

29. Clero regular y secular, 1793, Archivo General de la Nación, exp. 10, f. 201v–202, quoted in Gruzinski, "La 'segunda aculturación,'" 188.

30. Of course, not every creole or Spaniard saw the Indians as indecent, but exceptional was the individual who spoke publicly in their defense. One such instance was, however, recorded in Chiapas; see *Gazeta de Guatemala*, "Un ladino ilustrado defiende a los indios contra los que opinan que ellos son ocios y borrachos por naturaleza," Guatemala, October 15 and 22, 1801, reproduced as Documento 28 in Jan de Vos, *Vivir en frontera*, 245–247.

31. Gruzinski, "La 'segunda aculturación,'" 193.

32. See Foucault, "Right of Death and Power over Life," in Rabinow, *Foucault Reader*, 261.

33. See Colin M. MacLachlan and Jaime E. Rodríguez O., eds., "Rationalization, Reform, and Reaction," chap. 9 in *The Forging of the Cosmic Race: A Reinterpretation of Colonial Mexico* (Berkeley and Los Angeles: University of California Press, 1990).

34. See Hacking, "How Should We Do the History of Statistics?" in Burchell, Gordon, and Miller, *Foucault Effect*; and Hacking, *Taming of Chance*.

35. See Lafaye, *Quetzalcoatl and Guadalupe*, 109–112.

36. The Society of Jesus arrived in New Spain in 1570, just after the conquest and conversion period was considered to have ended, and their energies were there-

fore principally directed at the urban elite, although some Jesuits also set about the creation of missions in the still-untamed north of the colony.

37. See Lynch, *Bourbon Spain*, 280–290.

38. For an analytically comprehensive account of the historical project adopted by both scholars, see in particular chap. 4 of Pagden, *Spanish Imperialism*.

39. See Pagden, *Spanish Imperialism*, 104; and R. H. Barlow, "Some Remarks on the Term 'Aztec Empire,'" *The Americas* 1 (1945).

40. There was and is, of course, a limit to how much one can "write out" the present, and this was made clear first with the Indian uprising of June 1692 in Mexico City (after which the intellectually sensitive Sigüenza y Góngora wrote no more of the glorious Indian past), then later with the Hidalgo uprising. See Pagden, *Spanish Imperialism*, 97. The same might well be said of the rude awakening that the 1994 Zapatista uprising presented for those who have attempted to provide a first-world script for contemporary Mexico.

41. Quoted in David Brading, *The Origins of Mexican Nationalism* (Cambridge: Centre of Latin American Studies, 1985), 48.

42. Lafaye, *Quetzalcoatl and Guadalupe*, 306.

43. See a series of articles by Eric Van Young, "Millennium on the Northern Marches: The Mad Messiah of Durango and Popular Rebellion in Mexico, 1800–1815," *Comparative Studies in Society and History* 28, no. 3 (July 1986); "The Raw and the Cooked: Elite and Popular Ideology in Mexico, 1800–1821," in *The Middle Period in Latin America: Values and Attitudes in the 17th–19th Centuries*, ed. Mark D. Szuchman (Boulder: Lynne Rienner, 1989); and "Who Was That Masked Man, Anyway? Popular Symbols and Ideology in the Mexican Wars of Independence," in *Proceedings, Rocky Mountain Council on Latin American Studies, Annual Meeting*, 1:18–35 (Las Cruces, NM, 1984). Also see William B. Taylor, *Drinking, Homicide, and Rebellion in Colonial Mexican Villages* (Stanford: Stanford University Press, 1979).

44. Van Young, "Millennium," 386.

45. See Van Young, "Millennium," 406, and "Who Was That Masked Man, Anyway?" In this connection, we might also do well to ponder the mystique created around the figure of Mexico's current masked man, Subcomandante Marcos.

46. Brading, *Miners and Merchants*, 340.

47. See Farris, *Crown and Clergy*, 254–265, for an extensive list of the numbers of lower clergy who participated in the movement.

48. "Discourse of Morelos, Chilpancingo, 14 September 1813," in *Morelos Documentos*, 2:177–181, quoted in Wilbert H. Timmons, "The Political and Social Ideas of Morelos," in *Mexico: From Independence to Revolution, 1810–1910*, ed. W. Dirk Raat (Lincoln: University of Nebraska Press, 1982), 37. The original speech was apparently written by Carlos Bustamante.

49. Timmons, "Ideas of Morelos," 32.

50. Christon I. Archer, "'La Causa Buena': The Counterinsurgency Army of New Spain and the Ten Years' War," in *The Independence of Mexico and the Creation of the New Nation*, ed. Jaime E. Rodríguez O. (Berkeley and Los Angeles: University of California Press, 1989), 86.

51. Agustín de Iturbide, "Plan de Iguala," in Raat, *Mexico: From Independence to Revolution*, 46–48.

52. Foucault, "Governmentality," 87.

53. See Charles A. Hale, "Alamán, Antunano y la continuidad del liberalismo," *Historia Mexicana* 11, no. 2 (October–December 1961): 224–245; Hale, *Mexican Liberalism in the Age of Mora, 1821–1853* (New Haven: Yale University Press, 1968); Will Fowler, *The Liberal Origins of Mexican Conservatism, 1821–1832*, (occasional paper, Institute of Latin American Studies, Glasgow University, Glasgow, 1997); and Fowler, "Dreams of Stability: Mexican Political Thought during the 'Forgotten Years'; An Analysis of the Beliefs of the Creole Intelligentsia (1821–1853)," *Bulletin of Latin American Research* 14, no. 3 (1995): 287–312.

54. See Brian R. Hamnett, "Liberal Politics and Spanish Freemasonry, 1814–1820," *History: The Journal of the Historical Association* 69, no. 226 (June 1984); and Jean-Pierre Bastian, ed., *Protestantes, liberales y francmasones: Sociedades de ideas y modernidad en América Latina, siglo XIX* (Mexico City: Fondo de Cultura Económica, 1990). For evidence that secret societies were also influential in the case in the Audiencia of Guatemala and Chiapas, see García de León, *Resistencia y utopia*, 134–138.

55. Beatriz Urías Horcasitas, "El pensamiento económico moderno en el México independiente," in Rodriguez, *Independence of Mexico*, 266.

56. See David Harris, "European Liberalism and the State," in Lubasz, *Development of the Modern State*, 72–90.

57. See Hale, "Alamán, Antunano."

58. Ibid., 239.

59. See Miguel León-Portilla, *Pueblos originarios y globalización* (Mexico City: Colegio Nacional, 1997), 26–34; and Bartolomé Clavero, *Derecho indígena y cultura constitucional en América* (Mexico City: Siglo XXI Editores, 1994).

60. Hale, *Mexican Liberalism*, 221.

61. Ibid., 225. Also see Ivan Gomezcésar Hernández, "Los liberales mexicanos frente al problema indígena: La comunidad y la integración nacional," in *Diversidad étnica y conflicto en América Latina: El indio como metáfora en la identidad nacional*, ed. Raquel Barcelo, María Ana Portal, and Martha Judith Sánchez (Mexico City: Universidad Nacional Autónoma de México, 1995), for a further elaboration of this governmental stance.

62. Hale, *Mexican Liberalism*, 218.

63. José Luis Mora, *México y sus revoluciones*, 1836, quoted in Horcasitas, "El pensamiento económico," 274.

64. See Nelson Reed, *The Caste War of Yucatan* (Stanford: Stanford University Press, 1964); and Leticia Reina, "La rebelión campesina de Sierra Gorda," in *Sierra Gorda: Pasado y presente*, ed. Lino Gómez Canedo (Querétaro, Mexico: Fondo Editorial de Querétaro, 1994).

65. Hale, *Mexican Liberalism*, 223.

66. Gomezcésar Hernández, "Los liberales mexicanos," 83.

67. See Hale, *Mexican Liberalism*, 234. In this regard, we would do well to remember the manipulative use made of this creole fear of caste war in the state of Chiapas. See Jan Rus, "Whose Caste War? Indians, *Ladinos*, and the Chiapas 'Caste War' of 1869," in Gosner and Ouweneel, *Indigenous Revolts*.

68. See Barbara Tenenbaum, "Development and Sovereignty: Intellectuals and the Second Empire," in *Los intelectuales y el poder en México*, ed. Roderic A. Camp, Charles A. Hale, and Josefina Z. Vázquez (Mexico City: Colegio de México and UCLA Latin American Center Publications, 1991).

Chapter Three

1. Examples of these two interpretations are, respectively, Farris, *Crown and Clergy*, in particular the conclusion; and Jan Bazant, *A Concise History of Mexico: From Hidalgo to Cárdenas, 1805–1940* (Cambridge: Cambridge University Press, 1977).

2. See Daniel Cosío Villegas's section *El porfiriato* in the mammoth collaborative project *Historia moderna de México*, ed. Cosío Villegas, 7 vols. (Mexico City: Hermes, 1957–1972).

3. Hale, *Mexican Liberalism*, 5.

4. de Vos, *Vivir en frontera*, 178.

5. Rus, "Whose Caste War?" 64.

6. The invention seems to have first appeared in the account of Vicente Piñeda, *Historia de las sublevaciones indígenas habidas en el estado de Chiapas* (1888), as a means to once again ensure a tight grip on the Indian workforce some twenty years after the uprising. See Rus, "Whose Caste War?" 69–70.

7. See García de León, *Resistencia y utopia*, 150–151.

8. Thomas Benjamin, *A Rich Land, a Poor People: Politics and Society in Modern Chiapas*, rev. ed. (Albuquerque: University of New Mexico Press, 1996), 11.

9. See Wasserstrom, *Class and Society*, 108–112; and also Jan Rus and Robert Wasserstrom, "Civil-Religious Hierarchies in Central Chiapas: A Critical Perspective," *American Ethnologist* 7, no. 3 (August 1980): 469.

10. Rus and Wasserstrom, "Civil-Religious Hierarchies," 469.

11. Benjamin, *Rich Land*, 13–14.

12. See Wasserstrom, *Class and Society*, 119; and de Vos, *Vivir en frontera*, 169.

13. de Vos, *Vivir en frontera*, 169.

14. Ibid., 170.

15. See Robert Wasserstrom, "A Caste War That Never Was: The Tzeltal Conspiracy of 1848," *Peasant Studies* 7, no. 2 (1978): 73–85; also see the report by the priest of Ocosingo on the displacement of the Indians from the village of Chilon (1848), original document reproduced in de Vos, *Vivir en frontera*, 258–260.

16. de Vos, *Vivir en frontera*, 166.

17. See Wasserstrom, *Class and Society*, 130, 133.

18. Rus, "Whose Caste War?" 48.

19. Ibid., 46.

20. See Will Fowler, "The Repeated Rise of General Antonio López de Santa Anna in the So-called 'Age of Chaos' (Mexico 1821–1855)," in *Authoritarianism in Latin America since Independence*, ed. Will Fowler (Westport, CT: Greenwood Press, 1996).

21. For more on this period, see Richard Sinkin, *The Mexican Reform, 1855–1876: A Study in Liberal Nation-Building* (Austin: University of Texas Press, 1979); see also David Brading, "Liberal Patriotism and the Mexican Reforma," *Journal of Latin American Studies* 20, no. 1 (1988): 27–48.

22. A good overview of this period is also provided by Jan Bazant, "From Independence to the Liberal Republic, 1821–1867," in *Mexico since Independence*, ed. Leslie Bethell, 1–48 (Cambridge: Cambridge University Press, 1991).

23. Rus, "Whose Caste War?" 54.

24. Ibid., 55.

25. See Rus and Wasserstrom, "Civil-Religious Hierarchies."

26. Rus, "Whose Caste War?" 56.

27. de Vos, *Vivir en frontera*, 185.

28. de Vos, *Vivir en frontera*, 185.

29. Rus, "Whose Caste War?" 59.

30. Since the 1994 Zapatista uprising there have been attempts to draw parallels between the ladino Galindo and the mestizo Marcos, subcomandante of the EZLN. These misplaced comparisons have been employed in an attempt to suggest that the Indians are in some way easily influenced by ideologically driven non-Indians.

31. Rus, "Whose Caste War?" 63.

32. Ibid., 64, quoting San Cristóbal's conservative newspaper, *La Brújula*, June 25, 1868.

33. Pedro José Montesinos, as reported to his nephew José María Montesinos (1870), original document reproduced in de Vos, *Vivir en frontera*, 271–274. Translation quoted from Rus, "Whose Caste War?" 65–66.

34. Charles A. Hale, *The Transformation of Liberalism in Late Nineteenth-Century Mexico* (Princeton: Princeton University Press, 1989), 3.

35. While it has become quite common among Mexican and non-Mexican historians to write of a liberal continuity throughout Mexican history, it is my belief that such a nomenclature is not a useful means of discussing the intellectual and practical continuities that certainly do exist. Making liberalism a catch-all label merely obscures what might be called the essential tension within liberal thinking: the conflict between a political idea that wishes to restrict government in the name of individual liberty and a liberalism that needs to strengthen government to bring about the conditions necessary for that certain understanding of freedom to exist. The period of the Porfiriato dictatorship can thus be viewed as an unpleasant consequence of this tension. However, while some contemporary liberals would argue that liberalism is exactly the continued negotiation of this tension, to give in to one aspect is to enter into an authoritarianism that should not still be called liberalism. See Rorty, "Private Irony and Liberal Hope" (see introduction, note 32). I believe Hale's description of the period as one unified by a "liberal myth" also suggests the lack of liberalism itself. The *científicos* were, of course, aware of such a contradiction and attempted to resolve it by calling themselves "conservative liberals." See Hale, *Transformation of Liberalism*, 20. For an alternative interpretation, see Alan Knight, "El liberalismo mexicano desde la reforma hasta la revolución," *Historia Mexicana* 35, no. 1 (1985).

36. See Alfonso de María y Campos, "Los científicos: Actitudes de un grupo de intelectuales porfirianos frente al positivismo y la religión," in Camp, Hale, and Vázquez, *Los intelectuales y el poder en México*.

37. Hale, *Transformation of Liberalism*, 31–32.

38. See Hale, *Transformation of Liberalism*; for the continent-wide influence of such theoretical innovation, also see Hale, "Political and Social Ideas in Latin America, 1870–1930," in *The Cambridge History of Latin America*, ed. Leslie Bethell, vol. 4, *Ca. 1870 to 1930* (Cambridge: Cambridge University Press, 1986).

39. Comte's theoretical stance was made public through the publication of his lectures under the title *Course in Positive Philosophy* (Paris, 1830–1842), which appeared in six volumes. See volume 1 for the Law of Three Stages. For a revealing

insight into just how positivist thought and some of Comte's more spiritual conclusions are seen by a classic liberal, see John Stuart Mill, *Auguste Comte and Positivism* (Ann Arbor: University of Michigan Press, 1961).

40. See, for example, W. Dirk Raat, "Agustín Aragón and Mexico's Religion of Humanity," *Journal of Interamerican Studies and World Affairs* 11, no. 3 (July 1969). Also see Raat, *El positivismo durante el porfiriato* (Mexico City: SepSetentas, 1975), for an interesting account of the more spiritual aspects of Comte's work and the consequent split between "orthodox" and "heterodox" positivists.

41. See Hale, *Transformation of Liberalism,* chap. 5, 139–168.

42. Quoted in Hale, "Political and Social Ideas," 389.

43. Emilio Rabasa, *La constitución y la dictadura: Estudio sobre la organización política de México* (1912; repr., Mexico City: Talleras de Reproducciones OSVIC, 2002).

44. See Juan Felipe Leal, "Positivismo y liberalismo," in *El porfiriato,* ed. José Alfredo Castellanos, 211–224 (Mexico City: Universidad Autónoma Chapingo, 1988).

45. For more on the prolific Rabasa, see Carmen Ramos Escandón, "Emilio Rabasa: Su obra literaria como expresión política," in Camp, Hale, and Vázquez, *Los intelectuales y el poder en México,* 665–680.

46. Paul J. Vanderwood, *Disorder and Progress: Bandits, Police, and Mexican Development* (Wilmington, DE: Scholarly Resources, 1992), 67.

47. Quoted in Robert Freeman Smith, "The Diaz Era: Background to the Revolution of 1910," in Raat, *Mexico: From Independence to Revolution,* 195.

48. Ibid., 194.

49. For more on the extent and influence of foreign investment, see José Luis Ceceña, "El porfirismo," in Castellanos, *El porfiriato,* 49–64.

50. For more on this period, see Moisés González Navarro, "The Hours of Leisure," in *The Age of Porfirio Díaz,* ed. Carlos B. Gil, 123–128 (Albuquerque: University of New Mexico Press, 1977). A good counterbalance to this account of the *gente decente* (decent people) is William E. French, "Prostitutes and Guardian Angels: Women, Work and the Family in Porfirian Mexico," *Hispanic American Historical Review* 72, no. 4 (November 1992): 529–554.

51. Friedrich Katz, "The Liberal Republic and the Porfiriato, 1867–1910," in Bethell, *Mexico since Independence,* 94.

52. See Evelyn Hu-Dehart, "Pacification of the Yaquis," in Gil, *Age of Porfirio Diaz,* 129–138, in which Hu-Dehart estimates that some 15,000 Yaquis were deported. This concurs with Katz, who cites 15,700; see "Liberal Republic," 92.

53. Alan Knight, "Mexican Peonage: What Was It and Why Was It?" *Journal of Latin American Studies* 18, no. 1 (1986): 43.

54. He also established a state treasurers general office, introducing state audits for the first time; see Benjamin, *Rich Land,* 43. For more on the Seguridad Pública, see Vanderwood, *Disorder and Progress,* 119–130.

55. See Benjamin, *Rich Land,* 43.

56. See García de León, *Resistencia y utopia,* 219.

57. Benjamin, *Rich Land,* 48.

58. Wasserstrom, *Class and Society,* 113.

59. See T. G. Powell, "Mexican Intellectuals and the Indian Question, 1876–1911," *Hispanic American Historical Review* 48, no. 1 (1968).

60. Comment from an editorial in the Cristobalense newspaper *El Tiempo* in 1907, quoted in Benjamin, *Rich Land*, 77.

61. See Ricardo Pozas, "El trabajo en las plantaciones de café y el cambio socio-cultural del indio," *Revista Mexicana de Estudios Antropológicos* 13 (1952).

62. See Benjamin, *Rich Land*, 89.

63. See Thomas Benjamin, "El trabajo en las monterías de Tabasco y Chiapas, 1870–1946," *Historia Mexicana* 30 (April–June 1981): 506–529. Also consider B. Travern's provocative novels, e.g., *March to the Montería* (New York: Hill & Wang, 1971).

64. Letter from Francisco León to President Porfirio Díaz, December 20, 1898, reprinted in de Vos, *Vivir en frontera*, 278–281; quote from p. 279.

65. See Rus and Wasserstrom, "Civil-Religious Hierarchies," 472–473; and Frank Cancian, *Economics and Prestige in a Maya Community: The Religious Cargo System in Zinacantán* (Stanford: Stanford University Press, 1965).

66. Karena Shields, *The Changing Wind* (New York: Thomas Cromwell, 1959), 40, quoted in Benjamin, *Rich Land*, 88.

Chapter Four

1. See Hector Aguilar, *La frontera nomada: Sonora y la revolución mexicana* (Mexico City: Siglo XXI Editores, 1977).

2. See John Womack Jr., *Zapata and the Mexican Revolution* (New York: Vintage Books, 1968). The reform of article 27 was, of course, an important part of the neoliberal reform program pursued by President Salinas during his *sexenio*, or six-year term (1988–1994), and now also forms an important part of the contemporary Zapatista demands. This connection is one obvious reason for their choice of Zapata as a unifying symbol for their struggle. Womack, not surprisingly, has recently written his own (much criticized) short account of the ongoing Chiapan conflict, *Chiapas, el obispo de San Cristóbal y la revuelta zapatista* (Mexico City: Cal y Arena Editores, 1998). See the book review in *Proceso*, August 16, 1998, for a typical Mexican reception.

3. John Womack Jr., "The Mexican Revolution, 1910–1920," in Bethell, *Mexico since Independence*, 129. For a survey of the varied interpretations of the revolution, see Alan Knight, "The Mexican Revolution: Bourgeois? Nationalist? or Just a 'Great Rebellion'?" *Bulletin of Latin American Research* 4, no. 2 (1985).

4. Kevin J. Middlebrook, *The Paradox of Revolution: Labor, the State and Authoritarianism in Mexico* (Baltimore: Johns Hopkins University Press, 1995), 1.

5. Consider Ilene O'Malley, *The Myth of Revolution: Hero Cults and the Institutionalization of the Mexican State, 1920–1940* (Westport, CT: Greenwood Press, 1986); and Luis Javier Garrido, *El Partido de la Revolución Institucionalizada* (Mexico City: SEP, 1986).

6. Hale, "Political and Social Ideas," 397.

7. Ibid., 435.

8. This being, in fact, the central argument of his book; see Hale, *Transformation of Liberalism*, 245–261.

9. Hale, "Political and Social Ideas," 436; also see Hale, *Transformation of Liberalism*, 260.

10. See Arnaldo Cordova, "Espiritualismo o positivismo? La filosofía de la Revolución Mexicana" (Avances de Investigación 14, Centro de Estudios Latino-americanos, Universidad Nacional Autónoma de México, Mexico City, 1975). Also consider what Alan Knight refers to as "developmentalist liberalism" in "El liberalismo mexicano."

11. See Hale, "The Legacy," in *Transformation of Liberalism*, 245–261.

12. In this regard, we would do well to remember Emilio Rabasa, the young governor of Chiapas and the author of *La constitución y la dictadura*, whose influence can nevertheless be seen in the postrevolutionary constitution of 1917.

13. See Hale, "Political and Social Ideas," 419–421.

14. José Enrique Rodó, *Ariel* (1900), trans. Margaret Sayers Peden (Austin: University of Texas Press, 1988).

15. For more on *Ariel* and the use of the *Tempest* in Latin America, see Roberto Fernández Retamar, *Caliban and Other Essays* (Minneapolis: University of Minnesota Press, 1988).

16. Quoted in Hale, "Political and Social Ideas," 421.

17. José Vasconcelos, *The Cosmic Race*, trans. Didier Jaen (Los Angeles: California State University, 1979). In a contemporary light, it is possible to see the attempt to continue such theories, or even claim that they have been realized, in both the title and the content of MacLachlan and Rodríguez, *Forging of the Cosmic Race*.

18. See Mary Kay Vaughan, *The State, Education, and Social Class in Mexico, 1880–1928* (Dekalb: North Illinois University Press, 1982); and Vaughan, *Cultural Politics in Revolution: Teachers, Peasants, and Schools in Mexico, 1930–1940* (Tucson: University of Arizona Press, 1997).

19. See Jean Meyer, *Historia de los cristianos de América Latina, siglos XIX y XX.* (Mexico: Ediciones Vuelta, 1989).

20. From José Clemente Orozco, *Autobiografía* (Mexico City: Ediciones Occidente, 1945), quoted and translated in Jean Meyer, "Revolution and Reconstruction in the 1920s," in Bethell, *Mexico since Independence*, 209.

21. Octavio Paz, "Re/Visiones: La pintura mural," in *Los privilegios de la vista* (Mexico City: Fondo de Cultura Económica, 1987), 260.

22. Betty Ann Brown, "The Past Idealized: Diego Rivera's Use of Pre-Columbian Imagery," in *Diego Rivera: A Retrospective*, ed. Linda Downs (New York: W. W. Norton, 1986), 155.

23. See chap. 2.

24. Diego Rivera, "La lucha de clases y el problema indígena: Proyecto de tesis sobre el problema indígena en México y América Latina con relación a la cuestión agraria" (1938), in *Arte y política*, (Mexico City: , 1979), 187.

25. George W. Stocking Jr., "The Basic Assumptions of Boasian Anthropology," in *A Franz Boas Reader: The Shaping of American Anthropology, 1883–1911*, ed. George W. Stocking Jr. (Chicago: University of Chicago Press, 1974), 1.

26. British anthropology was, of course, particularly influenced by such race and evolutionary theories, which, placed in the context of British anthropology's relationship with British colonialism, should once again alert us to the highly political nature of "objective" social science. See Henrika Kuklick, "The Sins of the Fathers: British Anthropology and the African Colonial Administration," *Research in the Sociology of Knowledge, Science and Art* 1 (1978): 93–119; and Kuklick, *The Savage*

Within: The Social History of British Anthropology, 1885–1945 (Cambridge: Cambridge University Press, 1991).

27. See Matti Bunzl, "Franz Boas and the Humboldtian Tradition: From *Volksgeist* and *Nationalcharakter* to an Anthropological Concept of Culture," in *Volksgeist as Method and Ethic: Essays on Boasian Ethnography and the German Anthropological Tradition*, ed. George W. Stocking Jr. (Madison: University of Wisconsin Press, 1996). See also the introduction to chap. 2 of this volume for Humboldt's earlier influence on elite Mexican science.

28. Bunzl, "Franz Boas," 55, 68.

29. Stocking, *The Ethnographer's Magic, and Other Essays in the History of Anthropology* (Madison: University of Wisconsin Press, 1992), 112–113.

30. That he should have gone to Columbia University at all was due to the influence of Zelia Nutall, an American archaeologist already at work in Mexico. For more on this connection, see Helen Depler, *The Enormous Vogue of Things Mexican: Cultural Relations between the United States and Mexico, 1920–1935* (Tuscaloosa: University of Alabama Press, 1992), 96–97.

31. Alan Knight, "Racism, Revolution, and *Indigenismo*: Mexico, 1910–1940," in *The Idea of Race in Latin America, 1840–1940*, ed. Richard Graham (Austin: University of Texas Press, 1990), 77.

32. Initially the Dirección de Antropología was a dependency of Secretariat of Agricultura.

33. See David Brading, "Manuel Gamio and Official Indigenismo in Mexico," *Bulletin of Latin American Research 7*, no. 1 (1988): 75–89.

34. See Robert Redfield, *Tepotzlan: A Mexican Village* (Chicago: University of Chicago Press, 1930); and Redfield, *The Folk Culture of Yucatan* (Chicago: University of Chicago Press, 1940).

35. Jan Rus, "Managing Mexico's Indians: The Historical Context and Consequences of *Indigenismo*" (unpublished manuscript, 1976, Biblioteca Daniel Cosío Villegas, Colegio de México, Mexico City) 32; see also Redfield, *Tepotzlan*.

36. Rus, "Managing Mexico's Indians," 44.

37. See Rob Aitken, *Localizing Politics: Cardenismo, the Mexican State and Local Politics in Contemporary Michoacán* (Amsterdam: Centre for Latin American Research and Documentation, 1999).

38. See Arnaldo Cordova, *La política del masas del cardenismo* (Mexico City: Ediciones Era, 1976); and Alan Knight, "The Rise and Fall of Cardenismo," in Bethell, *Mexico since Independence.*

39. Jan Rus, "Managing Mexico's Indians," 20. Cárdenas's land reform alone saw the promise of article 27 reach the communities of some 726,000 *ejidatarios* (collective farmers), encompassing some 20,137,000 hectares, a figure that has to this day never been surpassed.

40. See Cordova, *Política del masas*, especially chap. 6.

41. For more on the complex relationship of the CTM with the federal government, see Middlebrook, *Paradox of Revolution.*

42. See Rosa Elena Montes de Oca, "The State and the Peasants," in *Authoritarianism in Mexico*, ed. José Luis Reyna and Richard G. Hellman (New York: Center for Inter-American Relations, 1978).

43. Cordova, *Política del masas*, 164.

44. Vaughan, *Cultural Politics in Revolution*, 65. See also Engracia Loyo, "Popular Reactions to the Educational Reforms of Cardenismo," in *Rituals of Resistance: Public Celebrations and Popular Culture in Mexico*, ed. William H. Beezley, Cheryl English Martin, and William E. French (Wilmington, DE: Scholarly Resources, 1994).

45. See chap. 2.

46. See Jan Rus and Robert Wasserstrom, "Evangelization and Political Control: The SIL in Mexico," in *Is God an American? An Anthropological Perspective on the Missionary Work of the Summer Institute of Linguistics*, ed. Søren Hvalkof and Peter Aaby, 163–172 (Copenhagen: International Work Group on Indigenous Affairs, 1981).

47. Leonel Durán, ed., *Lázaro Cárdenas, Ideario Político* (Mexico City: Ediciones Era, 1972), 173.

48. Thomas Benjamin, "Primera Viva Chiapas! Local Rebellions and the Mexican Revolution in Chiapas," *European Review of Latin American and Caribbean Studies* 49 (December 1990): 33.

49. On this rebellion, see García de León, *Resistencia y utopia*, 223–237.

50. Quoted in Benjamin, "Primera Viva Chiapas!" 44.

51. Benjamin, "Primer Viva Chiapas!" 45.

52. Ibid., 48.

53. Quoted in Benjamin, *Rich Land*, 170.

54. Andrés Aubry, *En la escuela y en la milpa la pláctica no es la misma: Historia Tzotzil de la Revolución Mexicana en Chiapas* (San Cristóbal de Las Casas: INAREMAC, 1984). This article has also been partially translated by Jan Rus in *Rebellion in Chiapas: An Historical Reader*, ed. John Womack Jr., 97–104 (New York: New York Press, 1999).

55. García de León, *Resistencia y utopia*, 226.

56. See Rus and Wasserstrom, "Civil-Religious Hierarchies," 473.

57. In fact, such was the insistence on community solidarity that a significant number of Chamulans were forced into exile (in a repeat of the expulsions that occurred after the "caste war" of 1867–1869), leading to the creation of a new community in the north of the state called Rincón Chamula. For more on this, see García de León, *Resistencia y utopia*, 235; and Gary H. Gossen, "La diáspora de San Juan Chamula: Los indios en el proyecto nacional mexicano," in *De palabra y obra en el Nuevo Mundo*, ed. M. Gutiérrez Estévez, M. León-Portilla, G. H. Gossen, and J. J. Klor de Avala (Madrid: Siglo XXI de España, 1992).

58. See Jan Rus, "The 'Comunidad Revolucionario Institucional': The Subversion of Native Government in Highland Chiapas, 1936–1968" (San Cristóbal de Las Casas: INAREMAC, 1992), 6. Reprinted in *Everyday Forms of State Formation: Revolution and the Negotiation of Rule in Modern Mexico*, ed. Gilbert M. Joseph and Daniel Nugent (Durham, NC: Duke University Press, 1994). Page references are to the INAREMAC edition.

59. Ibid.

60. See, for instance, the native testimony "Abtel ta pinka/Trabajo en las fincas," recorded in Womack, *Rebellion in Chiapas*, 111–118.

61. Rus, "Comunidad Revolucionario," 7.

62. Graham Greene, *The Lawless Roads* (1939; repr., London: Penguin Books, 1982), 184–192.

63. The Zinacantecos seem to be an exception to this, making claims as early as the 1920s. See Robert Wasserstrom, "Land and Labour in Central Chiapas: A Regional Analysis," *Development and Change* 8, no. 4 (1977): 449.

64. For more on this, see Benjamin, *Rich Land*, 183–194.

65. Quoted in Benjamin, *Rich Land*, 191.

66. Quoted in Rus, "Comunidad Revolucionario," 10.

67. Rus, "Comunidad Revolucionario," 17.

68. The politics of liquor became particularly insidious during this period, especially for the women of Chiapas. See Christine Eber, *Women and Alcohol in a Highland Maya Township* (Austin: University of Texas Press, 1995). For more on the continued struggle with alcohol, see Eber, "'Take My Water': Liberation through Prohibition in San Pedro Chenalhó, Chiapas, Mexico," *Social Science and Medicine* 53 (2001): 251–262.

69. Alan Knight, "Cardenismo: Juggernaut or Jalopy?" *Journal of Latin American Studies* 26, no. 1 (1994): 107.

70. Rus, "Comunidad Revolucionario," 37. See also Luz Olivia Pineda, "Maestros bilingües, burocracía y poder político en los Altos de Chiapas," in Viqueira and Ruz, *Chiapas*.

71. It is important to mention that Jan Rus and Robert Wasserstrom were among the last of these students. In all, the Harvard project produced twenty-one doctoral dissertations and twenty-seven monographs and edited volumes.

72. Rus, "Comunidad Revolucionario," 2. See also Pineda, "Maestros bilingües." On the idea of "closed corporate communities," see Eric Wolf, "Closed Corporate Peasant Communities in Mesoamerica and Central Java," *Southwestern Journal of Anthropology* 13 (1957): 1–18.

73. Rus, "Comunidad Revolucionaria," 2.

74. Ibid., 38.

Chapter Five

1. Carlos Montemayor, *Chiapas*, 66–80. See also Daniel Pereyra, *Del Moncada a Chiapas: Historia de la lucha armada en América Latina* (Madrid: Los Libros de la Catarata, 1994), 181–191.

2. To give some idea of the number of armed groups active throughout Mexico during the '60s and '70s, here are the names of ten out of an estimated twenty-four: Movimiento Revolucionario del Pueblo, Partido de los Pobres, Asociación Cívica Nacional Revolucionaria, Comando Urbano Lacandones "Patria Nueva," Frente Urbano Zapatista, Partido Revolucionario Obrero Clandestino Unión del Pueblo, Unión Campesina Independiente, Movimiento 23 de Septiembre, Liga Comunista Espartaco, Frente Revolucionario del Pueblo. See Montemayor, *Chiapas*, and Pereyra, *Del Moncada a Chiapas*.

3. A picture of these operations can nevertheless be garnered from the following studies: Gustavo Hirales, "La guerra secreta, 1970–1978," *Nexos*, no. 54 (June 1982): 20–35; Guillermo Boils, "Los militares en México, 1965–1985," *Revista Mexicana Sociología*, no. 47 (January–February 1985): 169–185; Lilia Bermudez Torres, *Guerra de baja intensidad: Reagan contra Centroamérica* (Mexico City: Siglo XXI Editores, 1987); Martha Patricia López Astrain, *La guerra de baja intensi-*

dad en México (Mexico City: Universidad Iberoamericana and Plaza y Valdés Editores, 1996).

4. While there was much written at the time, Elena Poniatowska's *Massacre in Mexico* (Columbia: University of Missouri Press, 1978) still stands out for its transcription of first-hand testimony. Only recently, however, has the full story of the massacre begun to be told; see Julio Scherer García and Carlos Monsivias, *Parte de guerra* (Mexico City: Aguilar, 1999), for the latest interpretation of events.

5. Hale, "Political and Social Ideas," 397.

6. See Bo Anderson and James D. Cockcroft, "Control and Coöptation in Mexican Politics," in *Latin American Radicalism*, ed. Irving Louis Horowitz, Josué de Castro, and John Gerassi (London: Jonathan Cape, 1969); and Susan Kaufman Purcell, "Mexico: Clientalism, Corporatism, and Political Stability," in *Political Clientism, Patronage, and Development*, ed. S. N. Eisenstadt and Rene Lemarchand (Beverly Hills: Sage, 1981).

7. According to one CIA operative in the 1970s, "Mexican security services are so effective in eradicating the extreme left that we don't have to worry about it. If the government was less effective, we would, of course, have to promote their repression." Philip Agee, *Inside the Company: CIA Diary* (New York: Penguin Books, 1975), quoted in Roger Bartra, "Revolutionary Nationalism and National Security in Mexico," in *Mexico: In Search of Security*, ed. Bruce Bagley and Sergio Aguayo Quezada (New Brunswick, NJ: Transaction, 1993), 143.

8. Quoted in Montemayor, *Chiapas*, 70.

9. Ibid.

10. Ibid.

11. Jan Rus, "Local Adaptation to Global Change: The Reordering of Native Society in Highland Chiapas, Mexico, 1974–1994," *European Review of Latin American and Caribbean Studies*, no. 58 (June 1995): 82.

12. Ibid., 81.

13. Neil Harvey, "Rebellion in Chiapas: Rural Reforms and Popular Struggle," *Third World Quarterly* 16, no. 1 (1995): 42.

14. See Jan Rus, ed., *Chamulas en California: El testimonio de Santos, Mariano y Juan Gómez López* (San Cristóbal de Las Casas: INAREMAC, 1995).

15. Rus, "Local Adaptation," 82. Also see Frank Cancian, *The Decline of Community in Zinacantán: Economy, Public Life, and Social Stratification, 1960–1987* (Stanford: Stanford University Press, 1992).

16. This particular parable has been repeated to me several times, but never more emotively than by the refugees from Chenalhó, who have been unable to return to their communities for fear of attacks by paramilitaries. "*Las abejas*" ("the bees," the collective name of the refugee group) spoke longingly about their unattended milpa and their consequent concerns for their children's upbringing. Interviews in Chiapas, June 1998. On Mayan Indian folklore, see Robert Laughlin, *Of Cabbages and Kings: Tales from Zinacantán* (Washington, DC: Smithsonian Institution, 1977); and Sna Jtz'ibajom theater and writing group, ed., *Cuentos de Chiapas* (San Cristóbal de Las Casas, Mexico: Sna Jtz'ibajom, 1990).

17. See Bricker, *Indian Christ*.

18. For an informed insight, see Jan Rus, "Antropología social en los Altos de Chiapas: Historia y bibliografía" (Apuntes de Lectura 3, INAREMAC, June 1977);

and Juan Pedro Viqueira, "La comunidad india en México en los estudios antropológicos e históricos," in *Anuario 1994* (San Cristóbal de Las Casas: Universidad de Ciencias y Arte del Estado de Chiapas, 1995).

19. The classic examples of this kind of work—typifying a structural functionalist mode of analysis—are Evon Vogt, *Zinacantán: A Maya Community in the Highlands of Chiapas* (Cambridge, MA: Harvard University Press, Belknap Press, 1969); and Cancian, *Economics and Prestige.*

20. Villa Rojas, "El nagualismo," 536.

21. Gossen, "From Olmecs to Zapatistas, 555.

22. The classic example is Calixta Gutieras-Holmes, *Perils of the Soul: The World View of a Tzotzil Indian* (Glencoe, IL: Free Press of Glencoe, 1961). See also Gary H. Gossen, "On the Human Condition and the Moral Order: A Testimony from the Chamula Tzotzil Maya of Chiapas, Mexico," in Gossen, *South and Meso-American Native Spirituality*; and Priscilla Rachun Linn, "Souls and Selves in Chamula: A Thought on Individuals, Fatalism, and Denial," in *Ethnographic Encounters in Southern Mesoamerica: Essays in Honor of Evon Zartman Vogt Jr.*, ed. Victoria R. Bricker and Gary H. Gossen, (Albany: University at Albany, 1989).

23. Also see George A. Collier, "The New Politics of Exclusion: Antecedents to the Rebellion in Mexico," *Dialectical Anthropology* 19, no. 1 (May 1994): 27–30.

24. See Rus, "Comunidad Revolucionario"; Rus, "Managing Mexico's Indians"; and Pineda, "Maestros bilingües."

25. What follows is based upon Gary H. Gossen's "Life, Death, and Apotheosis of a Chamula Protestant Leader: Biography as Social History," in Bricker and Gossen, *Ethnographic Encounters*, 217–229.

26. On the arrival of Protestantism in Chiapas, see Rus and Wasserstrom, "Evangelization and Political Control"; and for its more specific effects on women, see Susanna Rostas, "A Grass Roots View of Religious Change amongst Women in an Indigenous Community in Chiapas, Mexico," *Bulletin of Latin American Research* 18, no. 3 (July 1999): 327–341.

27. Rus, "Local Adaptation," 73.

28. See Peter H. Smith, "Leadership and Change: Intellectuals and Technocrats in Mexico," in *Mexico's Political Stability: The Next Five Years*, ed. Roderic Ai Camp, 101–117 (Boulder: Westview, 1986).

29. See Miguel Ángel Centeno and Sylvia Maxfield, "The Marriage of Finance and Order: Changes in the Mexican Political Elite," *Journal of Latin American Studies* 24 (1992).

30. Miguel Ángel Centeno, *Democracy within Reason: Technocratic Revolution in Mexico*, (University Park: Pennsylvania State University Press, 1994), 122.

31. See Wayne A. Cornelius, *Mexican Politics in Transition: The Breakdown of a One-Party-Dominant Regime*, Monograph Series 41 (San Diego: Center for U.S.–Mexican Studies, University of California, 1996), 5 n. 2, for evidence that the "crash" was in fact a manufactured case of computer fraud.

32. See Andrew Gamble, *Hayek: The Iron Cage of Liberty* (Cambridge, UK: Polity Press, 1996), 128–135.

33. Ibid., 21.

34. The most famous and influential works of Hayek's group are: Friedrich August von Hayek, *The Road to Serfdom* (London: Routledge, 1944); Hayek, *Individ-*

ualism and Economic Order (Chicago: University of Chicago Press, 1948); Hayek, *The Fatal Conceit: The Errors of Socialism* (Chicago: University of Chicago Press, 1988); Milton Friedman, *Free to Choose* (London: Secker & Warburg, 1980); Friedman, *Capitalism and Freedom* (Chicago: University of Chicago Press, 1962); and Ludwig von Mises, *The Free and Prosperous Commonwealth* (New York: Van Nostrand, 1962).

35. Hayek, *The Constitution of Liberty* (London: Routledge, 1966), 12.

36. See Nick Bosanquet, *After the New Right* (London: Heinemann, 1983).

37. See Elton Rayack, *Not So Free to Choose: The Political Economy of Milton Friedman and Ronald Reagan* (New York: Praeger, 1987).

38. From Ranelagh, *Thatcher's People*, quoted in Gamble, *Hayek*, 151.

39. Nowhere, of course, was the influence of Hayek more apparent than in Chile, where after the coup, General Pinochet decided to rewrite and rename the constitution, calling it "The Constitution of Liberty," after his beloved Hayek. See Phil O'Brien and Jackie Roddick, *Chile: The Pinochet Decade; The Rise and Fall of the Chicago Boys* (London: Latin American Bureau, 1983), 86–87. For an insider's criticism of Friedman and the "Chicago boys" who first implemented Chile's neoliberal experiment under the Pinochet regime, see Andre Gunder Frank, *Economic Genocide in Chile: Monetarist Theory versus Humanity; Two Open Letters to Milton Friedman and Arnold Harberger* (Nottingham, UK: Spokesman Books, 1976).

40. This is in fact the very principle upon which such monumental projects as the history of private life are based. See Duby, *History of Private Life*.

41. Nikolas Rose, "Government, Authority and Expertise in Advanced Liberalism," *Economy and Society* 22, no. 3 (August 1993): 29.

42. "Society" was, of course, a concept that the British prime minister, Margaret Thatcher, famously announced no longer existed in neoliberal Britain of the 1980s.

43. See David Williams, "Constructing the Economic Space: The World Bank and the Making of *Homo oeconomicus*," *Millennium: Journal of International Studies* 28, no. 1 (1999).

44. Quoted in Peter H. Smith, "Mexico since 1946: Dynamics of an Authoritarian Regime," in Bethell, *Mexico since Independence*, 384.

45. Ibid., 383–4.

46. Quoted in Centeno, *Democracy within Reason*, 191.

47. Centeno, *Democracy within Reason*, 198 (my emphasis).

48. See Laurence Whitehead, "Prospects for a 'Transition' from Authoritarian Rule in Mexico," in *The Politics of Economic Restructuring: State-Society Relations and Regime Change in Mexico*, ed. Maria Lorena Cook, Kevin J. Middlebrook, and Juan Molinar Horcasitas (San Diego: Center for U.S.–Mexican Studies, University of California, 1994).

49. The means by which he accomplished this are explained in Denise Dresser, *Neo-populist Solutions to Neoliberal Problems: Mexico's National Solidarity Program*, Monograph Series 24 (San Diego: Center for U.S.–Mexican Studies, University of California, 1991); also see Dresser's contribution "Bringing the Poor Back In: National Solidarity as a Strategy of Regime Legitimacy," in *Transforming State-Society Relations in Mexico: The National Solidarity Strategy*, ed. Wayne A. Cornelius, Ann L. Craig, and Jonathan Fox, 143–165 (San Diego: Center for U.S.–Mexican Studies, University of California, 1994). Also see Ann Varley, "Delivering the Goods: Solidarity, Land Regularisation and Urban Services," in *Dismantling the*

Mexican State? ed. Rob Aitken, Nikki Craske, Gareth A. Jones, and David E. Stansfield, 204–224 (London: Macmillan Press, 1996).

50. See Alan Knight, "Solidarity: Historical Continuities and Contemporary Implications," in Cornelius, Craig, and Fox, *Transforming State-Society Relations,* 29–45.

51. Dresser, "Bringing the Poor Back In," 163–165; also see Nikki Craske, "Dismantling or Retrenchment? Salinas and Corporatism," in Aitken et al., *Dismantling the Mexican State?* 89.

52. Judith A. Teichman, "Neoliberalism and the Transformation of Mexican Authoritarianism," *Mexican Studies/Estudios Mexicanos* 13, no. 1 (Winter 1997): 145. See also Robert Kaufman and Guillermo Trejo, "Regionalism, Regime Transformation, and PRONASOL: The Politics of the National Solidarity Programme in Four Mexican States," *Journal of Latin American Studies* 29 (1997).

53. Rose, "Advanced Liberalism," 294.

54. Neil Harvey, "The Difficult Transition: Neoliberalism and Neocorporatism in Mexico," in *Mexico: Dilemmas of Transition,* ed. Neil Harvey (London: Institute of Latin American Studies, 1993), 18.

55. Centeno, *Democracy within Reason,* 224.

56. Kathy Powell, "Neoliberalism and Nationalism," in Aitken et al., *Dismantling the Mexican State?* 43.

57. *Business Week,* June 15, 1992, 52, quoted in Centeno, *Democracy within Reason,* 24.

58. Duncan Green, *Silent Revolution: The Rise of Market Economics in Latin America* (London: Cassell, 1995), 13–32, 77–78.

59. See Francisco Javier Guerro Aguirre, "The North American Free Trade Agreement: An Analysis of the Process of Pre-negotiation in Mexico," *Paradigms* 9, no. 2 (Winter 1995).

60. The story of the formation of the Zapatistas has been repeated in several sources; one of the best accounts is by Subcomandante Marcos himself, retold in Montemayor, *Chiapas,* 135–140. Also see Yvon Le Bot, *Subcomandante Marcos: El sueño zapatista* (Barcelona: Plaza & Janes Editores, 1997); and for a more controversial and locally contested account of the Zapatistas, see Carlos Tello Díaz, *La rebelión de Las Cañadas* (Mexico City: Cal y Arena, 1995).

61. Andrés Aubry, "La historia de Chiapas identifica a los zapatistas" (Doc. 043–VI, INAREMAC, 1994), 9.

62. Rosalva Aída Hernández Castillo, "De la sierra a la selva: Identidades étnicas y religiosas en la frontera sur," in Viqueira and Ruz, *Chiapas,* 408–411.

63. See Rus and Wasserstrom, "Evangelization and Political Control."

64. Hernández Castillo, "De la sierra," 411–415.

65. Ibid., 411–414. See also David G. Scotchmer, "Life of the Heart: A Maya Protestant Spirituality," in Gossen, *South and Meso-American Native Spirituality.*

66. See Leonardo Boff, *When Theology Listens to the Poor* (San Francisco: Harper & Row, 1988); and Gustavo Gutiérrez, *A Theology of Liberation* (New York: Orbis Books, 1971).

67. Present at both Vatican II and the Medellin Council of Latin American Bishops in 1968, Msgr. Samuel Ruiz, bishop of the Diocese of San Cristóbal de Las Casas since 1960, had initially come to Chiapas with the intention of converting

the Indians, but he ended up himself—like Salvadorian archbishop Oscar Romero, with whom he is often compared—"being converted by the Indians." For the full story, see Carlos Fazio, *Samuel Ruiz: El Caminante* (Mexico City: Espasa Calpe, 1994); for the story in abbreviated form, see Andrés Aubry, "El 1968 de la iglesia latinoamericana," *Masiosare*, supplement to *La Jornada*, October 25, 1998. More generally on the relationship between revolutionaries and liberation theologists, see Mary Christine Morkovsky, "*Guerrilleros*, Political Saints, and the Theology of Liberation," in Gossen, *South and Meso-American Native Spirituality*. Undoubtedly, however, the clearest statement of Ruiz's diocesan policy is to be found in his open pastoral letter to Pope John Paul II, *En esta hora de gracia: Carta pastoral con motivo del saludo de SS el papa Juan Pablo II a los indígenas del continente* (Mexico City: Ediciones Dabar, 1993).

68. See Tello Díaz, *Rebelión de Las Cañadas*, 73–78, for an account of the consequences of Ruiz's chance meeting with Orive in Torreón. See also *Proceso*, no. 1107, January 18, 1998, 12–17.

69. The Machiavellian character of Adolfo Orive is perhaps worthy of an article in itself. First, his role as economics professor at the Universidad Nacional Autónoma de Mexico (UNAM) during the period when a group of wealthy students known as *los tóficos* (which included a young Carlos Salinas de Gortari) can be seen as influential in the creation of a governing mentality premised on economics. Second, in light of his activism in Chiapas throughout the 1970s and '80s, many have viewed his appointment as chief adviser to the Mexican minister of the interior in January 1998 as a sinister betrayal of the grassroots union that he helped found. Some have even gone further, suggesting that through judicious use of his Chiapan contacts, Orive, with the full support of the interior ministry, has been actively creating the political matrix that can support the ever-growing groups of paramilitary squads that conduct a low-intensity war against the Zapatistas and the communities that form their civilian support base. See *Masiosare*, supplement to *La Jornada*, no. 9, January 18, 1998, 3–6; and no. 21, April 19, 1998, 3–5.

70. Jan de Vos, "El Lacandon: Una introducción historica," in Viqueira and Ruz, *Chiapas*, 358. See also Xochitl Leyva Solano, "Militancia político-religiosa e identidad en la Lacandona," *Espiral: Estudios sobre estado y sociedad* (Universidad de Guadalajara) 1, no. 2 (January–April 1995): 59–88; and Neil Harvey, "La Unión de Uniones de Chiapas y los retos políticos del desarrollo de base," in *Autonomía y nuevos sujetos en el desarrollo social*, ed. J. Moguel, C. Botey, and L. Hernández, 219–232 (Mexico City: Siglo XXI Editores and CELAM, 1992).

71. See Nicholas P. Higgins and Marta Durán de Huerta, "An Interview with Subcomandante Insurgente Marcos, Spokesperson and Military Commander of the Zapatista National Liberation Army (EZLN)," *International Affairs* 75, no. 2 (April 1999): 269–279.

72. See Xochitl Leyva Solano, "Catequistas, misioneros y tradiciones en Las Cañadas," in Viqueira and Ruz, *Chiapas*, 395. Also see Solano's more recent "Regional, Communal, and Organisational Transformations in Las Cañadas" *Latin American Perspectives* 28, no. 117, no. 2 (March 2001): 20–44.

73. Hernández Castillo, "De la sierra a la selva," 422. Here Hernández Castillo writes about the implications of such cultural change for the role of women in the Indian community. Also see Hernández Castillo, "Cultura, género y poder en Chi-

apas: Las voces de las mujeres en el análisis antropológico," in *Anuario 1996* (San Cristóbal de Las Casas: Universidad de Ciencias y Artes del Estado de Chiapas, 1997), 220–242; and June Nash, "The Reassertion of Indigenous Identity: Mayan Responses to State Intervention in Chiapas," *Latin American Research Review* 30, no. 3 (1995): 7–41.

74. Hernández Castillo, "De la sierra a la selva," 419.

75. de Vos, "El Lacandon," 353.

76. Neil Harvey, *The Chiapas Rebellion: The Struggle for Land and Democracy* (Durham: Duke University Press, 1998), 79–80.

77. Ronald Wright, *Time among the Maya* (London: Abacus, 1989), 275.

78. Harvey, *Chiapas Rebellion*, 149.

79. Ibid., 160. Also see Tello Díaz, *La rebelión de Las Cañadas*, 102, for the claim that Castellanos Domínguez was responsible for 153 politically motivated killings during his term.

80. Harvey, "Rebellion in Chiapas," 45.

81. Ibid.

82. Such tactics were not, however, limited to Chiapas. See Neil Harvey, "The Limits of Concertation in Rural Mexico," in Harvey, *Mexico: Dilemmas of Transition*, 206, where he writes, "according to human rights monitors in Mexico, 14 leaders of regional peasant organisations were killed between December 1988 and November 1990."

83. It was as a direct result of such reform that the Diocese of San Cristóbal set up a human rights center, the Centro de Derechos Humanos Fray Bartolomé de Las Casas, in 1990. For more on the reform itself, see Womack, "Governor González's Penal Code: Tuxtla Gutiérrez, 1990," in Womack, *Rebellion in Chiapas*, 227–233.

84. Collier, "New Politics of Exclusion," 18.

85. James F. Rochlin, *Redefining Mexican "Security": Society, State and Region under NAFTA* (Boulder: Lynne Rienner, 1997), 61.

86. Harvey, "Rebellion in Chiapas," 46.

87. *La Jornada*, January 19, 1994, reprinted and translated in *Zapatistas!* 62.

88. *Macropolis*, January 1, 1994, reprinted and translated in *Zapatistas!* 71.

Chapter Six

1. Subcomandante Insurgente Marcos, January 18, 1994, letter to the national and international press, reprinted in *Zapatistas!* 108–109.

2. See EZLN, "Demands Submitted during the Dialogue," in *Zapatistas!* 238–243.

3. Recognizing the Zapatistas as a belligerent force would imply the recognition of international treaties regulating armed conflicts, treaties with which the Mexican government clearly does not wish to comply. For a succinct explanation of this issue, see Carlos Montemayor, "Administrando la guerra," *Proceso*, no. 1113, March 1, 1998, 40–41.

4. For more on this situation, see Nicholas P. Higgins, "Mexico's Stalled Peace Process: Prospects and Challenges," *International Affairs* 77, no. 4 (October 2001): 888–903.

5. See Bertrand de la Grange and Maite Rico, *Marcos: La genial impostura* (Mexico City: Aguilar, 1997), 24–28.

6. See Carlos Tello Díaz, *La rebelión de Las Cañadas*, which tells the story of the Fuerzas de Liberación Nacional (Forces of National Liberation, FLN) and their transformation into the EZLN. Marcos refers to Díaz as a historian who has studied history with the CISEN (Centro de Investigación y Seguridad Nacional, the national intelligence service). For academic responses that support such an accusation of Díaz's work, see *Proceso*, no. 977, July 24, 1995.

7. In particular, see Michel Foucault, "Politics and the Study of Discourse," in Burchell, Gordon, and Miller, *Foucault Effect*, 53–72; Ian Hacking, "Language, Truth and Reason," in *Rationality and Relativism*, ed. Martin Hollis and Steven Lukes, 48–66 (Oxford: Basil Blackwell, 1982); and Paul Rabinow, "Representations Are Social Facts."

8. See Subcomandante Insurgente Marcos, *Cuentos para una soledad desvelada* (Mexico City: Ediciones del Frente Zapatista de Liberación Nacional, 1998); *La historia de las preguntas* (Mexico City: Offset Industrial, 1998); *La historia de los colores* (Mexico City: Offset Industrial, 1997); and *Relatos de El Viejo Antonio*, with a prologue by Armando Bartra (San Cristóbal de Las Casas: Centro de Información y Análisis de Chiapas, 1998).

9. See Marcos, "Resistir con poesía," in *Cuentos para una soledad desvelada*, 169.

10. See, for example, the collections translated in *Zapatistas!* and in *Shadows of Tender Fury: The Letters and Communiqués of Subcomandante Marcos and the Zapatista Army of National Liberation* (New York: Monthly Review Press, 1995).

11. This situation may soon change, however, as a new road is currently being constructed in the zone under the auspices of a government-backed "development program." See Neil Harvey, "Balas de azúcar," *La Jornada*, August 29, 1999, for a more revealing analysis of the project.

12. The story told here is principally based on Marcos's own version of events as they have been recorded in interviews. See Marta Durán de Huerta, comp., *Yo Marcos* (Mexico City: Ediciones del Milenio, 1994); Yvon Le Bot, *Subcomandante Marcos*; and Carmen Castillo and Tessa Brisac, "Historia de Marcos y de los hombres de la noche," in *Discusión sobre la historia*, by Adolfo Gilly, Carlo Ginzburg, and Subcomandante Marcos, 131–142 (Mexico City: Taurus, 1995).

13. Le Bot, *Subcomandante Marcos*, 133.

14. Castillo and Brisac, "Historia," 133. On this period, also see Durán de Huerta, *Yo Marcos*, 83–98.

15. Le Bot, *Subcomandante Marcos*, 150.

16. Castillo and Brisac, "Historia," 137–138.

17. Ibid.

18. Subcomandante Insurgente Marcos, "Problems," 1987, published on March 15, 1994, as part of a communiqué to the press, reprinted in *Documentos y comunicados del EZLN* (Mexico City: Ediciones Era, 1995), 2:198–200.

19. Castillo and Brisac, "Historia," 133.

20. Le Bot, *Subcomandante Marcos*, 146–147.

21. Ibid., 147–148.

22. Ibid., 149–150.

23. Castillo and Brisac, "Historia," 138.

24. Ibid., 134. In this regard, also see Gary H. Gossen's somewhat overly structural approach to a nevertheless interesting question, "Who Is the Comandante of Subcomandante Marcos?" in Gosner and Ouweneel, *Indigenous Revolts*, 107–120.

25. Castillo and Brisac, "Historia," 134.

26. Subcomandante Insurgente Marcos, "a gift and a lesson in politics," March 24, 1994, trans. Watsonville Human Rights Committee, in *Shadows of Tender Fury*, 188.

27. Le Bot, *Subcomandante Marcos*, 154.

28. These stories have been collected and retold by Subcomandante Marcos in *Relatos de El Viejo Antonio, La historia de las preguntas*, and *La historia de los colores*.

29. Castillo and Brisac, "Historia," 135.

30. Le Bot, *Subcomandante Marcos*, 145–146.

31. Subcomandante Insurgente Marcos, December 16, 1995, dedicated to Olivier Cyran, in *Cuentos para una soledad desvelada*, 24.

32. Xochitl Leyva Solano, "Lacandonia Babilonia en las postrimerias del siglo," *Ojarasca* 24 (September 1993): 23–28. Also see Hernández Castillo, "De la sierra a la selva."

33. de Vos, "El Lacandon," 335.

34. Andrés Aubry, *Historia de Chiapas*, 9. This was especially the case for Indian women; see Rosalva Aida Hernández Castillo, "Reinventing Tradition: The Women's Law," *Akwe:kon Journal* 11, no. 2 (Summer 1994): 67–70.

35. See chap. 5.

36. See Harvey, *Chiapas Rebellion*.

37. Le Bot, *Subcomandante Marcos*, 195–196.

38. EZLN, "An Interview with the CCRI-CG," in *Zapatistas!* 131–139.

39. This expression belongs to Carlos Montemayor, whose analysis of the Mexican government's strategy is incisive. See his regular contributions to *Proceso*, especially "Administrando la guerra," no. 1113, March 1, 1998, and no. 1126, May 31, 1998, as well as his useful monograph *Chiapas*.

40. See Jesus Ramírez Cuevas, "Un soldado por familia," *Masiosare*, supplement to *La Jornada*, January 25, 1998, 8–10, in which Cuevas claims there is now a soldier for each family in the jungle region.

41. On the paramilitary groups, see Andrés Aubry and Angelica Inda, "La paramilitarización en el nuevo paisaje social de las guerras campesinas," *Del Campo*, supplement to *La Jornada*, February 25, 1998, 1–4; and the special reports in the Mexican weekly *Proceso*, especially no. 1104, December 28, 1997, and no. 1104, January 4, 1998. Also see Marta Durán de Huerta and Massimo Boldrini, *Acteal, navidad en el infierno* (Mexico City: Times Editores, 1998); and the special report published by the Centro de Derechos Humanos Fray Bartolomé de Las Casas, *Camino a la masacre* (Mexico City: Centro de Derechos Humanos Fray Bartolomé de Las Casas, 1998), for detailed accounts of the paramilitary role in the Acteal massacre.

42. For example, see "De acá a allá, y volvemos a empezar," March 8, 1997, in Marcos, *Cuentos para una soledad desvelada*, 205–209.

43. Durán de Huerta, *Yo Marcos*, 21–22.

44. See the examples collected in Marcos, *Cuentos para una soledad desvelada,* or at the Internet site http://www.civila.com/hispania/autonomia/durito.htm.

45. Le Bot, *Subcomandante Marcos,* 356.

46. Ibid.

47. See Higgins and Durán de Huerta, "An Interview with Subcomandante Insurgente Marcos," esp. 275.

48. This description first appeared in the *New York Times,* January 1994.

Conclusion

1. The definition is, of course, Weber's. See Max Weber, *Economy and Society,* trans. and ed. Guenther Roth and Claus Wittich (New York: Bedminster Press, 1968), 1:56.

2. Skinner, *Foundations of Modern Political Thought,* 1:x.

3. Foucault, "Governmentality," 103.

4. This approach might better be described, in William E. Connolly's terms, as an "ontalogy," calling attention to the ambiguities, incommensurabilities, and play of *différence* that lie beneath our practices of coherence at any one time. See Connolly, *Augustinian Imperative,* 150; and my own "Question of Style."

5. Weber, *Economy and Society,* 1:56.

6. For more on this process, see Colin Gordon, "Governmental Rationality: An Introduction," in Burchell, Gordon, and Miller, *Foucault Effect,* 1–51. Foucault himself called this process a "daemonic" coupling of "city game" and "shepherd game" to form a "secular political pastorate." Foucault, *"Omnes et Singulatim."*

7. See John Gledhill, "Neoliberalism and Ungovernability: Caciquismo, Militarisation and Popular Mobilisation in Zedillo's Mexico," in *Encuentros Antropológicos: Power, Identity and Mobility,* ed. Valentina Napolitano and Xochitl Leyva Solano (London: ILAS, 1998); and Rochlin, *Redefining Mexican "Security."*

8. For more on the Fox administration and the possibilities for a historic resolution of the demands raised by the Zapatista rebels, see Higgins, "Mexico's Stalled Peace Process."

9. See Chris Brown, "Cultural Diversity and International Political Theory: From the *Requirement* to 'Mutual Respect'?" *Review of International Studies* 26, no. 2 (2000): 199–213; and David Campbell and Michael J. Shapiro, eds., introduction to *Moral Spaces: Rethinking Ethics and World Politics* (Minneapolis: University of Minnesota Press, 1999).

10. Much of this work in international relations is labeled postmodern or poststructuralist. However, the label obscures more than it reveals. Consider instead the variety of engagements embodied in the work of Richard Ashley, R. B. J. Walker, Michael Shapiro, David Campbell, Roland Bleiker, Christine Sylvester, Cynthia Enloe, and Vivienne Jabri—where a critical concern for the power invested in language, subjectivity, political practice, and ethics remains a more common problematique than loyalty to any one approach or theory.

11. Excerpt from the opening ceremony of the Zapatista Encuentro, in The Zapatistas, *Zapatista Encuentro: Documents from the 1996 Encounter for Humanity and Against Neoliberalism* (New York: Seven Stories Press, 1998), 24.

12. A very useful analysis of the nature of Zapatista democracy can be found in Gustavo Esteva and Madhu Suri Prakash, *Grassroots Post-Modernism: Remaking the Soil of Cultures* (London: Zed Books, 1998).

13. See Judith Shklar, *After Utopia: The Decline of Political Faith* (Princeton: Princeton University Press, 1969). Also consider David Owen, *Nietzsche, Politics and Modernity: A Critique of Liberal Reason,* (London: Sage, 1995). Owen's notion of "agonistic perspectivism" is perhaps better suited to the general sweep of this argument than Shklar's formulation.

14. See Comisión Nacional Organizadora del FZLN, "Organizing the Zapatista Front: Principles, Proposals, and Virtual Force, August 1997," with an introduction by John Womack Jr., in Womack, *Rebellion in Chiapas,* 327–339; and Higgins and Durán de Huerta, "Interview with Subcomandante Insurgente Marcos."

15. Marcos's ch'ulel (twin animal spirit or soul) is said to be a *culebra,* or cobra snake, which is claimed to be so frightening that it keeps the Mexican troops confined to their barracks and leads them to defy their officers when ordered to enter the jungle to track down the EZLN commander. See the testimony of Mariano Pérez Tzu, "Conversaciones ininterrumpidas: Las voces indígenas del mercado de San Cristóbal," trans. from the Tzotzil by Jan Rus in *Democracía en tierras indígenas: Las elecciones en los Altos de Chiapas, 1991–1998,* ed. Juan Pedro Viqueira and Willibald Sonnleitner (Mexico City: Colmex/CIESAS, forthcoming).

16. Again consider the Indian testimony of Mariano Pérez Tzu, "The First Two Months of the Zapatistas: A Tzotzil Chronicle," trans. from the Tzotzil by Jan Rus, in Gosner and Ouweneel, *Indigenous Revolts.* Also consider the suggested interpretation of Marcos as the reincarnation of Juan López—the "king" of the Indians during the 1712 Cancuc rebellion—in de Vos, *Vivir en frontera,* 186–188; and Montemayor, *Chiapas,* 117–130. Also consider the claim that the original Emiliano Zapata escaped his assassins in 1915 and continues to roam the Chiapan mountains; see Enrique Rajchenberg and Catherine Héau-Lambert, "History and Symbolism in the Zapatista Movement," in *Zapatista! Reinventing Revolution in Mexico,* ed. John Holloway and Eloína Peláez, (London: Pluto Press, 1998), 20.

17. Consider, for example, the appearance of the "holy child of Lomantán" in January 1994; see John Ross, "The EZLN: A History; Miracles, Coyunturas, Communiqués," in *Shadows of Tender Fury,* 7–8.

18. For more on this, see Nicholas P. Higgins, "Image and Identity: Mexican Indians and Photographic Art," *Social Alternatives* 20, no. 4 (October 2001): 22–36.

19. Rigoberta Menchú, *I, Rigoberta Menchú: An Indian Woman in Guatemala,* ed. Elisabeth Burgos-Debray, trans. Ann Wright (London: Verso, 1984), 20. The nahual is defined as "the double, the alter-ego, be it an animal or any other living thing, which according to Indian belief, all human beings possess. There is a relationship between the *nahual* and a person's personality. The designation of the *nahual* means the new-born child is recognised as a member of the community." See *Latin American Perspectives* Special Issue.

20. Rigoberta Menchú, *Crossing Borders,* trans. and ed. Ann Wright (London: Verso, 1998), 226–227.

21. Gossen, "From Olmecs to Zapatistas."

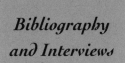

Bibliography
and Interviews

Interviews

Most interviews were conducted in confidentiality, and the names of interviewees are withheld by mutual agreement.

August 1997   Members of Indian and religious groups in Mexico City.

September 1997   Members of the Zapatista Army of National Liberation (EZLN). Representatives of Indian groups at the Congreso Nacional Indígena (CNI). Founding members of the Zapatista Front of National Liberation (FZLN).

October 1997   Representatives of the Diocese of San Cristóbal de Las Casas, Chiapas. Representatives of the Instituto Nacional Indigenista (INI), Centro Coordinador Tzeltal-Tzotzil, Chiapas. Representatives of the Centro de Derechos Humanos Fray Bartolomé de Las Casas, Chiapas. Representatives of Alianza Cívica, Chiapas.

January 1998   Rodolfo Stavenhagen, chairman of the official peace accords implementation-observer group (COSEVER), Mexico City.

February–March 1998   Refugees and survivors from the massacre at Acteal, Chenalhó, in Nuevo Primavera and Don Bosco, Chiapas. Representatives of Las Abejas (nonviolent Zapatista-supporting community organization), Chiapas. Members of expelled evangelical groups, La Hormiga, San Cristóbal de Las Casas, Chiapas. Director of the Instituto de Asesoría Antropológica para la Región Maya (INAREMAC). Members of the Sna Jtz'ibajom Indian theater and writing group, Chiapas. Representatives of the highland Indian communities of Tenejapa, Chamula, Zinacantán, and San Andrés. Work with Chamula Indian Mariano Calixto López on the project "Consejos de Los Ancianos" (Advice of the Indian Elders), Los Altos, Chiapas.

June 1998   Representatives and members of the autonomous Zapatista community of Oventic, Chiapas. Members of "las abejas." Archivists at the Archivo de la Catedral, Chiapas. Director of the Centro de Investigaciones Humanísticas de Mesoamerica y el Estado de Chiapas (CIHMECH).

November 1998   Members of the Zapatista command at the encounter between "civil society" and the EZLN, San Cristóbal de Las Casas, Chiapas. Representatives of national and local civil organizations. Members of human rights observation brigades, Chiapas.

February 2000   Don Samuel Ruiz, former bishop of San Cristóbal de Las Casas, official mediator in government-rebel peace talks, Glasgow and Edinburgh, Scotland.

February–March 2001   Members of the Zapatista command of the "March for Indigenous Dignity," San Cristóbal de Las Casas–Mexico City. Members of the National Indigenous Congress, Nurío, Michoacán.

August–September 2002   Representatives of the Centro de Derechos Humanos Fray Bartolomé de Las Casas, Chiapas. Representatives of the ruling council of Las Abejas, Acteal, and Los Chorros, Chiapas.

Published Materials

Aguilar, Hector. *La frontera nomada: Sonora y la revolución mexicana.* Mexico City: Siglo XXI Editores, 1977.

Aitken, Rob. *Localizing Politics: Cardenismo, the Mexican State and Local Politics in Contemporary Michoacán.* Amsterdam: Centre for Latin American Research and Documentation, 1999.

Aitken, Rob, Nikke Craske, Gareth A. Jones, and David E. Stansfield, eds. *Dismantling the Mexican State?* London: Macmillan Press, 1996.

Anderson, Bo, and James D. Cockcroft. "Control and Coöptation in Mexican Politics." In *Latin American Radicalism,* edited by Irving Louis Horowitz, Josué de Castro, and John Gerassi. London: Jonathan Cape, 1969.

Archer, Christon I. " 'La Causa Buena': The Counterinsurgency Army of New Spain and the Ten Years' War." In Rodríguez, *Independence of Mexico.*

Aristotle. *Politics.* Translated by Stephen Everson. Cambridge: Cambridge University Press, 1996.

Aubry, Andrés. *En la escuela y en la milpa la pláctica no es la misma: Historia Tzotzil de la Revolución Mexicana en Chiapas.* San Cristóbal de Las Casas: INAREMAC, 1984. Translated in part by John Womack Jr., with help from Andrés Aubry, in Womack, *Rebellion in Chiapas,* 97–104.

———, ed. "Extractos de una carta pastoral IX, San Cristóbal 1698, por Fr. Francisco Obispo de Chiapa." *Boletín del Archivo Histórico Diocesano* (San Cristóbal de Las Casas, Chiapas), June 1983.

———. "La historia de Chiapas identifica a los zapatistas." Doc. 043–VI, INAREMAC, 1994.

———. "El 1968 de la iglesia latinoamericana." *Masiosare,* supplement to *La Jornada,* October 25, 1998.

Aubry, Andrés, and Angelica Inda. "La paramilitarización en el nuevo paisaje social de las guerras campesinas." *Del Campo,* supplement to *La Jornada,* February 25, 1998, 1–4.

Avalos, Eugenio Maurer. "The Tzeltal Maya-Christian Synthesis." In Gossen, *South and Meso-American Native Spirituality,* 228–250.

Banks, Michael. "The Evolution of International Relations Theory." In *Conflict in World Society: A New Perspective on International Relations*, edited by Michael Banks, 3–21. Brighton: Wheatsheaf Books, 1984.

———. "The Inter-Paradigm Debate." In *International Relations: A Handbook of Current Theory*, edited by Margot Light and A. J. R. Groom, 7–26. London: Pinter, 1985.

Barlow, R. H. "Some Remarks on the Term 'Aztec Empire.'" *The Americas* 1 (1945).

Barry, Andrew, Thomas Osborne, and Nikolas Rose, eds. *Foucault and Political Reason: Liberalism, Neo-Liberalism and Rationalities of Government*. London: UCL Press, 1996.

Bartelson, Jens. *A Genealogy of Sovereignty*. Cambridge: Cambridge University Press, 1995.

Bartra, Roger. "Revolutionary Nationalism and National Security in Mexico." In *Mexico: In Search of Security*, edited by Bruce Bagley and Sergio Aguayo Quezada, 143–169. New Brunswick, NJ: Transaction, 1993.

Bastian, Jean-Pierre, ed. *Protestantes, liberales y francmasones: Sociedades de ideas y modernidad en América Latina, siglo XIX*. Mexico City: Fondo de Cultura Económica, 1990.

Bazant, Jan. *A Concise History of Mexico: From Hidalgo to Cárdenas, 1805–1940*. Cambridge: Cambridge University Press, 1977.

———. "From Independence to the Liberal Republic, 1821–1867." In Bethell, *Mexico since Independence*, 1–48.

Beck, Hanno. *Alexander von Humboldt*. 2 vols. Wiesbaden, Germany: F. Steiner, 1959–1961.

Benjamin, Thomas. "Primera Viva Chiapas! Local Rebellions and the Mexican Revolution in Chiapas." *European Review of Latin American and Caribbean Studies* 49 (December 1990): 33–53.

———. *A Rich Land, a Poor People: Politics and Society in Modern Chiapas*. Rev. ed. Albuquerque: University of New Mexico Press, 1996.

———. "El trabajo en las monterías de Tabasco y Chiapas, 1870–1946." *Historia Mexicana* 30 (April–June 1981): 506–529.

Bermudez Torres, Lilia. *Guerra de baja intensidad: Reagan contra Centroamérica*. Mexico City: Siglo XXI Editores, 1987.

Bethell, Leslie, ed. *Mexico since Independence*. Cambridge: Cambridge University Press, 1991.

Bireley, Robert. *The Counter-Reformation Prince: Anti-Machiavellianism or Catholic Statecraft in Early Modern Europe*. Chapel Hill: University of North Carolina Press, 1990.

Bloom, Harold. *Shakespeare: The Invention of the Human*. New York: Riverhead Books, 1998.

Boff, Leonardo. *When Theology Listens to the Poor*. San Francisco: Harper & Row, 1988.

Boils, Guillermo. "Los militares en México, 1965–1985." *Revista Mexicana Sociología*, no. 47 (January–February 1985): 169–185.

Bonaccorsi, Nelida. *El trabajo obligatorio indígena en Chiapas, siglo XVI*. Mexico City: Universidad Nacional Autónoma de Mexico, 1990.

Booth, Ken. "Discussion: A Reply to Wallace." *Review of International Studies* 23, no. 3 (1997): 371–377.

Bosanquet, Nick. *After the New Right.* London: Heinemann, 1983.

Bowen, Margaret. *Empiricism and Geographical Thought: From Francis Bacon to Alexander von Humboldt.* Cambridge: Cambridge University Press, 1981.

Brading, David A. *Church and State in Bourbon Mexico: The Diocese of Michoacán, 1749–1810.* Cambridge: Cambridge University Press, 1994.

——. "Liberal Patriotism and the Mexican Reforma." *Journal of Latin American Studies* 20, no. 1 (1988): 27–48.

——. "Manuel Gamio and Official Indigenismo in Mexico." *Bulletin of Latin American Research* 7, no. 1 (1988): 75–89.

——. *Miners and Merchants in Bourbon Mexico, 1763–1810.* Cambridge: Cambridge University Press, 1971.

——. *The Origins of Mexican Nationalism.* Cambridge: Centre of Latin American Studies, 1985.

——. "Tridentine Catholicism and Enlightened Despotism in Bourbon Mexico." *Journal of Latin American Studies* 15, no. 1 (1983): 1–22.

Breton, Alain, and Jacques Arnauld, coords. *Los mayas: La pasión por los antepasados, el deseo de perdurar.* Mexico City: Editorial Grijalbo, 1994.

Bricker, Victoria. *The Indian Christ, the Indian King: The Historical Substrate of Maya Myth and Ritual.* Austin: University of Texas Press, 1981.

Bricker, Victoria, and Gary H. Gossen, eds. *Ethnographic Encounters in Southern Mesoamerica: Essays in Honor of Evon Zartman Vogt Jr.* Albany: University at Albany, 1989.

Brown, Betty Ann. "The Past Idealized: Diego Rivera's Use of Pre-Columbian Imagery." In *Diego Rivera: A Retrospective,* edited by Linda Downs. New York: W. W. Norton, 1986.

Brown, Chris. "Cultural Diversity and International Political Theory: From the *Requirement* to 'Mutual Respect'?" *Review of International Studies* 26, no. 2 (2000): 199–213.

——. "Turtles All the Way Down: Anti-foundationalism, Critical Theory and International Relations." *Millennium* 23, no. 2 (Summer 1994): 213–236.

Brown Scott, James. *The Spanish Origin of International Law: Francisco de Vitoria and His Law of Nations.* Vol. 1. Oxford: Oxford University Press, 1934.

Bunzl, Matti. "Franz Boas and the Humboldtian Tradition: From *Volksgeist* and *Nationalcharakter* to an Anthropological Concept of Culture." In *Volksgeist as Method and Ethic: Essays on Boasian Ethnography and the German Anthropological Tradition,* edited by George W. Stocking Jr. Madison: University of Wisconsin Press, 1996.

Burchell, Graham, Colin Gordon, and Peter Miller, eds. *The Foucault Effect: Studies in Governmentality.* Chicago: University of Chicago Press, 1991.

Burkhart, Louise M. *The Slippery Earth: Nahua-Christian Moral Dialogue in Sixteenth-Century Mexico.* Tucson: University of Arizona Press, 1989.

Buzan, Barry. "The Timeless Wisdom of Realism?" In *International Theory: Positivism and Beyond,* edited by Steve Smith, Ken Booth, and Marysia Zalewski, 47–65. Cambridge: Cambridge University Press, 1996.

Camp, Roderic A., Charles A. Hale, and Josefina Z. Vázquez, eds. *Los intelectuales y el poder en México.* Mexico City: Colegio de México and UCLA Latin American Center Publications, 1991.

Campbell, David. "Contra Wight: The Errors of Premature Writing." *Review of International Studies* 25, no. 2 (1999): 317–321.

Campbell, David, and Michael J. Shapiro, eds. Introduction to *Moral Spaces: Rethinking Ethics and World Politics.* Minneapolis: University of Minnesota Press, 1999.

Cancian, Frank. *The Decline of Community in Zinacantán: Economy, Public Life, and Social Stratification, 1960–1987.* Stanford: Stanford University Press, 1992.

———. *Economics and Prestige in a Maya Community: The Religious Cargo System in Zinacantán.* Stanford: Stanford University Press, 1965.

Cardinal, Marie. *In Other Words.* Translated by Amy Cooper. London: The Women's Press, 1996.

———. *The Words to Say It.* London: The Women's Press, 1993.

Carr, Edward H. *The Twenty Years' Crisis, 1919–1939.* 1940. Reprint, New York: Harper & Row, 1968.

———. *What Is History?* 1961. 2nd ed., with an introduction by R. W. Davies. London: Macmillan, 1986.

Carroll, Michael P. *The Cult of Virgin Mary: Psychological Origins.* Princeton: Princeton University Press, 1992.

Castillo, Carmen, and Tessa Brisac. "Historia de Marcos y de los hombres de la noche." In *Discusión sobre la historia,* by Adolfo Gilly, Carlo Ginzburg, and Subcomandante Marcos, 131–142. Mexico City: Taurus, 1995.

Ceceña, José Luis. "El porfirismo." In *El porfiriato,* edited by José Alfredo Castellanos, 49–64. Mexico City: Universidad Autónoma Chapingo, 1988.

Centeno, Miguel Ángel. *Democracy within Reason: Technocratic Revolution in Mexico.* University Park: Pennsylvania State University Press, 1994.

Centeno, Miguel Ángel, and Sylvia Maxfield. "The Marriage of Finance and Order: Changes in the Mexican Political Elite." *Journal of Latin American Studies* 24 (1992).

Centro de Derechos Humanos Fray Bartolomé de Las Casas. *Camino a la massacre.* Mexico City: Centro de Derechos Humanos Fray Bartolomé de Las Casas, 1998.

Chiappelli, Fredi, ed. *First Images of America: The Impact of the New World on the Old.* 2 vols. Berkeley and Los Angeles: University of California Press, 1976.

Clavero, Bartolomé. *Derecho indígena y cultura constitucional en América.* Mexico City: Siglo XXI Editores, 1994.

Clendinnen, Inga. "'Fierce and Unnatural Cruelty': Cortes and the Conquest of Mexico." In Greenblatt, *New World Encounters,* 12–47.

Coates, Wilson, Hayden White, and J. Salwyn Schapiro. *The Emergence of Liberal Humanism.* New York: McGraw-Hill, 1966.

Collier, George A. "The New Politics of Exclusion: Antecedents to the Rebellion in Mexico." *Dialectical Anthropology* 19, no. 1 (May 1994): 1–44.

Comisión Nacional Organizadora del FLZN. "Organizing the Zapatista Front: Principles, Proposals, and Virtual Force, August 1997." With an introduction by John Womack Jr. In Womack, *Rebellion in Chiapas,* 327–339.

Connolly, William E. *The Augustinian Imperative.* New York: Sage, 1995.

Cordova, Arnaldo. "Espiritualismo o positivismo? La filosofía de la Revolución Mexicana." Avances de Investigación 14, Centro de Estudios Latinoamericanos, Universidad Nacional Autónoma de México, Mexico City, 1975.

———. *La política del masas del cardenismo.* Mexico City: Ediciones Era, 1976.

Cornelius, Wayne A. *Mexican Politics in Transition: The Breakdown of a One-Party-Dominant Regime.* Monograph Series 41. San Diego: Center for U.S.–Mexican Studies, University of California, 1996.

Cornelius, Wayne A., Ann L. Craig, and Jonathan Fox, eds. *Transforming State-Society Relations in Mexico: The National Solidarity Strategy.* San Diego: Center for U.S.–Mexican Studies, University of California, 1994.

Corro, Salvador. "El gobierno fracasó en su estrategia de desgaste en Chiapas, pero aún administra una guerra despiada: Carlos Montemayor." *Proceso,* no. 1126, May 31, 1998, 22–26.

Cosío Villegas, Daniel. *El porfiriato.* In *Historia moderna de México,* edited by Daniel Cosío Villegas. 7 vols. Mexico City: Hermes, 1957–1972.

Craske, Nikki. "Dismantling or Retrenchment? Salinas and Corporatism." In Aitken et al., *Dismantling the Mexican State?*

Cuevas, Jesus Ramírez. "Un soldado por familia." *Masiosare,* supplement to *La Jornada,* January 25, 1998, 8–10.

Davidson, Donald. "Causal Relations." In *Causation and Conditionals,* edited by E. Sosa. Oxford: Oxford Readings, 1975.

———. "A Coherence Theory of Truth and Knowledge." In *Truth and Interpretation: Perspectives on the Philosophy of Donald Davidson,* edited by E. Lepore. Oxford: Blackwell, 1986.

———. *Inquiries into Truth and Interpretation.* Oxford: Oxford University Press, 1984.

———. "Mental Events." In *Essays on Actions and Events.* Oxford: Oxford University Press, 1985.

———. "Myth of the Subjective." In *Relativism: Interpretation and Confrontation,* edited by Michael Krausz. Notre Dame: University of Notre Dame Press, 1989.

de la Grange, Bertrand, and Maite Rico. *Marcos: La genial impostura.* Mexico City: Aguilar, 1997.

Depler, Helen. *The Enormous Vogue of Things Mexican: Cultural Relations between the United States and Mexico, 1920–1935.* Tuscaloosa: University of Alabama Press, 1992.

Der Derian, James. *On Diplomacy: A Genealogy of Western Estrangement.* Oxford: Basil Blackwell, 1987.

———. "The Pen, The Sword, and the Smart Bomb: Criticism in the Age of Video." *Alternatives* 19 (1994).

de Vos, Jan. *La batalla del Sumidero: Historia de la rebelión de los chiapanecas, 1532–1534, a través de testimonios españoles e indígenas.* Mexico City: Editorial Katun, 1985.

———. "El Lacandon: Una introducción histórica." In Viqueira and Ruz, *Chiapas,* 331–361.

———. *Vivir en frontera: La experiencia de los indios de Chiapas.* Mexico City: CIESAS and Instituto Nacional Indigenista, 1994.

Dresser, Denise. "Bringing the Poor Back In: National Solidarity as a Strategy of Regime Legitimacy." In Cornelius, Craig, and Fox, *Transforming State-Society Relations*, 143–165.

———. *Neo-populist Solutions to Neoliberal Problems: Mexico's National Solidarity Program*. Monograph Series 24. San Diego: Center for U.S.–Mexican Studies, University of California, 1991.

Duby, Georges, ed. *A History of Private Life*. 5 vols. Cambridge, MA: Harvard University Press, Belknap Press, 1987.

Duffy, Eamon. *Madonnas that Maim? Christianity and the Cult of the Virgin*. Glasgow: Blackfriars, 1999.

Dunn, Mary Maples. Introduction to *Political Essay on the Kingdom of New Spain*, by Alexander von Humboldt. New York: Alfred A. Knopf, 1972.

Durán, Leonel, ed. *Lázaro Cárdenas, Ideario Político*. Mexico City: Ediciones Era, 1972.

Durán de Huerta, Marta, comp. *Yo Marcos*. Mexico City: Ediciones del Milenio, 1994.

Durán de Huerta, Marta, and Massimo Boldrini. *Acteal, navidad en el infierno*. Mexico City: Times Editores, 1998.

Eber, Christine. "Take My Water: Liberation through Prohibition in San Pedro Chenalhó, Chiapas, Mexico." *Social Science and Medicine* 53 (2001): 251–262.

———. *Women and Alcohol in a Highland Maya Township*. Austin: University of Texas Press, 1995.

Edgerton, S. Y., Jr. "From Mental Matrix to *Mappamundi* to Christian Empire: The Heritage of Christian Cartography in the Renaissance" In *Art and Cartography*, edited by D. Woodward, 10–50. Chicago: University of Chicago Press, 1987.

Edmonson, Munro S. "The Maya Faith." In Gossen, *South and Meso-American Native Spirituality*, 65–85.

Elliot, J. H. *Imperial Spain*. London: Pelican, 1970.

———. "A World United." In *Circa 1492: Art in the Age of Exploration*, edited by Jay A. Levenson, 647–652. New Haven: Yale University Press, 1991.

Elliott, Dyan. *Fallen Bodies: Pollution, Sexuality, and Demonology in the Middle Ages*. Philadelphia: University of Pennsylvania Press, 1998.

Escalante, Pablo. "Sentarse, guardar la compostura y llorar: Entre los antiguos Nahuas, el cuerpo y el proceso de civilización." In *Familia y vida privada en la historia de IberoAmérica*, edited by Pilar Gonzalbo Aizpuru and Cecilia Rebell Romero. Mexico City: Colegio de Mexico and Universidad Nacional Autónoma de México, 1996.

Esteva, Gustavo. "The Meaning and Scope of the Struggle for Autonomy." *Latin American Perspectives* 28, no. 117, no. 2 (March 2001): 120–148.

Esteva, Gustavo, and Madhu Suri Prakash. *Grassroots Post-Modernism: Remaking the Soil of Cultures*. London: Zed Books, 1998.

EZLN. "Demands Submitted during the Dialogue." In *Zapatistas!* 238–243.

———. "An Interview with the CCRI-CG." In *Zapatistas!* 131–139.

———. "V declaración de la Selva Lacandona." *Perfil*, supplement to *La Jornada*, July 21, 1998.

Farris, Nancy. *Crown and Clergy in Colonial Mexico, 1759–1821: The Crisis of Ecclesiastical Privilege.* London: Athlone Press, 1968.

Fazio, Carlos. *Samuel Ruiz: El Caminante.* Mexico City: Espasa Calpe, 1994.

Fernández-Santamaría, J. A. *The State, War and Peace: Spanish Political Thought in the Renaissance, 1516–1559.* Cambridge: Cambridge University Press, 1977.

Foucault, Michel. "Afterword: The Subject and Power." In *Michel Foucault: Beyond Structuralism and Hermeneutics,* by Hubert L. Dreyfus and Paul Rabinow. Hemel Hempstead: Harvester Wheatsheaf, 1982.

———. *Birth of the Clinic.* Translated by Alan Sheridan. London: Tavistock, 1976.

———. *Discipline and Punish: Birth of the Prison.* Translated by Alan Sheridan. New York: Vintage Books, 1979.

———. "The Ethics of Concern for the Self as a Practice of Freedom." In *Ethics: Subjectivity and Truth,* edited by Paul Rabinow, translated by R. Hurley. New York: Free Press, 1997.

———. "Foucault at the Collège de France I: A Course Summary." Translated and introduced by James Bernauer. *Philosophy and Social Criticism* 8, no. 2 (Summer 1981).

———. "Foucault at the Collège de France II: A Course Summary." Translated and introduced by James Bernauer. *Philosophy and Social Criticism* 8, no. 3 (Fall 1981).

———. "Governmentality" Translated by R. Braidotti. In Burchell, Gordon, and Miller, *Foucault Effect.*

———. *The History of Sexuality.* Vol. 1, *An Introduction.* Translated by Robert Hurley. London: Allen Lane, 1979.

———. *The History of Sexuality.* Vol. 2, *The Use of Pleasure.* Translated by Robert Hurley. New York: Vintage, 1986.

———. *The History of Sexuality.* Vol. 3, *The Care of the Self.* Translated by Robert Hurley. London: Allen Lane, 1986.

———. "Is It Useless to Revolt?" Translated and introduced by James Bernauer. *Philosophy and Social Criticism* 8, no. 1 (Spring 1981).

———. *Madness and Civilization: A History of Insanity in the Age of Reason.* Translated by Richard Howard. New York: Random House, 1973.

———. "*Omnes et Singulatim:* Towards a Criticism of 'Political Reason.'" In *The Tanner Lectures on Human Values.* Vol. 2, edited by Sterling McMurrin. Cambridge: Cambridge University Press, 1981.

———. "On Governmentality." *Ideology and Consciousness,* no. 6 (1979): 5–21.

———. "On the Genealogy of Ethics: An Overview of Work in Progress." In Rabinow, *Foucault Reader.*

———. *The Order of Things: An Archaeology of the Human Sciences.* London: Tavistock, 1970.

———. "Polemics, Politics, and Problematizations." In Rabinow, *Foucault Reader.*

———. "Politics and the Study of Discourse." In Burchell, Gordon, and Miller, *Foucault Effect,* 53–72.

———. *Power/Knowledge: Selected Interviews and Other Writings, 1972–1977.* Edited by Colin Gordon. Hemel Hempstead: Harvester Wheatsheaf, 1980.

———. "Right of Death and Power over Life." In Rabinow, *Foucault Reader.*

————. "What Is Enlightenment?" Translated by C. Porter. In Rabinow, *Foucault Reader*.

Fowler, Will. "Dreams of Stability: Mexican Political Thought during the 'Forgotten Years'; An Analysis of the Beliefs of the Creole Intelligentsia, (1821–1853)." *Bulletin of Latin American Research* 14, no. 3 (1995): 287–312.

————. *The Liberal Origins of Mexican Conservatism, 1821–1832.* Occasional paper, Institute of Latin American Studies, Glasgow University, Glasgow 1997.

————. "The Repeated Rise of General Antonio López de Santa Anna in the So-called 'Age of Chaos' (Mexico 1821–1855)." In *Authoritarianism in Latin America since Independence*, edited by Will Fowler. Westport, CT: Greenwood Press, 1996.

Fox-Genovese, Elizabeth. *The Origins of Physiocracy: Economic Revolution and Social Order in Eighteenth-Century France.* Ithaca: Cornell University Press, 1976.

Fraser, Nancy. "From Irony to Prophecy to Politics: A Response to Richard Rorty." In Goodman, *Pragmatism: A Contemporary Reader.*

————. "Michel Foucault: A 'Young Conservative'?" *Ethics* 96 (1985).

————. *Unruly Practices: Power, Discourse, and Gender in Contemporary Social Theory.* Cambridge, UK: Polity Press, 1989.

French, William E. "Prostitutes and Guardian Angels: Women, Work and the Family in Porfirian Mexico." *Hispanic American Historical Review* 72, no. 4 (November 1992): 529–554.

Friedman, Milton. *Capitalism and Freedom.* Chicago: University of Chicago Press, 1962.

————. *Free to Choose.* London: Secker & Warburg, 1980.

Frost, Elsa Celia. "Indians and Theologians: Sixteenth-Century Spanish Theologians and Their Concept of the Indigenous Soul." In Gossen, *South and Meso-American Native Spirituality.*

Gagliardo, John G. *Enlightened Despotism.* London: Routledge & Kegan Paul, 1968.

Gamble, Andrew. *Hayek: The Iron Cage of Liberty.* Cambridge, UK: Polity Press, 1996.

Gane, Mike, and Terry Johnson, eds. *Foucault's New Domains.* London: Routledge, 1993.

García de León, Antonio. *Resistencia y utopia: Memorial de agravios y crónica de revueltas y profecías de Chiapas durante los últimos quinientos años de su historia.* 2nd ed. Mexico City: Ediciones Era, 1998.

Garrido, Luis Javier. *El Partido de la Revolución Institucionalizada.* Mexico City: SEP, 1986.

Gazeta de Guatemala. "Un ladino ilustrado defiende a los indios contra los que opinan que ellos son ocios y borrachos por naturaleza." Guatemala, October 15 and 22, 1801. Reproduced as Documento 28 in de Vos, *Vivir en frontera*, 245–247.

Geertz, Clifford. *The Interpretation of Cultures: Selected Essays.* New York: Basic Books, 1973.

Gide, Charles, and Charles Rist, eds. *A History of Economic Doctrines: From the Time of the Physiocrats to the Present Day.* Translated by R. Richards. London: George G. Harap, 1915. 7th ed., 1950.

Gilmore, Myron P. *The World of Humanism, 1453–1517.* New York: Harper & Row, 1962.

Gledhill, John. "Neoliberalism and Ungovernability: Caciquismo, Militarisation and Popular Mobilisation in Zedillo's Mexico." In *Encuentros Antropológicos: Power, Identity and Mobility*, edited by Valentina Napolitano and Xochitl Leyva Solano. London: Institute of Latin American Studies, 1998.

Gomezcésar Hernández, Ivan. "Los liberales mexicanos frente al problema indígena: La comunidad y la integración nacional." In *Diversidad étnica y conflicto en América Latina: El indio como metáfora en la identidad nacional*, edited by Raquel Barcelo, María Ana Portal, and Martha Judith Sánchez. Mexico City: Universidad Nacional Autónoma de México, 1995.

Gómez Gutiérrez, Domingo. *Letras mayas contemporáneos*. Mexico City: Instituto Nacional Indigenista, 1992.

González Navarro, Moisés. "The Hours of Leisure." In *The Age of Porfirio Díaz*, edited by Carlos B. Gil, 123–128. Albuquerque: University of New Mexico Press, 1977.

Goodman, Russell B., ed. *Pragmatism: A Contemporary Reader*. London: Routledge, 1995.

Gordon, Colin. "Governmental Rationality: An Introduction." In Burchell, Gordon, and Miller, *Foucault Effect*, 1–51.

————. "The Soul of the Citizen: Max Weber and Michel Foucault on Rationality and Government." In *Michel Foucault: Critical Assessments*, edited by Barry Smart, vol. 4. London: Routledge, 1995.

Gosner, Kevin. "Historical Perspectives on Maya Resistance: The Tzeltal Revolt of 1712." In Gosner and Ouweneel, *Indigenous Revolts*.

————. *Soldiers of the Virgin: The Moral Economy of a Colonial Maya Rebellion*. Tucson: University of Arizona Press, 1992.

Gosner, Kevin, and Arij Ouweneel. *Indigenous Revolts in Chiapas and the Andean Highlands*. Amsterdam: Centre for Latin American Research and Documentation, 1996.

Gossen, Gary H. "La diáspora de San Juan Chamula: Los indios en el proyecto nacional mexicano." In *De palabra y obra en el Nuevo Mundo*, edited by M. Gutiérrez Estévez, M. León-Portilla, G. H. Gossen, and J. J. Klor de Avala. Madrid: Siglo XXI de España, 1992.

————. "From Olmecs to Zapatistas: A Once and Future History of Souls." *American Anthropologist* 96, no. 3 (1994): 553–570.

————. "Life, Death, and Apotheosis of a Chamula Protestant Leader: Biography as Social History." In Bricker and Gossen, *Ethnographic Encounters*, 217–229.

————. "On the Human Condition and the Moral Order: A Testimony from the Chamula Tzotzil Maya of Chiapas, Mexico," in Gossen, *South and Meso-American Native Spirituality*.

————, ed. *South and Meso-American Native Spirituality: From the Cult of the Feathered Serpent to the Theology of Liberation*. In collaboration with Miguel León-Portillo. New York: Crossroad Publishing, 1993.

————. "Translating Cuscat's War: Understanding Maya Oral History." *Journal of Latin America Lore*, no. 3 (1977).

————. "Who Is the Comandante of Subcomandante Marcos?" In Gosner and Ouweneel, *Indigenous Revolts*, 107–120.

Grafton, Anthony. *New Worlds, Ancient Texts: The Power of Tradition and the Shock of Discovery.* Cambridge, MA: Harvard University Press, Belknap Press, 1992.

Green, Duncan. *Silent Revolution: The Rise of Market Economics in Latin America.* London: Cassell, 1995.

Greenblatt, Stephen, ed. *New World Encounters.* Berkeley and Los Angeles: University of California Press, 1993.

Greene, Graham. *The Lawless Roads.* 1939. Reprint, London: Penguin Books, 1982.

Grisel, Etienne. "The Beginnings of International Law and General Public Law Doctrine: Francisco de Vitoria's *De Indiis prior.*" In Chiappelli, *First Images of America,* 1:305–326.

Gruzinski, Serge. *The Conquest of Mexico: The Incorporation of Indian Societies into the Western World, 16th–18th Centuries.* Cambridge, UK: Polity Press, 1993.

———. "Individualization and Acculturation: Confession among Nahuas of Mexico from the Sixteenth to the Eighteenth Century." In *Sexuality and Marriage in Colonial Latin America,* edited by Asunción Lavría. Lincoln: University of Nebraska Press, 1989.

———. "La 'segunda aculturación': El estado ilustrado y la religiosidad indígena en Nueva España (1775–1800)." Estudios de Historia NovHispania 8. Mexico City: Universidad Nacional Autónoma de México, 1985.

Guerro Aguirre, Francisco Javier. "The North American Free Trade Agreement: An Analysis of the Process of Pre-negotiation in Mexico." *Paradigms* 9, no. 2 (Winter 1995).

Gunder Frank, Andre. *Economic Genocide in Chile: Monetarist Theory versus Humanity; Two Open Letters to Milton Friedman and Arnold Harberger.* Nottingham, UK: Spokesman Books, 1976.

Gutieras-Holmes, Calixta. *Perils of the Soul: The World View of a Tzotzil Indian.* Glencoe, IL: Free Press of Glencoe, 1961.

Gutiérrez, Gustavo. *A Theology of Liberation.* New York: Orbis Books, 1971.

Haber, Honi. "Richard Rorty's Failed Politics." *Social Epistemology* 7, no. 1 (1993).

Hacking, Ian. "The Archaeology of Foucault." In *Foucault: A Critical Reader,* edited by David Couzens Hoy. Oxford: Basil Blackwell, 1986.

———. *The Emergence of Probability.* Cambridge: Cambridge University Press, 1975.

———. "Five Parables." In *Philosophy in History: Essays on the Historiography of Philosophy,* edited by Richard Rorty, Quentin Skinner, and J. B. Schneewind. Cambridge: Cambridge University Press, 1984.

———. "How Should We Do the History of Statistics?" In Burchell, Gordon, and Miller, *Foucault Effect.*

———. "Language, Truth and Reason." In *Rationality and Relativism,* edited by Martin Hollis and Steven Lukes, 48–66. Oxford: Basil Blackwell, 1982.

———. "Making People Up." In *Reconstructing Individualism: Autonomy, Individuality, and the Self in Western Thought,* edited by Thomas Heller, Morton Sosna, and David Wellbery. Stanford: Stanford University Press, 1986.

———. *Rewriting the Soul: Multiple Personality and the Sciences of Memory.* Princeton: Princeton University Press, 1995.

———, ed. *Scientific Revolutions.* Oxford: Oxford University Press, 1981.

————. *The Taming of Chance.* Cambridge: Cambridge University Press, 1990.

Hale, Charles A. "Alamán, Antunano y la continuidad del liberalismo." *Historia Mexicana* 11, no. 2 (October–December 1961): 224–245.

————. *Mexican Liberalism in the Age of Mora, 1821–1853.* New Haven: Yale University Press, 1968.

————. "Political and Social Ideas in Latin America, 1870–1930." In *The Cambridge History of Latin America,* edited by Leslie Bethell, vol. 4, *Ca. 1870 to 1930.* Cambridge: Cambridge University Press, 1986.

————. *The Transformation of Liberalism in Late Nineteenth-Century Mexico.* Princeton: Princeton University Press, 1989.

Hamilton, Bernard. *Medieval Inquisition: Foundations of Medieval History.* London: Holmes & Meier, 1981.

Hamnett, Brian R. "Liberal Politics and Spanish Freemasonry, 1814–1820." *History: The Journal of the Historical Association* 69, no. 226 (June 1984).

————. "The Mexican Bureaucracy before the Bourbon Reforms, 1700–1770: A Study in the Limitations of Absolutism." Institute of Latin American Studies Occasional Papers 26, Glasgow University, Glasgow, 1979.

Hanke, Lewis. *Aristotle and the American Indians: A Study in Race Prejudice in the Modern World.* London: Hollis and Carter, 1959.

————. "The Dawn of Conscience in America: Spanish Experiments and Experiences with Indians in the New World." *Proceedings of the American Philosophical Society* 107, no. 2 (1963).

Harris, David. "European Liberalism and the State." In Lubasz, *Development of the Modern State,* 72–90.

Harris, Olivia. "'The Coming of the White People': Reflections on the Mythologisation of History in Latin America." *The Bulletin of Latin American Research* 14, no. 1 (1995): 9–24.

Harvey, Neil. "Balas de azúcar." *La Jornada,* August 29, 1999.

————. *The Chiapas Rebellion: The Struggle for Land and Democracy.* Durham: Duke University Press, 1998.

————. "The Difficult Transition: Neoliberalism and Neocorporatism in Mexico." In Harvey, *Mexico: Dilemmas of Transition.*

————. "The Limits of Concertation in Rural Mexico." In Harvey, *Mexico: Dilemmas of Transition.*

————, ed. *Mexico: Dilemmas of Transition.* London: Institute of Latin American Studies, 1993.

————. "Rebellion in Chiapas: Rural Reforms and Popular Struggle." *Third World Quarterly* 16, no. 1 (1995).

————. "La Unión de Uniones de Chiapas y los retos políticos del desarrollo de base." In *Autonomía y nuevos sujetos en el desarrollo social,* edited by J. Moguel, C. Botey, and L. Hernández, 219–232. Mexico City: Siglo XXI Editores and CEHAM, 1992.

Hayek, Friedrich August von. *The Constitution of Liberty.* London: Routledge, 1966.

————. *The Fatal Conceit: The Errors of Socialism.* Chicago: University of Chicago Press, 1988.

————. *Individualism and Economic Order.* Chicago: University of Chicago Press, 1948.

———. *The Road to Serfdom.* London: Routledge, 1944.

Hernández Castillo, Rosalva Aída. "Between Civil Disobedience and Silent Rejection: Differing Responses by Mam Peasants to the Zapatista Rebellion." *Latin American Perspectives* 28, no. 117, no. 2 (March 2001): 98–119.

———. "Cultura, género y poder en Chiapas: Las voces de las mujeres en el análisis antropológico." In *Anuario 1996,* 220–242. San Cristóbal de Las Casas: Universidad de Ciencias y Artes del Estado de Chiapas, 1997.

———. "De la sierra a la selva: Identidades étnicas y religiosas en la frontera sur." In Viqueira and Ruz, *Chiapas,* 402–423.

———. "Reinventing Tradition: The Women's Law." *Akwe:kon Journal* 11, no. 2 (Summer 1994): 67–70.

Herr, Richard. *The Eighteenth-Century Revolution in Spain.* Princeton: Princeton University Press, 1958.

Higgins, Nicholas P. "Image and Identity: Mexican Indians and Photographic Art." *Social Alternatives* 20, no. 4 (October 2001): 22–36.

———. "An Interview with Comandante David, Leader of the Zapatista Delegation to Mexico City, March 2001." *Alternatives* 26, no. 3 (October 2001): 373–382.

———. "Mexico's Stalled Peace Process: Prospects and Challenges." *International Affairs* 77, no. 4 (October 2001): 888–903.

———. "The Politics of Humanitarian Intervention: The Ethiopian-Eritrean Experience." In *New Thinking in Politics and International Relations,* edited by Hazel Smith. Kent Papers in Politics and International Relations, series 5, no. S2, University of Kent at Canterbury, 1996.

———. "A Question of Style: The Politics and Ethics of Cultural Conversation in Rorty and Connolly." *Global Society* 10, no. 1 (1996): 25–42.

———."Richard Rorty and William E. Connolly: Contested Concepts of Politics and Culture for International Relations." In *Theorising in International Relations: Contemporary Theorists and Their Critics,* edited by Stephen Chan and Jarrod Wiener. New York: Edwin Mellen Press, 1997.

———. "'Supposing Truth to Be a Woman?' Pragmatism and the Feminist Problematique." In *Women, Culture, and International Relations,* edited by Vivienne Jabri and Eleanor O'Gorman, 137–163. London: Lynne Rienner, 1999.

———. "The Zapatista Conflict and the Poetics of Cultural Resistance." *Alternatives: Social Transformation and Humane Governance* 25, no. 3 (2000): 359–374.

Higgins, Nicholas P., and Marta Durán de Huerta. "An Interview with Subcomandante Insurgente Marcos, Spokesperson and Military Commander of the Zapatista National Liberation Army (EZLN)." *International Affairs* 75, no. 2 (April 1999): 269–279.

Hirales, Gustavo. "La guerra secreta, 1970–1978." *Nexos,* no. 54 (June 1982): 20–35.

Holscher, Ludger. *The Reality of the Mind: Augustine's Philosophical Arguments for the Human Soul as a Spiritual Substance.* London: Routledge & Kegan Paul, 1986.

Horcasitas, Beatriz Urías. "El pensamiento económico moderno en el México independiente." In Rodríguez, *The Independence of Mexico and the Creation of the New Nation.*

Hu-Dehart, Evelyn. "Pacification of the Yaquis." In *The Age of Porfirio Díaz,* edited by Carlos B. Gil, 129–138. Albuquerque: University of New Mexico Press, 1977.

Humboldt, Alexander von. *Atlas géographique et physique des regions equinoxiales du nouveau continent.* Paris: Libraire de Gide, 1814–1834. .

———. *Examen critique de l'histoire de la géographie du nouveau continent.* 1813.

———. *Political Essay on the Kingdom of New Spain.* Edited by Mary Maples Dunn. Based on the original four-volume translation by John Black in 1811. New York: Alfred A. Knopf, 1972.

———. *Vues des cordillères et monuments des peuples indigènes de l'Amérique.* Paris, 1810.

Iturbide, Agustín de. "Plan de Iguala." In Raat, *Mexico: From Independence to Revolution.*

Jornada, La. "Testimonies from the First Day." January 19, 1994. Reprinted and translated in *Zapatistas!* 62.

Katz, Friedrich. "The Liberal Republic and the Porfiriato, 1867–1910." In Bethell, *Mexico since Independence.*

Kaufman, Robert, and Guillermo Trejo. "Regionalism, Regime Transformation, and PRONASOL: The Politics of the National Solidarity Programme in Four Mexican States." *Journal of Latin American Studies* 29 (1997).

Kaufman Purcell, Susan. "Mexico: Clientalism, Corporatism, and Political Stability." In *Political Clientism, Patronage, and Development,* edited by S. N. Eisenstadt and Rene Lemarchand. Beverly Hills: Sage, 1981.

Keith, Robert G. "Encomienda, Hacienda and Corregimiento in Spanish America: A Structural Analysis." *Hispanic American Historical Review* 51, no. 3 (August 1971).

Knight, Alan. "Cardenismo: Juggernaut or Jalopy?" *Journal of Latin American Studies* 26, no. 1 (1994): 73–107.

———. "El liberalismo mexicano desde la reforma hasta la revolución." *Historia Mexicana* 35, no. 1 (1985).

———. "Mexican Peonage: What Was It and Why Was It?" *Journal of Latin American Studies* 18, no. 1 (1986): 41–74.

———. "The Mexican Revolution: Bourgeois? Nationalist? or Just a 'Great Rebellion'?" *Bulletin of Latin American Research* 4, no. 2 (1985).

———. "Racism, Revolution, and *Indigenismo*: Mexico, 1910–1940." In *The Idea of Race in Latin America, 1840–1940,* edited by Richard Graham. Austin: University of Texas Press, 1990.

———. "The Rise and Fall of Cardenismo." In Bethell, *Mexico since Independence.*

———. "Solidarity: Historical Continuities and Contemporary Implications." In Cornelius, Craig, and Fox, *Transforming State-Society Relations,* 29–45.

Knutsen, Torbjørn L. *A History of International Relations Theory.* 2nd ed. Manchester: Manchester University Press, 1997.

Krishna, Sankaran. "The Importance of Being Ironic: A Postcolonial View on Critical International Relations Theory." *Alternatives* 18, no. 3 (Summer 1993).

Kuhn, Thomas. *The Essential Tension.* Chicago: University of Chicago Press, 1977.

———. *The Structure of Scientific Revolutions.* Chicago: University of Chicago Press, 1962.

Kuklick, Henrika. *The Savage Within: The Social History of British Anthropology, 1885–1945.* Cambridge: Cambridge University Press, 1991.

————. "The Sins of the Fathers: British Anthropology and the African Colonial Administration." *Research in the Sociology of Knowledge, Science and Art* 1 (1978): 93–119.

Lafaye, Jacques. *Quetzalcoatl and Guadalupe: The Formation of Mexican National Consciousness, 1531–1831.* Chicago: University of Chicago Press, 1976.

Las Casas, Bartolomé de. *Historia de Las Indies.* Edited by Augustín Milares Carlo. With a preliminary study by Lewis Hanke. 2 vols. Mexico City: Fondo de Cultura Económica, 1965.

Laughlin, Robert. *Of Cabbages and Kings: Tales from Zinacantán.* Washington, DC: Smithsonian Institution, 1977.

Leal, Juan Felipe. "Positivismo y liberalismo." In *El porfiriato*, edited by José Alfredo Castellanos, 211–224. Mexico City: Universidad Autónoma Chapingo, 1988.

Le Bot, Yvon. *Subcomandante Marcos: El sueño zapatista.* Barcelona: Plaza & Janes Editores, 1997.

Leclerq, Dom Jean, et al., eds. *A History of Christian Spirituality.* Vol. 2, *The Spirituality of the Middle Ages.* New York: Seabury Press, 1982.

Lefebvre, Georges. "Enlightened Despotism." In Lubasz, *Development of the Modern State.*

León-Portilla, Miguel. "El Nuevo Mundo, 1492–1992: Una disputa interminable?" In *Raíces indígenas: Presencia hispánica*, edited by Miguel León-Portilla. Mexico City: Colegio Nacional, 1993.

————. *Pueblos originarios y globalización.* Mexico City: Colegio Nacional, 1997.

————. *Time and Reality in the Thought of the Maya.* 2nd ed. Norman: University of Oklahoma Press, 1988.

López Astrain, Martha Patricia. *La guerra de baja intensidad en México.* Mexico City: Universidad Iberoamericana and Plaza y Valdés Editores, 1996.

Loyo, Engracia. "Popular Reactions to the Educational Reforms of Cardenismo." In *Rituals of Resistance: Public Celebrations and Popular Culture in Mexico*, edited by William H. Beezley, Cheryl English Martin, and William E. French. Wilmington, DE: Scholarly Resources, 1994.

Lubasz, Heinz. *The Development of the Modern State.* London: MacMillan, 1964.

Lynch, John. *Bourbon Spain, 1700–1808.* Oxford: Basil Blackwell, 1989.

MacLachlan, Colin M., and Jaime E. Rodríguez O., eds. *The Forging of the Cosmic Race: A Reinterpretation of Colonial Mexico.* Berkeley and Los Angeles: University of California Press, 1990.

MacLeod, Murdo J. "Papel social y económica de las cofradías indígenas de la colonia en Chiapas." *Mesoamerica* 5 (1983).

Marcos, Subcomandante Insurgente. *Cuentos para una soledad desvelada.* Mexico City: Ediciones del Frente Zapatista de Liberación Nacional, 1998.

————. "De acá a allá, y volvemos a empezar." March 8, 1997. In Marcos, *Cuentos para una soledad desvelada*, 205–209.

————. "A gift and a lesson in politics." March 24, 1994. Translated in *Shadows of Tender Fury*, 188.

————. *La historia de las preguntas.* Mexico City: Offset Industrial, 1998.

————. *La historia de los colores.* Mexico City: Offset Industrial, 1997.

————. Letter to the national and international press. *La Jornada*, January 18, 1994. Reprinted in *Zapatistas!*

————. Poem. December 16, 1995. Dedicated to Olivier Cyran. In Marcos, *Cuentos para una soledad desvelada*, 24.

————. "Problems." 1987. Published on March 15, 1994, as part of a communiqué to the press. Reprinted in *Documentos y comunicados del EZLN*, 2:198–200. Mexico City: Ediciones Era, 1995.

————. *Relatos de El Viejo Antonio*. With a prologue by Armando Bartra. San Cristóbal de Las Casas: Centro de Información y Análisis de Chiapas, 1998.

————. "Los siete arcoiris." In *Acuerdos de San Andrés*, edited by Luis Hernández Navarro and Ramón Vera Herrera. Mexico City: Ediciones Era, 1998.

María y Campos, Alfonso de. "Los científicos: Actitudes de un grupo de intelectuales porfirianos frente al positivismo y la religion." In Camp, Hale, and Vázquez, *Los intelectuales y el poder en México*.

Markman, Sidney David. *Architecture and Urbanization in Colonial Chiapas, Mexico*. Philadelphia: American Philosophical Society, 1984.

Masden, William. "Religious Syncretism." In *Handbook of Middle American Indians*, vol. 6, *Social Anthropology*, edited by Manning Nash, 369–391. Austin: University of Texas Press, 1967.

Masiosare. Supplement to *La Jornada*. No. 9, January 18, 1998.

————. No. 21, April 19, 1998.

Menchú, Rigoberta. *Crossing Borders*. Translated and edited by Ann Wright. London: Verso, 1998.

————. *I, Rigoberta Menchú: An Indian Woman in Guatemala*. Edited by Elisabeth Burgos-Debray. Translated by Ann Wright. London: Verso, 1984.

Meras, Luisa Martin. *Cartografía marítima hispana: La imagen de América*. Madrid: Lunwerg Editores, 1993.

Meyer, Jean. *Historia de los cristianos de América Latina, siglos XIX y XX*. Mexico City: Ediciones Vuelta, 1989.

————. "Revolution and Reconstruction in the 1920s." In Bethell, *Mexico since Independence*.

Middlebrook, Kevin J. *The Paradox of Revolution: Labor, the State and Authoritarianism in Mexico*. Baltimore: Johns Hopkins University Press, 1995.

Mill, John Stuart. *Auguste Comte and Positivism*. Ann Arbor: University of Michigan Press, 1961.

————. *The Subjection of Women*. 1869.

Millet, Kate. *The Loony Bin Trip*. London: Virago Press, 1991.

————. *Sexual Politics*. London: Virago Press, 1970.

Mises, Ludwig von. *The Free and Prosperous Commonwealth*. New York: Van Nostrand, 1962.

Montaigne, Michel de. *The Complete Essays*. Translated by M. A. Screech. London: Penguin Books, 1991.

Montemayor, Carlos. "Administrando la guerra." *Proceso*, no. 1113, March 1, 1998, 40–41.

————. *Chiapas: La rebelión indígena de México*. Mexico City: Editorial Joaquin Mortiz, 1997.

Montes de Oca, Rosa Elena. "The State and the Peasants." In *Authoritarianism in Mexico*, edited by José Luis Reyna and Richard G. Hellman. New York: Center for Inter-American Relations, 1978.

Morgenthau, Hans J. *Politics among Nations*. New York: Knopf, 1978.

Morkovsky, Mary Christine. "*Guerrilleros*, Political Saints, and the Theology of Liberation." In Gossen, *South and Meso-American Native Spirituality.*

Morris, John N. *Versions of the Self: Studies in English Autobiography from John Bunyan to Stuart Mill.* New York: Basic Books, 1966.

Nagel, Thomas. *The View from Nowhere.* Oxford: Oxford University Press, 1986.

Nash, June. *Maya Visions: The Quest for Autonomy in an Age of Globalisation.* London: Routledge, 2001.

————. "The Reassertion of Indigenous Identity: Mayan Responses to State Intervention in Chiapas." *Latin American Research Review* 30, no. 3 (1995): 7–41.

Nauert, Charles G., Jr. *Humanism and the Culture of Renaissance Europe.* Cambridge: Cambridge University Press, 1995.

Nicholson, Michael. "Imaginary Paradigms: A Sceptical View of the Inter-Paradigm Debate in International Relations." Kent Papers in Politics and International Relations, series 1, no. 7, University of Kent at Canterbury, 1992.

————. "What's the Use of International Relations?" *Review of International Relations* 26, no. 2 (April 2000): 183–198.

Nietzsche, Friedrich. "On the Uses and Disadvantages of History for Life." Chap. 2 in *Untimely Meditations*, translated by R. J. Hollingdale. Cambridge: Cambridge University Press, 1983.

Norris, Christopher. *What's Wrong with Postmodernism: Critical Theory and the Ends of Philosophy.* New York: Harvester Wheatsheaf, 1990.

O'Brien, Phil, and Jackie Roddick. *Chile: The Pinochet Decade; The Rise and Fall of the Chicago Boys.* London: Latin American Bureau, 1983.

O'Connor, D. J. *The Correspondence Theory of Truth.* London: Hutchinson, 1975.

O'Gorman, Edmundo. *La invención de América.* Mexico City: Fondo de Cultura Económica, 1984.

Olschki, Leonardo. "What Columbus Saw on Landing in the West Indies." *Proceedings of the American Philosophical Society*, no. 84 (1941): 633–659.

O'Malley, Ilene. *The Myth of Revolution: Hero Cults and the Institutionalization of the Mexican State, 1920–1940.* Westport, CT: Greenwood Press, 1986.

Orozco, Jose Clemente. *Autobiografía.* Mexico City: Ediciones Occidente, 1945. Quoted in Jean Meyer, "Revolution and Reconstruction," 209.

Owen, David. *Nietzsche, Politics and Modernity: A Critique of Liberal Reason.* London: Sage, 1995.

Pagden, Anthony. *European Encounters with the New World: From Renaissance to Romanticism.* New Haven: Yale University Press, 1993.

————. "*Ius et Factum:* Text and Experience in the Writings of Bartolomé de Las Casas." In Greenblatt, *New World Encounters*, 85–100.

————. *Spanish Imperialism and the Political Imagination: Studies in European and Spanish-American Social and Political Theory, 1513–1830.* New Haven: Yale University Press, 1990.

Paz, Octavio. "Re/Visiones: La pintura mural." In *Los privilegios de la vista.* Mexico City: Fondo de Cultura Económica, 1987.

Pereyra, Daniel. *Del Moncada a Chiapas: Historia de la lucha armada en América Latina.* Madrid: Los Libros de la Catarata, 1994.

Pérez Tzu, Mariano. "Conversaciones ininterrumpidas: Las voces indígenas del mercado de San Cristóbal." Translated from the Tzotzil by Jan Rus. In *Democracia en tierras indígenas: Las elecciones en los Altos de Chiapas, 1991–1998*, edited by Juan Pedro Viqueira and Willibald Sonnleitner. Mexico City: Colmex/ CIESAS, forthcoming.

―――. "The First Two Months of the Zapatistas: A Tzotzil Chronicle." Translated from the Tzotzil by Jan Rus. In Gosner and Ouweneel, *Indigenous Revolts*.

Peters, Edward M. *Inquisition*. London: Free Press, 1988.

Phelan, John Leddy. "Authority and Flexibility in the Spanish Imperial Bureaucracy." *Administrative Science Quarterly* 5 (June 1960): 47–66.

―――. *The Millennial Kingdom of the Franciscans in the New World*. Berkeley and Los Angeles: University of California Press, 1956.

Pineda, Luz Olivia. "Maestros bilingües, burocracía y poder político en los Altos de Chiapas." In Viqueira and Ruz, *Chiapas*.

Poniatowska, Elena. *Massacre in Mexico*. Columbia: University of Missouri Press, 1978.

Porter, Bruce D. *War and the Rise of the State: The Military Foundations of Modern Politics*. New York: Free Press, 1994.

Powell, Kathy. "Neoliberalism and Nationalism." In Aitken et al., *Dismantling the Mexican State?*

Powell, T. G. "Mexican Intellectuals and the Indian Question, 1876–1911." *Hispanic American Historical Review* 48, no. 1 (1968).

Pozas, Ricardo. "El trabajo en las plantaciones de café y el cambio sociocultural del indio." *Revista Mexicana de Estudios Antropológicos* 13 (1952).

Priestley, H. I. *José de Gálvez, Visitador-General of New Spain, 1765–1771*. Philadelphia: Porcupine Press, 1916. 2nd ed., 1980.

Proceso. No. 1104, January 4, 1998.

―――. No. 1107, January 18, 1998.

―――. No. 977, July 24, 1995.

―――. No. 1104, December 28, 1997.

Raat, W. Dirk. "Agustín Aragón and Mexico's Religion of Humanity." *Journal of Interamerican Studies and World Affairs* 11, no. 3 (July 1969).

―――, ed. *Mexico: From Independence to Revolution, 1810–1910*. Lincoln: University of Nebraska Press, 1982.

―――. *El positivismo durante el porfiriato*. Mexico City: SepSetentas, 1975.

Rabasa, Emilio. *La constitución y la dictadura: Estudio sobre la organización política de México*. 1912. Reprint, Mexico City: Talleras de Reproducciones OSVIC, 2002.

Rabinow, Paul, ed. *The Foucault Reader*. 3rd ed. London: Penguin Books, 1991.

―――. "Representations Are Social Facts: Modernity and Post-Modernity in Anthropology." In *Writing Culture: The Poetics and Politics of Ethnography*, edited by James Clifford and George E. Marcus, 234–261. Berkeley and Los Angeles: University of California Press, 1986.

Rachun Linn, Priscilla. "Souls and Selves in Chamula: A Thought on Individuals, Fatalism, and Denial." In Bricker and Gossen, *Ethnographic Encounters*.

Rajchenberg, Enrique, and Catherine Héau-Lambert. "History and Symbolism in the Zapatista Movement." In *Zapatista! Reinventing Revolution in Mexico*, edited by John Holloway and Eloína Peláez. London: Pluto Press, 1998.

Ramos Escandón, Carmen. "Emilio Rabasa: Su obra literaria como expresión política." In Camp, Hale, and Vázquez, *Los intelectuales y el poder en México*, 665–680.

Rayack, Elton. *Not So Free to Choose: The Political Economy of Milton Friedman and Ronald Reagan.* New York: Praeger, 1987.

Redfield, Robert. *The Folk Culture of Yucatan.* Chicago: University of Chicago Press, 1940.

———. *Tepotzlan: A Mexican Village.* Chicago: University of Chicago Press, 1930.

Reed, Nelson. *The Caste War of Yucatan.* Stanford: Stanford University Press, 1964.

Reina, Leticia. "La rebelión campesina de Sierra Gorda." In *Sierra Gorda: Pasado y presente,* edited by Lino Gómez Canedo. Querétaro, Mexico: Fondo Editorial de Querétaro, 1994.

Retamar, Roberto Fernández. *Caliban and Other Essays.* Minneapolis: University of Minnesota Press, 1988.

Rivera, Diego. "La lucha de clases y el problema indígena: Proyecto de tesis sobre el problema indígena en México y América Latina con relación a la cuestión agraria." 1938. In *Arte y política.* Mexico City: Grijalbo, 1979.

Rochlin, James F. *Redefining Mexican "Security": Society, State and Region under NAFTA.* Boulder: Lynne Rienner, 1997.

Rodó, José Enrique. *Ariel.* 1900. Translated by Margaret Sayers Peden. Austin: University of Texas Press, 1988.

Rodríguez O., Jaime E., ed. *The Independence of Mexico and the Creation of the New Nation.* Berkeley and Los Angeles: University of California Press, 1989.

Rorty, Richard. *Consequences of Pragmatism.* Minneapolis: University of Minnesota Press, 1982.

———. *Contingency, Irony, and Solidarity.* Cambridge: Cambridge University Press, 1989.

———. "Feminism and Pragmatism." In Goodman, *Pragmatism: A Contemporary Reader.*

———. "Human Rights, Rationality and Sentimentality." In *On Human Rights: The 1993 Oxford Amnesty Lectures.* New York: Basic Books, 1993.

———. "Method, Social Science, Social Hope." In *Philosophical Papers.* Vol. 1, *Objectivity, Relativism, and Truth,* 203–208.

———. "Moral Identity and Private Autonomy: The Case of Foucault." In *Philosophical Papers.* Vol. 2, *Essays on Heidegger and Others.*

———. *Philosophical Papers.* Vol. 1, *Objectivity, Relativism, and Truth.* Cambridge: Cambridge University Press, 1991.

———. *Philosophical Papers.* Vol. 2, *Essays on Heidegger and Others.* Cambridge: Cambridge University Press, 1991.

———. *Philosophical Papers.* Vol. 3, *Truth and Progress.* Cambridge: Cambridge University Press, 1999.

———. *Philosophy and the Mirror of Nature.* Oxford: Blackwell, 1980.

———. "Postmodern Bourgeois Liberalism." In *Philosophical Papers.* Vol. 1, *Objectivity, Relativism, and Truth.*

———. "Priority of Democracy to Philosophy." In *Philosophical Papers.* Vol. 1, *Objectivity, Relativism, and Truth.*

———. "Private Irony and Liberal Hope." In *Contingency, Irony, and Solidarity,* 73–95.

Rose, Nikolas. "Assembling the Modern Self." In *Rewriting the Self: Histories from the Renaissance to the Present,* edited by Roy Porter. London: Routledge, 1997.

————. "Authority and the Genealogy of Subjectivity." In *De-traditionalization: Authority and Self in an Age of Cultural Change*, edited by P. Healas, P. Morris, and S. Lash. Oxford: Blackwell, 1996.

————. *Governing the Soul: The Shaping of the Private Self.* London: Routledge, 1990.

————. "Government, Authority and Expertise in Advanced Liberalism." *Economy and Society* 22, no. 3 (August 1993).

————. *Inventing Ourselves: Psychology, Power and Personhood.* New York: Cambridge University Press, 1996.

————. *Powers of Freedom: Reframing Political Thought.* Cambridge: Cambridge University Press, 1999.

————. *The Psychological Complex: Psychology, Politics and Society in England, 1869–1939.* London: Routledge, 1985.

————. "Towards a Critical Sociology of Freedom." Inaugural lecture, Goldsmiths College, London, May 5, 1992. Folio paper, Goldsmiths College, University of London, 1993.

Ross, John. "The EZLN: A History; Miracles, *Coyunturas*, Communiqués." In *Shadows of Tender Fury.*

Rostas, Susanna. "A Grass Roots View of Religious Change amongst Women in an Indigenous Community in Chiapas, Mexico." *Bulletin of Latin American Research* 18, no. 3 (July 1999): 327–341.

Roys, Ralph L., trans. *The Book of Chilam Balam of Chumayel.* Washington, DC: Carnegie Institution of Washington, 1933.

Ruiz, Samuel. *En esta hora de gracia: Carta pastoral con motivo del saludo de SS el papa Juan Pablo II a los indígenas del continente.* Mexico City: Ediciones Dabar, 1993.

Rus, Jan, trans. "Abtel ta pinka/Trabajo en las fincas." In Womack, *Rebellion in Chiapas*, 111–118.

————. "Antropología social en los Altos de Chiapas: Historia y bibliografía." Apuntes de Lectura 3, INAREMAC, June 1977.

————, ed. *Chamulas en California: El testimonio de Santos, Mariano y Juan Gómez López* San Cristóbal de Las Casas: INAREMAC, 1995.

————. "The 'Comunidad Revolucionario Institucional': The Subversion of Native Government in Highland Chiapas, 1936–1968." San Cristóbal de Las Casas: INAREMAC, 1992. Reprinted in *Everyday Forms of State Formation: Revolution and the Negotiation of Rule in Modern Mexico*, edited by Gilbert M. Joseph and Daniel Nugent. Durham, NC: Duke University Press, 1994. Page references are to the INAREMAC edition.

————. "Local Adaptation to Global Change: The Reordering of Native Society in Highland Chiapas, Mexico, 1974–1994." *European Review of Latin American and Caribbean Studies*, no. 58 (June 1995): 21–89.

————. "Managing Mexico's Indians: The Historical Context and Consequences of *Indigenismo*." Unpublished manuscript, 1976. Biblioteca Daniel Cosío Villegas, Colegio de México, Mexico City.

————. "Whose Caste War? Indians, *Ladinos*, and the Chiapas 'Caste War' of 1869." In Gosner and Ouweneel, *Indigenous Revolts.*

Rus, Jan, and Robert Wasserstrom. "Civil-Religious Hierarchies in Central Chiapas: A Critical Perspective." *American Ethnologist* 7, no. 3 (August 1980).

————. "Evangelization and Political Control: The SIL in Mexico." In *Is God an American? An Anthropological Perspective on the Missionary Work of the Summer Insti-*

tute of Linguistics, edited by Søren Hvalkof and Peter Aaby, 163–172. Copenhagen: International Work Group on Indigenous Affairs, 1981.

Sacristán, María Cristina. *Locura e inquisición en Nueva España, 1571–1760*. Mexico City: Fondo de Cultura y Económica, 1992.

Scaglione, Aldo. "A Note on Montaigne's *Des Cannibales* and the Humanist Tradition." In Chiappelli, *First Images of America*, vol. 1.

Schedel, Hartman. *Liber chronicarum* [the Latin version of the *Nuremberg Chronicle*]. Nuremberg, 1493.

Scherer García, Julio, and Carlos Monsivais. *Parte de guerra*. Mexico City: Aguilar, 1999.

Scotchmer, David G. "Convergence of the Gods: Comparing Traditional Maya and Christian Maya Cosmologies." In *Symbol and Meaning beyond the Closed Community: Essays in MesoAmerican Ideas*, edited by Gary H. Gossen, 197–226. Albany: University at Albany, Institute for MesoAmerican Studies, 1986.

———. "Life of the Heart: A Maya Protestant Spirituality." In Gossen, *South and Meso-American Native Spirituality*.

Sellars, Wilfred. *Science, Perception, and Reality*. London: Routledge & Kegan Paul, 1963.

Shadows of Tender Fury: The Letters and Communiqués of Subcomandante Marcos and the Zapatista Army of National Liberation. New York: Monthly Review Press, 1995.

Shklar, Judith. *After Utopia: The Decline of Political Faith*. Princeton: Princeton University Press, 1969.

Simpson, Leslie Byrd. *The Encomienda in New Spain: The Beginning of Spanish Mexico*. Berkeley and Los Angeles: University of California Press, 1950.

Sinkin, Richard. *The Mexican Reform, 1855–1876: A Study in Liberal Nation-Building*. Austin: University of Texas Press, 1979.

Skinner, Andrew S. "Adam Smith: The French Connection." University of Glasgow Discussion Papers in Economics, no. 9703, 1997.

Skinner, Quentin. *The Foundations of Modern Political Thought*. 2 vols. Cambridge: Cambridge University Press, 1978.

———. *Liberty before Liberalism*. Cambridge: Cambridge University Press, 1998.

Smith, Peter H. "Leadership and Change: Intellectuals and Technocrats in Mexico." In *Mexico's Political Stability: The Next Five Years*, edited by Roderic Ai Camp, 101–117. Boulder: Westview, 1986.

———. "Mexico since 1946: Dynamics of an Authoritarian Regime." In Bethell, *Mexico since Independence*.

Smith, Robert Freeman. "The Diaz Era: Background to the Revolution of 1910." In Raat, *Mexico: From Independence to Revolution*.

Smith, Steve. "The Forty Years' Detour: The Resurgence of Normative Theory in International Relations." *Millennium* 21, no. 3 (1992): 489–506.

———. "Power and Truth: A Reply to William Wallace." *Review of International Studies* 23, no. 4 (1997): 507–516.

———. "The Self-Images of a Discipline: A Genealogy of International Relations Theory." In *International Relations Theory*, edited by Ken Booth and Steve Smith, 1–37. Cambridge, UK: Polity Press, 1995.

Sna Jtz'ibajom theater and writing group, ed. *Cuentos de Chiapas*. San Cristóbal de Las Casas: Sna Jtz'ibajom, 1990.

Solano, Xochitl Leyva. "Catequistas, misioneros y tradiciones en Las Cañadas." In Viqueira and Ruz, *Chiapas*.

———. "Lacandonia Babilonia en las postrimerias del siglo." *Ojarasca* 24 (September 1993): 23–28.

———. "Militancia politico-religiosa e identidad en la Lacandona." *Espiral: Estudios sobre estado y sociedad* (Universidad de Guadalajara) 1, no. 2 (January–April 1995): 59–88.

———. "Regional, Communal, and Organisational Transformations in Las Cañadas." *Latin American Perspectives* 28, no. 117, no. 2 (March 2001): 20–44.

Stocking, George W., Jr. "The Basic Assumptions of Boasian Anthropology." In *A Franz Boas Reader: The Shaping of American Anthropology, 1883–1911,* edited by George W. Stocking Jr. Chicago: University of Chicago Press, 1974.

———. *The Ethnographer's Magic, and Other Essays in the History of Anthropology.* Madison: University of Wisconsin Press, 1992.

Sylvester, Christine. *Feminist Theory and International Relations in a Postmodern Era.* Cambridge: Cambridge University Press, 1994.

Taussig, Michael. *Memesis and Alterity.* Chicago: University of Chicago Press, 1992.

———. *Shamanism, Colonialism, and the Wild Man.* Chicago: University of Chicago Press, 1987.

Taylor, William B. *Drinking, Homicide, and Rebellion in Colonial Mexican Villages.* Stanford: Stanford University Press, 1979.

Tedlock, Barbara. "Mayans and Mayan Studies from 2000 B.C. to A.D. 1992." *Latin American Research Review* 28/3 (1993): 153–173.

Tedlock, Dennis, trans. *Popol Vuh: The Mayan Book of the Dawn of Life.* New York: Touchstone, 1996.

Teichman, Judith A. "Neoliberalism and the Transformation of Mexican Authoritarianism." *Mexican Studies/Estudios Mexicanos* 13, no. 1 (Winter 1997).

———. *Privatization and Political Change in Mexico.* Pittsburgh: University of Pittsburgh Press, 1995.

Tello Díaz, Carlos. *La rebelión de Las Cañadas.* Mexico City: Cal y Arena, 1995.

Tenenbaum, Barbara. "Development and Sovereignty: Intellectuals and the Second Empire." In Camp, Hale, and Vázquez, *Los intelectuales y el poder en México.*

Thompson, J. Eric S. *The Rise and Fall of Maya Civilization.* Norman: University of Oklahoma Press, 1954.

Timmons, Wilbert H. "The Political and Social Ideas of Morelos." In Raat, *Mexico: From Independence to Revolution.*

Todorov, Tzvetan. *The Conquest of America: The Question of the Other.* New York: Harper & Row, 1984.

———. *Le jardin imparfait: La pensée humaniste en France.* Paris: Bernard Grasset, 1998.

Toulmin, Stephen. *Cosmopolis: The Hidden Agenda of Modernity.* Chicago: University of Chicago Press, 1990.

———. "The Recovery of Practical Philosophy." *American Scholar* 57, no. 3 (Summer 1988): 337–352.

Toulmin, Stephen, and Albert R. Jonsen. *The Abuse of Casuistry.* Berkeley and Los Angeles: University of California Press, 1988.

Travern, B. *March to the Montería.* New York: Hill & Wang, 1971.

Tully, James. "The Pen Is a Mighty Sword: Quentin Skinner's Analysis of Politics." *British Journal of Political Science* 13 (1983).

Valdellano, Luis de. "Historia de las instituciones españoles de los orígenes al final de la Edad Media." *Revista de Occidente* (1968).

Vanderwood, Paul J. *Disorder and Progress: Bandits, Police, and Mexican Development.* Wilmington, DE: Scholarly Resources, 1992.

Van Young, Eric. "Millennium on the Northern Marches: The Mad Messiah of Durango and Popular Rebellion in Mexico, 1800–1815." *Comparative Studies in Society and History* 28, no. 3 (July 1986).

———. "The Raw and the Cooked: Elite and Popular Ideology in Mexico, 1800–1821." In *The Middle Period in Latin America: Values and Attitudes in the 17th–19th Centuries,* edited by Mark D. Szuchman. Boulder: Lynne Rienner, 1989.

———. "Who Was That Masked Man, Anyway? Popular Symbols and Ideology in the Mexican Wars of Independence." In *Proceedings, Rocky Mountain Council on Latin American Studies, Annual Meeting,* 1:18–35. Las Cruces, NM, 1984.

Varley, Ann. "Delivering the Goods: Solidarity, Land Regularisation and Urban Services." In Aitken et al., *Dismantling the Mexican State?* 204–224.

Vasconcelos, José. *The Cosmic Race.* Translated by Didier Jaen. Los Angeles: California State University, 1979.

Vaughan, Mary Kay. *Cultural Politics in Revolution: Teachers, Peasants, and Schools in Mexico, 1930–1940.* Tucson: University of Arizona Press, 1997.

———. *The State, Education, and Social Class in Mexico, 1880–1928.* Dekalb: Northern Illinois University Press, 1982.

Villa Rojas, Alfonso. "El nagualismo como recurso de control social entre los grupos Mayanses de Chiapas, Mexico." In *Estudios Etnológicos: Los Mayas.* Mexico City: Universidad Nacional Autónoma de México, 1985.

Viqueira, Juan Pedro. "La comunidad india en México en los estudios antropológicos e históricos." In *Anuario 1994.* San Cristóbal de Las Casas: Universidad de Ciencias y Arte del Estado de Chiapas, 1995.

———. *Indios rebeldes e idólatras: Dos ensayos históricos sobre la rebelión india de Cancuc, Chiapas, acaecida en el año de 1712.* Mexico City: CIESAS, 1997.

———. *María de la Candelaria, india natural de Cancuc.* Mexico City: Fondo de Cultura Económica, 1993.

———. "Matrimonio y sexualidad en los confesionarios en lenguas indígenas." *Cuicuilco: Revista de la ENAH* (Mexico), no. 12 (January 1984).

Viqueira, Juan Pedro, and Mario Humberto Ruz, eds. *Chiapas: Los rumbos de otra historia.* Mexico City: Universidad Nacional Autónoma de México, 1998.

Vogt, Evon. *Zinacantán: A Maya Community in the Highlands of Chiapas.* Cambridge, MA: Harvard University Press, Belknap Press, 1969.

Walker, Ralph. *The Coherence Theory of Truth.* London: Routledge, 1989.

Wallace, William. "Truth and Power, Monks and Technocrats: Theory and Practice in International Relations." *Review of International Studies* 22, no. 3 (1996).

Waltz, Kenneth N. *Theory of International Politics.* Reading, MA: Addison-Wesley, 1979.

Warner, Marina. *Alone of All Her Sex: The Myth and the Cult of the Virgin Mary.* London: Picador, 1985.

Wasserstrom, Robert. "A Caste War That Never Was: The Tzeltal Conspiracy of 1848," *Peasant Studies* 7, no. 2 (1978): 73–85.

———. *Class and Society in Central Chiapas.* Berkeley and Los Angeles: University of California Press, 1983.

———. "Land and Labour in Central Chiapas: A Regional Analysis." *Development and Change* 8, no. 4 (1977).

———. "Spaniards and Indians in Colonial Chiapas, 1528–1790." In *Spaniards and Indians in Southeastern Mesoamerica: Essays on the History of Ethnic Relations,* edited by Murdo J. MacLeod and Robert Wasserstrom. Lincoln: University of Nebraska Press, 1983.

Watanabe, John M. "In the World of the Sun: A Cognitive Model of Mayan Cosmology." *Man* 18 (1983): 710–728.

Weber, Max. *Economy and Society.* Translated and edited by Guenther Roth and Claus Wittich. 3 vols. New York: Bedminster Press, 1968.

White, Hayden. "The Noble Savage: Theme as Fetish." In Chiappelli, *First Images of America,* 1:121–135.

Whitehead, Laurence. "Prospects for a 'Transition' from Authoritarian Rule in Mexico." In *The Politics of Economic Restructuring: State-Society Relations and Regime Change in Mexico,* edited by Maria Lorena Cook, Kevin J. Middlebrook, and Juan Molinar Horcasitas. San Diego: Center for U.S.–Mexican Studies, University of California, 1994.

Wight, Colin. "MetaCampbell: The Epistemological Problematics of Perspectivism." *Review of International Studies* 25, no. 2 (1999).

Wight, Martin. *Systems of States.* Leicester: Leicester University Press, 1977.

Williams, David. "Constructing the Economic Space: The World Bank and the Making of *Homo oeconomicus.*" *Millennium: Journal of International Studies* 28, no. 1 (1999).

Wolf, Eric. "Closed Corporate Peasant Communities in Mesoamerica and Central Java." *Southwestern Journal of Anthropology* 13 (1957): 1–18.

Womack, John, Jr. *Chiapas, el obispo de San Cristóbal y la revuelta zapatista.* Mexico City: Cal y Arena Editores, 1998.

———. "Governor González's Penal Code: Tuxtla Gutiérrez, 1990." In Womack, *Rebellion in Chiapas,* 227–233.

———. "The Mexican Revolution, 1910–1920." In Bethell, *Mexico since Independence.*

———, ed. *Rebellion in Chiapas: An Historical Reader.* New York: New York Press, 1999.

———. *Zapata and the Mexican Revolution.* New York: Vintage Books, 1968.

Wortman, Miles L. *Government and Society in Central America, 1680–1840.* New York: Columbia University Press, 1982.

Wright, Ronald. *Time among the Maya.* London: Abacus, 1989.

Zamora, Margarita. "Christopher Columbus's 'Letter to the Sovereigns': Announcing the Discovery." In Greenblatt, *New World Encounters.*

Zapatistas! Documents of the New Mexican Revolution. New York: Autonomedia, 1994.

Zapatistas, The. *Zapatista Encuentro: Documents from the 1996 Encounter for Humanity and Against Neoliberalism.* New York: Seven Stories Press, 1998.

Zavala, Silvio. *El castellano, lengua obligatoria?* Mexico City: Centros de Estudios de Historia de México, Condumex, 1977.

———. *Sir Thomas More in New Spain: A Utopian Adventure of the Renaissance.* Cambridge, UK: W. Heffer & Sons, 1955.

Index